Advance Praise for *The Power of Black Excellence*

"Long seen as engines of economic progress for Black Americans, HBCUs are also—according to Deondra Rose's informed and timely book—engines of engaged, impactful Black citizenship. A vital contribution to both political science scholarship and America's fraught conversation about multiracial democracy."

> —**Jacob S. Hacker**, Stanley B. Resor Professor of Political Science, Yale University

"Rose's book makes a groundbreaking case that HBCUs matter as both centers of Black American higher education and social mobility, but also as places where the promise of American democracy is both contested and reaffirmed. Counter to most histories of Black higher education and theories of American political development, Rose highlights the key role that the federal government has played in establishing these bulwarks of opportunity. In light of the US's most recent racial reckoning, Rose demonstrates how these centers of Black excellence have fostered generations of civically engaged graduates and Black elite leadership who continually fought for a more inclusionary American democracy."

> —**Kimberley Johnson**, Professor of Social & Cultural Analysis, NYU College of Arts & Sciences

"*The Power of Black Excellence* is an important exploration of the significant role played by Historically Black Colleges and Universities in American public life. Based on quantitative and qualitative primary data, Rose argues that these institutions have been and remain 'pathways to democratic engagement.' Rose shows in extraordinary detail how HBCUs produced generations of educators, physicians, and leaders capable of addressing the needs of Black communities at the local and national level. Without HBCUs' cultivation of Black leaders Rose explains, there would be no Thurgood Marshall, Ella Baker, Andrew Young, or Martin Luther King. Rose's powerful work provides an unusual analysis and understanding of their institutional roles in advancing the political interests of African Americans. It is a work of outstanding importance."

—**Dianne Pinderhughes**, Rev. Edmund P. Joyce C.S.C. Professor of Africana Studies and Political Science, University of Notre Dame

"*The Power of Black Excellence* is a groundbreaking study of HBCUs and their political significance. The book is deeply researched and written to be accessible to a wide audience. Its chapters are brimming with insights into race, public policy, and the importance of higher education for democracy and inequality in America. Deondra Rose is an expert storyteller and an incisive political analyst, with a humane appreciation for the complex conditions that shape people's lives and choices. She has brought all of these talents and more to bear in a project that illuminates grinding injustices and inspiring achievements in equal measure. I highly recommend it."

—**Joe Soss**, Inaugural Cowles Chair for the Study of Public Service, University of Minnesota

The Power of Black Excellence

HBCUs AND THE FIGHT FOR AMERICAN DEMOCRACY

DEONDRA ROSE

OXFORD
UNIVERSITY PRESS

Oxford University Press is a department of the University of Oxford. It furthers
the University's objective of excellence in research, scholarship, and education
by publishing worldwide. Oxford is a registered trade mark of Oxford University
Press in the UK and certain other countries.

Published in the United States of America by Oxford University Press
198 Madison Avenue, New York, NY 10016, United States of America.

Library of Congress Cataloging-in-Publication Data
Names: Rose, Deondra, author.
Title: The power of Black excellence : HBCUs and the fight
for American democracy / Deondra Rose.
Description: New York, NY : Oxford University Press, [2024] |
Series: Studies in postwar American political development |
Includes bibliographical references.
Identifiers: LCCN 2024003210 (print) | LCCN 2024003211 (ebook) |
ISBN 9780197776599 (hardback) | ISBN 9780197776612 (epub)
Subjects: LCSH: Historically Black colleges and universities—Political aspects. |
African Americans—Education (Higher)—History—20th century. |
Education, Higher—Political aspects—United States. |
Democracy and education—United States.
Classification: LCC LC2781.R656 2024 (print) | LCC LC2781 (ebook) |
DDC 378.1/982996073—dc23/eng/20240507
LC record available at https://lccn.loc.gov/2024003210
LC ebook record available at https://lccn.loc.gov/2024003211

DOI: 10.1093/oso/9780197776599.001.0001

Printed by Sheridan Books, Inc., United States of America

For my grandmother, Shirley Ann Lynch, RN.

CONTENTS

———⬥⬥⬥———

ACKNOWLEDGMENTS

THIS BOOK HAS BEEN A labor of true love; and as my work comes to an end, I find myself overwhelmed with gratitude and affection for the many people who helped make *The Power of Black Excellence* possible.

This project would not exist without the work of generations of Black Americans and their allies who built, sustained, and powered HBCUs and shaped them into institutions that celebrate and champion Black excellence. For that reason, 50 percent of the royalties from this book will go to the Thurgood Marshall College Fund in honor of HBCUs, their extraordinary legacy, and the crucial democracy work that they continue to do.

I offer heartfelt thanks to the National Academy of Education (NAEd)/ Spencer Foundation for a generous postdoctoral fellowship that provided me with valuable time to invest in this project and a vibrant community of interlocutors who share my passion for higher education. It is a true privilege to be a part of the NAEd/Spencer Foundation's extraordinary community of education scholars, and I will be forever grateful for their generous support.

I am in awe of and in eternal debt to the many people who made time to share their higher educational experiences with me by completing surveys and/or by participating in interviews for this study. To the many people who shared their lives with me and entrusted me with candid accounts of their college years—triumphs, hopes, dreams, trials, tribulations, lessons learned, heartbreaks, joys, and more—I hope that I have done justice to the data, including the priceless memories and deep insights, that they shared with me. I also offer a very special thanks to Yelberton Watkins; Paul Braithwaite; Dr. Michael Lomax; Ms. Kassandra A. Ware and the Spelman College Archives Department; the Staff at Howard University's Founders Library; and the HBCU leaders and advocates who spoke with me for their kindness, generosity, and the insights that they shared as I developed this project.

For excellent research assistance, I thank a veritable panoply of former students: Camille Ampey, Brian Englar, Katherine Gan, Sofia Girvin, Jenny Hausman, Kendrick Icenhour, Sam Kahane, Mehdina Koelini, Kalito Luna, Ehime Ohue, Joey Rausch, Arturo Reyes, Matthew Tran, Trinity Wenzel-Wertheim, and Nicole Yoon.

Duke University and the Sanford School of Public Policy offered a vibrant intellectual home as I dreamed up, developed, and completed this project. I am especially grateful to the brilliant Kristin Goss and the brilliant Chris Lura for their thoughtful and valuable feedback that had a tremendous impact on this project. I'm also grateful to Professor Walter Allen for serving as discussant for an early presentation of the research at an NAEd/Spencer symposium in Washington, DC; and to my colleagues Charlie Clotfelter, Kerry Haynie, Bruce Jentleson, Anirudh Krishna, Paula McClain, Billy Pizer, Lisa Garcia-Bedolla, Suzanne Mettler, Michael Jones-Correa, Dianne Pinderhughes, Theda Skocpol, Sid Milkis, Elizabeth Sanders, Thavolia Glymph, Bob Korstad, Ed Balleisen, Karin Shapiro, Joe Soss, Peter Enns, Mary Summers, Rucker Johnson, Linda Burton, and so many others who have greatly influenced my thinking on race, educational opportunity, democracy, policy feedback, and American political development.

I am very grateful to the remarkable Steven M. Teles and David McBride at Oxford University Press for their interest in this project and for inviting me back to the Series on Postwar American Political Development and to Emily Benitez and the entire OUP team for marshaling the project through the production process. I would also like to offer my deepest thanks to the anonymous reviewers whose thoughtful, generous, and spot-on feedback helped me do greater justice to this topic.

My final thanks go to my dear family and friends for endless love and support. I'm especially grateful to my mother, Donna Rose-Gresham, and Kelton; my grandmother Shirley Lynch; my aunt Dionne Rose-Johnson and James; my uncle Don Rose, Kym, Destiny Fae, and Jonathan Rose; my sister Mercedes and nephew Aiden; my sister Brandy, Brandon, and niece Braylee ("Little Cupcake"); and to the Waltons, Wilsons, Snells, Walkers, Williamses, and the amazing group of aunts, uncles, cousins (with special thank-yous to Mekia Snell, Alexcia Johnson, Tanisha Walker Wilson, and Mario Walker), and loved ones who light up my life every day. I don't know what I would do without my kindred friends and colleagues: Jaimie Bleck, Chris Zepeda-Millan, Phillip Ayoub, Sree Muppirisetty, Igor Logvinenko, Natalie Hengstebeck, Mac McCorkle, Lynette Edgerton, Ruth Solom, Kristin Goss, Kate Whetten, Heather Bree, Jay Pearson, Nick Carnes, Joel Fleishman, Jacqueline Looney, Carolyn Barnes, Sally Nuamah, Suzanne Katzenstein, Stan Paskoff, Subhrendu Pattanayak, Susan Hoerger, Jenni Owen, Catherine Admay, Mallory SoRelle, Sarah Bermeo, Manoj Mohanan, Stephen Buckley, Erika Weinthal, Karin Reuter-Rice, Tyson Brown, Lindsey Haynes-Maslow, Sarah Verbiest, Meg Bittle, Quazha Nettles, Eric Shipley, Brandon Britt, Adam Hollowell, Lalita Kaligotla, Diane Weddington, Ajenai Clemmons, Asher Hildebrand, Miriam Sapiro, Sumetrice Porter, Josh Bond, Quentin Pell, Leslie Babinski, Tyson Brown, Abdullah Antepli, Christina Gibson-Davis, Don Taylor, Peter Ubel, David Schanzer, Gunther Peck, Eric Mlyn, Andrew Nurkin, Diane Wong, Samantha Fiske, Susan George James, Kylie Snyder, Minerva Dantzler, Shana Lassiter, Zach Johnson, Mary Lindsley, Erin Kramer, Heather Griswold, Chris Simmons, Mike Schoenfeld, Jeff Harris, Nancy Ward, Steven McHale, Matt Bunyi, Jenn Chambers, Diva Thomas, Loren Aguillard-Carcassole, and to my Spencer crew—Claudia Cervantes-Soon, Ozan Jaquette, Anna Kaiper-Marquez, Darris Means, Nicole Panorkou, Luis Poza, Niral Shah, and Amanda Tachine.

This book is dedicated to my grandmother, Shirley Ann Lynch, RN, an exemplar of all things excellent, whose brilliance, grace, beauty, hard work, determination, generosity, and kindness bless all who know her. This book simply would not exist were it not for the pep talks, phone conversations, prayers, hilarious stories, and endless encouragement that sustained and energized me. I offer endless gratitude and a high salute to an absolute legend.

Deondra Rose
Durham, North Carolina
September 2023

Introduction

HBCUs and the Politics of Black Education

IN THE IMMEDIATE AFTERMATH OF the 2020 election, as news outlets began to announce Joe Biden's victory over incumbent president Donald Trump, the significant role that higher education—and particularly Historically Black Colleges and Universities (HBCUs)—had played during the intense election became a trending topic. On November 7, 2020, Duke University Computer Science professor Dr. Nicki Washington (@ dr_nickiw) tweeted a list of HBCU graduates whose support was critical to Biden's campaign:

> *A FAMU grad (@KeishaBottoms) endorsed Biden in '19. A SCSU grad (@WhipClyburn) saved him in SC. A Spelman grad (@staceyabrams) galvanized votes in ATL/GA to flip the state blue. Now, a Howard grad (@KamalaHarris) will be VP. . . . The lesson: Stop sleepin on #HBCUs! #BlackHistory.*

Washington's post acknowledged the important role that endorsements from Florida A&M University alumna and Atlanta mayor Keisha Lance Bottoms and South Carolina State University alumnus Rep. James Clyburn (D-SC), Spelman College alumna Stacey Abrams's voter mobilization efforts, and Howard University alumna Kamala Harris's role as his running mate had played in securing Joe Biden's victory.

The next day, Travis Stroud (@golferswimmer), a North Carolina middle school educator, similarly underscored the role that Black HBCU alumnae in particular played in the 2020 election by sharing a post from an Instagram account known as @officialcocoadiaries. The post highlighted the work of Stacey Abrams, Keisha Lance Bottoms, and Kamala Harris, proclaiming that:

> *A Black woman from Spelman helped get out the vote in a city ran by a Black woman from FAMU to push a ticket with a Black woman from Howard over the top. Thank you Black women and thank you HBCUs!*

The comments that Stroud, Washington, and others shared on Twitter after the election accurately point to the important impact of HBCU graduates on the 2020 election. However, it is important to note that HBCUs and their graduates have long played a central role in shaping the American political landscape. As many scholars have noted, since their inception in the 1800s, HBCUs (which the 1965 Higher Education Act defined as any "college or university that was established prior to 1964, whose principal mission was, and is, the education of Black Americans") have provided Black Americans with access to knowledge, skills, and opportunities needed to drive socioeconomic progress and democratic citizenship.[1]

The first colleges and universities dedicated to providing Black Americans with access to higher education emerged during the mid-nineteenth century. The 1837 founding of Pennsylvania's Institute for Colored Youth (later known as Cheyney University) marked the birth of Black colleges in the United States. From that year through 1964, Black clergymen and military veterans, philanthropists, and federal and state lawmakers established 138 colleges and universities that provided higher educational opportunity to Black students whose postsecondary learning opportunities were restricted by Jim Crow and racial segregation. Prior to the passage of the Civil Rights Act of 1964, southern colleges and universities routinely barred Black students from admission, while many northern institutions invoked quotas to limit the number of Black students who would gain entry. A full 90 percent of HBCUs are located in the South, and 75 percent of them were established during a post–Civil War, Reconstruction-era college boom between 1865 and 1899.[2]

Racism and widespread institutional discrimination, however, continued to severely limit Black Americans' access to education well into the twentieth century.[3] In the face of that discrimination, Black colleges took on a powerful social role, providing generations of citizens with one of the few reliable pathways to personal and familial advancement. As the number of colleges and universities supporting Black Americans' access to higher education grew in the nineteenth and twentieth centuries, they also provided crucial support for collective advancement. They provided valuable resources for Black communities, including networks of educational and professional opportunity; access to cultural programming, guest speakers, and conversations that highlighted Black excellence and grappled with complex questions regarding race, citizenship, and justice; and hubs for community service and civic engagement. In their history of developing unique and transformative educational cultures that celebrated and cultivated Black excellence, HBCUs have long embodied the kind of disruptive educational approach that Derrick Bell, a pioneering scholar of critical race theory, describes as necessary for revolutionizing a culture.[4] Beginning in the nineteenth century, Black colleges and the intellectuals who built their careers in them engaged in the kind of scholarly resistance to racism and radical assessment of American society that were the first steps toward boldly disrupting the system of racial stratification that had relegated Black people to the bottom tiers of society.[5]

As education scholars Gloria Ladson-Billings and William F. Tate note, scholars like Carter G. Woodson and W. E. B. Du Bois, who were both products of and faculty ensconced in HBCUs, contested received notions of Black inferiority and worked to establish the study of race, including the study of African Americans, as a respected area of intellectual inquiry.[6] Black colleges were essential institutional structures that made scholarly resistance to racism possible. In doing so, HBCUs also fostered the development of figures who would assume positions at the vanguard of the civil rights movement—including the Reverend Dr. Martin Luther King Jr., Rosa Parks, and Supreme Court Justice Thurgood Marshall. As Black colleges expanded, they served as a home to tens of thousands of Black student activists who would go on to participate on the front lines of demonstrations driving the movement for desegregation and civil rights.[7]

In addition to cultivating leaders who would help to change the meaning of citizenship and civil rights in the United States, HBCUs have played a key role in providing protected spaces for Black citizens when the nation's governing institutions have fallen short of their responsibility to provide equal protection to all. During racial segregation, for example, HBCUs provided Black students with a respite from the harsh reality of racial apart-heid that existed outside of the college grounds. In his book *Shelter in a Time of Storm*, historian Jelani M. Favors offers powerful insight into how HBCUs offered a refuge from Jim Crow oppression and fostered Black political activism during the mid-twentieth century.[8] On-campus dining, residence halls, shopping, entertainment, and security made it unnecessary for Black college students to venture into often hostile surrounding areas for the necessities of life. Instead of having to occupy balcony seating at local movie theaters, students could watch movies or theater performances on campus. In this way, HBCUs have served as valuable substitutes for the state, protecting and empowering some of the nation's most vulnerable populations as they seek the citizenship-enhancing knowledge and skills that typically accompany higher education. By providing social spaces that were not only safe but empowering, HBCUs generated critical resources that supported the political agency of emerging citizens and future leaders.

In addition to expanding people's economic and professional opportunities, educational attainment is a central determinant of political engagement. Those with more education are significantly more likely to engage in activities like voting, contacting elected officials, contributing money to a political candidate, and protesting. Not only are they more likely to be invited to participate in such activities by political parties, or-ganizations, and candidates, but they are also significantly more likely to seek and hold political office.[9] Although scholars have recognized the sig-nificance of HBCUs for providing Black Americans with valuable higher educational opportunity, political scientists have yet to consider the vital role that HBCUs have played in American political development, their unique impact on the discourse around rights and citizenship, and their work to promote democratic inclusion for Black Americans. But as this book explains, HBCUs have been essential for empowering Black citizens and helping to reshape the distribution of political power in the United States.

Drawing on over six years of archival, qualitative interview, and statis-tical research, this book brings into view the historic impact that HBCUs have had on the American political landscape and the "friend"/"foe" re-lationship that government has had with them since their inception. It highlights how a changing political landscape in which Black Americans exerted unprecedented political influence both as voters and as elected officials during the late nineteenth century figured prominently in the development of policy changes that strengthened and supported HBCUs. Moreover, it underscores how HBCUs have acted as uniquely powerful incubators of democratic citizenship, playing a pivotal role in driving the movement for Black civil rights and cultivating the development of leaders who would play a central role in the long fight against injustice and for an inclusive, multiracial American democracy.[10] HBCUs have educated a stunningly high percentage of Black political elites. For example, a full 40 percent of Black members of Congress were educated at HBCUs, as were 50 percent of Black lawyers and a whopping 80 percent of Black judges.[11]

Rejecting a view of education as narrowly aimed at the production of workers, HBCUs historically have been committed to the holistic development and empowerment of citizens, which has had important implications for American democracy. Taking this approach to education, HBCUs have fostered the development of highly engaged citizens through a unique combination of academic programming, politically relevant cocurricular and extracurricular activities, distinct campus cultures that are particularly shaped by their faculty, and a strong commitment to community service.

By bringing into view the impetus for and impact of HBCUs' work, this book challenges the conventional wisdom that, prior to the late twentieth century, the federal government took a laissez-faire approach to education. As this study demonstrates, the emergence and early development of Black colleges during the nineteenth century occurred as a direct response to government interventions that necessitated a unique approach to Black education and empowerment. In the United States, "education policy" is frequently understood to be determined by local and state governments. But the history of Black higher education in the United States shows that this understanding is insufficient, and that it is important to expand what we think of as "education policy." Indeed, the history of Black higher education points to unique ways that education and democracy are closely intertwined, underscoring how higher educational institutions can be crucial partners in democracy work. Policymakers can promote democracy by supporting HBCUs and their unique approach to postsecondary education and empowerment that includes transmitting politically relevant knowledge, helping to build politically relevant skills, promoting political efficacy, and fostering a commitment to civic engagement.

Because of the empowering educational experience that HBCUs provide, public policies that have supported them—for instance, the Morrill

Land-Grant Acts of 1862 and 1890, and indirect support via financial aid programs like Pell Grants and federal student loans—have yielded important policy feedback effects that have helped to alter the racial dynamics of political power in the United States. Drawing on the knowledge and skills gained in Black colleges, HBCU graduates have reshaped the contours of American social, economic, and political life. These institutions have offered a space where Black intellectuals were empowered to think critically about race and citizenship; and to grapple with the hypocrisies of a national creed that propounded values like equality, freedom, and meritocracy while society was rife with segregation, discrimination, and White supremacy.

The political impact of HBCUs is particularly salient in the context of the civil rights movement of the mid-twentieth century, one of the most transformative moments in US political history. By empowering Black Americans to inhabit their roles as citizens, HBCUs played a fundamental role in setting the stage for the civil rights movement, producing many of its leaders. These leaders, in turn, would help to set a new agenda for government and public policy. Moreover, HBCUs have provided many Black Americans with a valuable resource—higher educational attainment derived from an empowering institutional setting—that significantly increases the probability that they will engage in politics. Arguably no other institutions in the history of the United States have made the same investment in developing Black American citizens.

This book draws on extensive archival research, interviews with Black HBCU and Predominantly White Institution (PWI) graduates, and survey data to examine the distinctive higher educational experiences that HBCUs have provided, and to better understand how such experiences have helped foster the development of citizens who are highly engaged in politics. Evidence suggests that a unique combination of academic programming, politically relevant cocurricular and extracurricular activities, distinct campus cultures, commitment to community service, and distinctive town/gown relations are central to the HBCU experience and contribute to their impact on the democratic landscape. This book also looks at the way that federal policymakers have acted as both friends and foes of HBCUs, shaping their creation and operation in ways that have contributed to important feedback effects for the distribution of political power in the United States. Ultimately, as this book documents, HBCUs—shaped by direct and indirect government interventions since the end of the Civil

War, and with their unique approach to promoting strong political and civic engagement—have directly influenced the structure, discourse, and trajectory of American democracy.

Opening Doors for Black Americans through Higher Education

HBCUs have served as powerful mechanisms for increasing educational attainment and building human capital since their founding. The close association between educational attainment and indicators of social, economic, and political empowerment are well known.[12] In addition to providing access to knowledge and skills that open doors to more prestigious occupations, higher income, and rich social networks, earning a college degree significantly increases the probability that people will engage in political and civic activities. For nearly two centuries, HBCUs have provided Black Americans—a population whose pursuit of educational opportunity in the United States has otherwise been met by exclusion, discrimination, and even violence—with one of the most reliable pathways to higher educational opportunity. They worked to counteract a long history of racial stratification in education, from legally sanctioned illiteracy for enslaved people to school segregation during the Jim Crow era to discriminatory admissions policies and unequal access to high-quality education at the elementary and secondary levels.

Today, HBCUs have a robust place in the landscape of American education. In 2020, there were 101 HBCUs operating in the United States, serving 327,000 students in institutions located in nineteen states, Washington, DC, and the US Virgin Islands.[13] Alabama boasts the largest number of HBCUs, with fourteen operating in the state, while North Carolina is the state with the largest number of undergraduate students enrolled in HBCUs.[14] Fifty-one percent of HBCUs are public, 49 percent are private; and they include both four-year and two-year institutions.[15] During the 2018–2019 academic year, HBCUs enrolled approximately 9 percent of Black college students in the United States and nearly 2 percent of all US college students.[16] They also conferred more than 48,000 degrees—11 percent of which were associate's degrees, 68 percent were bachelor's degrees, 15 percent were master's degrees, and 5 percent were doctoral degrees. In 2019, HBCUs awarded 13 percent of the bachelor's degrees, 6 percent of master's degrees, and 10 percent of doctoral degrees conferred to Black students.[17] While HBCUs award degrees in the full range of academic areas, their impact for diversifying STEM fields is particularly impressive.

A full 25 percent of Black Americans who graduate with degrees in STEM fields are HBCU alumni.[18]

A powerful example of the impact HBCUs have on the educational landscape is the role that they are playing in helping to address the decline in Black teachers that the United States has seen in recent decades. In 1971, 8.1 percent of teachers in US public schools were Black. By 1986, that share had dropped to 6.9 percent; and in 2019, the share of Black teachers in public schools had declined to 6.7 percent.[19] This decline has important implications for the nation's progress toward becoming a truly multiracial democracy, as research has shown that Black students who have at least one Black teacher are more likely to graduate from high school and are less likely to be expelled.[20] Persisting to graduation and avoiding expulsion are two factors that promote higher overall levels of educational attainment, which is positively associated with participation in political and civic activities.

In recent years, HBCUs and the federal government have launched initiatives demonstrating intentional effort to increase the number of Black teachers in schools. At the institutional level, HBCUs like Bowie State University have developed education programs that offer valuable curricular opportunities such as student teacher programs that help prepare their students for teaching careers. State governments have also worked to increase the number of Black teachers by offering special programs. During the 1980s, for example, North Carolina established the NC Teaching Fellows program, which provided funding to help thousands of aspiring educators hone their skills in certain colleges and universities throughout the state. North Carolina A&T, an HBCU, was included in the original set of schools where teaching fellows could use their funds. In recent years, volatile state politics has played an important role in both promoting and undermining such state-level efforts, as shifts in party control of the legislature have prompted expansions and contractions of state support.

In addition to the work that individual HBCUs and states are doing to address the decline of Black teachers, the federal government is also working to reverse the trend. In 2023, the US Department of Education announced the availability of $18 million in grants for HBCUs and other minority-serving institutions (MSIs), highlighting the important role they play in helping build a diverse teaching force. As these examples illustrate, HBCUs and government actors are thinking seriously about how HBCUs can continue their legacy of producing Black teachers and, in doing so, how they can help address the nation's shortage of Black teachers.

As HBCUs have continued to make valuable contributions to the educational landscape, they have also undergone a variety of changes over time. For example, they have seen changes in the composition of their student bodies. Before 1964, HBCUs educated a supermajority of Black college students in the United States—as many as 90 percent, by some estimations.[21] After the passage of the 1964 Civil Rights Act and the end of legal racial segregation, the proportion of Black college students attending historically Black colleges declined, dipping to 17 percent of Black college students in 1980, 13 percent in 2000, and 9 percent in 2015.[22] While HBCUs were founded with the central purpose of providing Black Americans with postsecondary educational opportunity, they nevertheless pioneered egalitarian admissions policies that extended admission to applicants without regard to race, national origin, gender, or other identity factors frequently restricted by historically White colleges and universities. They have also helped promote education for Black women and, in 2019, a full 63 percent of students enrolled in HBCUs were women, compared to 53 percent in 1976. While the percentages of non-Black students enrolled in HBCUs have grown in recent years (in 2019, non-Black students represented 24 percent of HBCU students, up from 15 percent in 1976[23]), HBCUs continue to serve a powerful and well-established role for the educational advancement of Black Americans today.

This is particularly true in a higher educational landscape where the failure to guarantee Black and Brown students equitable access to public flagship colleges and universities has placed even greater strain on HBCU resources. In June 2023, the US Supreme Court outlawed the use of race-based affirmative action in college admissions, overturning nearly a half century of legal precedent established by *Regents of University of California v. Bakke* (1978), *Grutter v. Bollinger* (2003), and *Fisher v. University of Texas* (2016), which held that colleges and universities were justified in considering race in admissions decisions because colleges and universities have a vital interest in building diverse student bodies. Such diversity was intended to help rectify the historical discrimination against racial and ethnic minorities that has led to their underrepresentation in various professions and in positions of leadership in society.[24]

This dramatic policy change will have important implications for the higher educational landscape and for HBCUs in particular. Researchers have shown that when they are in operation, affirmative action programs help to increase the number of Black and Brown students at more-selective PWIs. As education scholar Walter R. Allen and his colleagues have shown, African American students' representation in flagship public colleges and universities has "remained persistently low" over the last half century.[25] They go on to note that there are stubborn declines in the enrollment of African American undergraduate and graduate students "in states where anti–affirmative action litigation, policies, and practices were adopted."[26] A powerful example of this has been the sharp decrease in the proportion of Black and Brown students studying in University of California system schools after 1996 when state lawmakers passed Proposition 209 outlawing the use of race in college admissions.[27] A decline in accessibility to PWIs will place additional demands on HBCUs, which have demonstrated an unstinted commitment to providing an increasingly diverse population of young people with access to college education. Maintaining this commitment will be especially challenging as other higher educational institutions restrict opportunity and while the nation sees demographic shifts that will produce larger numbers of Black and Brown students seeking college education by the year 2050.

From their founding through the mid-twentieth century, HBCUs provided a crucial pathway to college degrees when segregation placed strict confines on higher educational opportunity for African Americans. HBCUs have provided—and continue to provide—a cost-effective option for higher education that promotes significant expansions of educational opportunity for low-income and first-generation college students. Studies have shown that African Americans who attend HBCUs have been more likely to pursue graduate and professional degrees than their counterparts who are educated at predominantly White colleges and universities.[28] Scholars have devoted considerable attention to the extent to which HBCUs have provided an unrivaled source of empowerment for Black Americans, their families, and their communities. According to Cynthia Jackson and Eleanor Nunn, "[i]t would be difficult to find a Black family in the United States with college graduates who does not have an HBCU graduate in its lineage."[29] Arguably no other institutions in the history of the United States have provided Black Americans with the same reliable pathway to social, economic, and political capital that are part and parcel of first-class citizenship.

Education, HBCUs, and the Distribution of Political Power in the United States

The pivotal role that HBCUs have played in providing higher educational opportunity for Black Americans has been well documented. But we have yet to fully examine the complex relationship between HBCUs and the state, and the role that HBCUs have played in American political development. The historic debate between Booker T. Washington and W. E. B. Du Bois regarding the best way to achieve racial uplift and advancement for African Americans offers valuable clues as to the motives behind government actions shaping HBCUs and Black people's access to higher education. For Washington, the primary value of education for African Americans was to promote economic stability by providing skills that would make it possible to perform available jobs well, thereby becoming indispensable participants in the economy.[30] Thus, he regarded industrial forms of education that provided training for trades, agricultural work, and domestic jobs to be the most logical form of training for Black people. Du Bois, on the other hand, argued that the advancement of African Americans required an academic approach to education that could cultivate a class of Black leaders who could be trusted to guide Black advancement, which White leaders often fell short in doing.[31] He viewed a liberal arts education as the most reliable pathway for achieving racial uplift.

This debate raised questions about the appropriate scope and form that Black education should take; and depending on the answer, certain policy approaches became more favorable than others as mechanisms for promoting Black advancement. During the Reconstruction period, when Black Americans became citizens as guaranteed by the Fourteenth Amendment to the US Constitution, Black colleges represented a focal point of state effort to habilitate recently emancipated citizens. Industrial forms of education that resonated with Washington's belief in Black education as a means for achieving individual economic stability and broader societal wealth aligned with the interests of White industrialists from the North who enjoyed greater influence in the South after the Civil War. This approach also appealed to southern Whites who aimed to retain as much power as they could in the region during that period.[32] The availability of Black workers who would do the manufacturing, agricultural, and domestic work required to rebuild the southern economy was imperative to their ability to transform the region.

On the other hand, Du Bois advanced a vision of Black education that would offer students the opportunity to engage in serious academic study that included contemplation of the civic and political norms of the nation and a system of institutions built around segregation and racial stratification. In the South, where White planters dominated local governments, efforts to promote academic-style universal education that included Black children and adults were met with staunch opposition because they threatened to disrupt an economic order that had long counted on the availability of low-wage Black workers.[33] A classic, academic approach to education, Du Bois argued, had the power to contest that racial order, as schools providing this form of instruction held particular promise for preparing Black students to become leaders in the civil rights movement and the broader struggle for social justice. State and federal support for Black colleges offering liberal arts education contributed to the empowerment of generations of Black Americans who had long been disempowered by American public policy.[34]

The long history of Black marginalization in American education—into which HBCUs have worked to intervene—is the direct result of the equally lengthy history of Black Americans' systematic exclusion from full citizenship and equal access to political power. When delegates to the 1787 Constitutional Convention gathered to design the infrastructure for a purportedly democratic system of government, they institutionalized slavery and racial discrimination in the nation's blueprint. Equating each African American life to three-fifths of a human being, the framers of the Constitution made clear Black Americans' exemption from the vaunted principles of equality and freedom that the document promised to White men.[35] For the next seventy-seven years, the founders' laws enabled forced and unremunerated servitude of enslaved people and discrimination against free Black people.

Black Americans' slow movement toward full citizenship began with the end of the Civil War and the beginning of the Reconstruction era when new laws extended unprecedented access to political power to Black citizens. From 1865 through 1877, the federal government worked to enforce the Reconstruction Amendments to the US Constitution, which aimed to usher Black Americans into full citizenship.[36] During that time, Black Americans began to exercise political rights from which they had long been deprived. Black men participated in mass-level political activities such as voting and participating in state constitutional conventions. They also moved into positions of political leadership, serving at all levels of government, from city council seats to state legislatures to the halls of the US Congress.

However, this nineteenth-century period of Black participation in American political institutions—which White supremacists saw as a threat to their social status—was short lived, and a violent, repressive backlash emerged among southern Whites that would dismantle Black progress, codify White supremacists' racial logic into new laws, and usher in the discriminatory Jim Crow era. From the post-Reconstruction era and Jim Crow to the present era, HBCUs have provided crucial educational opportunity for Black Americans and have served as a critical part of the nation's educational infrastructure.[37] As Walter R. Allen, Joseph O. Jewell, Kimberly A. Griffin, and De'Sha S. Wolf note, "[h]istorically Black colleges and universities exist at the intersection where the 'American Dream' of unbridled possibilities meets the 'American Nightmare' of persistent racial-ethnic subordination."[38] From this perspective, gaining a clear sense of the contemporary value of HBCUs requires that we first achieve a deep understanding of their complex history.

Higher education was first established in North America in the British colonies in 1636. From that time, all the way until the 1964 Civil Rights Act outlawed race-based discrimination in colleges and universities, public and private higher educational institutions excluded or otherwise discriminated against Black Americans. Black colleges were created as a response to this deep structural racism that pervaded the nation's postsecondary institutions. From before the Civil War all the way until the 1964 Civil Rights Act ended racial segregation and discriminatory admissions policies, even as Black Americans contributed to the tax bases that funded state colleges that they were prohibited from attending, HBCUs offered nearly all of the educational opportunity afforded to African Americans. This was especially true in the South. Indeed, HBCUs pioneered egalitarian higher education, as they were some of the first postsecondary institutions to open their doors to students without regard to race, gender, nationality, or religious faith.[39]

Political scientists and historians have considered the development of higher education in the United States and have made compelling arguments demonstrating its significance for promoting democratic citizenship. In *Soldiers to Citizens: The G.I. Bill and the Making of the Greatest Generation* (2005), Suzanne Mettler demonstrated the important role that the G.I. Bill played in expanding higher educational access to middle- and low-income veterans during the post–World War II era and, in doing so, fostering high levels of civic and political engagement over the course of their lives.[40] In *Citizens By Degree: Higher Education Politics and the Changing Gender Dynamics of American Politics* (2018), I examined the role that landmark higher education programs like the 1965 Higher Education Act and Title IX of the 1972 Education Amendments played in expanding women's access to college degrees and a range of social, economic, and political benefits.[41] Yet the policy feedback literature does not yet consider the crucial role that HBCUs—and the policies that have shaped them—have played in American political development by way of promoting democratic citizenship. This book takes a step in that direction, considering the political development of HBCUs and the impact that these distinctive institutions have had on political and civic engagement and the fight for American democracy.

During the Reconstruction period, as Black Americans inhabited their new roles as citizens as guaranteed by the Fourteenth Amendment, Black colleges represented a focal point of state effort to habilitate recently emancipated citizens. State support for educational institutions during this era marked not only the designation of education as the chosen mechanism for cultivating citizens, but also the growth of the education state. As a particular form of the welfare state, the education state has favored support for work and investment in human capital as the preferred mechanisms for social support, in contrast with traditional forms of social support—such as support for soldiers, widows, and mothers—to whom the state provided support as a reward or in recognition of their identities and sacrifices.

Formerly enslaved people were not given direct reparations in acknowledgment of their previous situations or sacrifices. Rather than directly providing Black citizens with resources akin to the pensions that soldiers and widows would receive or income support for mothers—in the form of, say, "forty acres and a mule"—lawmakers instead targeted resources through educational institutions, enlisting them in the task of providing marginalized populations with the tools necessary to achieve stability and to make meaningful contributions to society. As Black citizens joined the ranks of American elected officials during this period, this unprecedented representation of Black interests—before the brutal backlash that resulted in the launching of the Jim Crow era—helped to anchor education as a focal point for promoting the advancement of Black citizens. Indeed, for Black Americans, higher educational institutions represented some of the principal mechanisms for transmitting civil rights, and I would argue that it was the delegation of responsibility to HBCUs for building Black citizens at this moment that marked the establishment of educational institutions as a central focal point for battles over civil rights.

In addition to using HBCUs to cultivate Black citizens, the state used them to placate White citizens who objected to the idea of integrating existing higher educational institutions. Embracing them as a mechanism for sustaining racial segregation in the United States, federal and state lawmakers provided support to HBCUs in hopes of maintaining the racial social order, particularly in the southern states where the majority of HBCUs were located. Moreover, for some White government officials, industrialists, and philanthropists who were among the earliest supporters of HBCUs, placing an emphasis on industrial education, as opposed to liberal arts education, was a priority. Many in this group saw industrial education for Black Americans as less potentially disruptive to the nation's economic order that relied on racial hierarchy and the subjugation of Black Americans who were expected to perform agricultural, industrial, and domestic labor.[42] In the twentieth century, after the 1964 Civil Rights Act made it illegal for colleges to discriminate on the basis of race, state interest in supporting HBCUs began to wane.

HBCUs, Policy Feedback, and the Advancement of Black Americans

In recent years, students of political science have paid increasing attention to the impact that public policy can have on the political landscape. Policy feedback theory—the notion that government programs have the capacity to reshape politics by altering the costs associated with political activities and individuals' inclination to participate in politics—has provided especially valuable insight into the role that social policies have played in fostering or suppressing political and civic engagement. Policy feedback theory centers on the idea that public policies have the capacity to act as both outputs of and inputs into the political process. As such, policies can alter citizens as well as the political environment by reshaping citizens' social and economic orientations, as well as their rates of involvement in politics and what they come to expect from the government.[43] Programs like Social Security retirement benefits and federal financial aid policies can shape politics through resource effects—extending resources, such as cash payments or access to education, that enhance people's ability to engage in activities like voting, contacting elected officials, volunteering for campaigns and other political causes, and engaging in protests or demonstrations.[44]

Policies can also operate through interpretive (or cognitive) effects, providing experiences and political learning that shape program beneficiaries' inclination to engage in political activities. The G.I. Bill operated in this way, providing recipients of the program with generous support for higher educational pursuits, home ownership, and relief during periods of unemployment. In addition to providing valuable resources, the landmark policy was administered in a way that provided recipients with a concierge-style experience of engaging with the government, sending a clear message that its benefits were offered in gratitude for the service that veterans had provided to the nation. Beneficiaries gained the sense that government viewed them as valued, first-class citizens, and the high levels of efficacy that this fostered helped to generate remarkably high levels of civic and political engagement.[45]

What role has the government played in the development of HBCUs? Since the nineteenth century, policymakers have acted in ways that have both supported and undermined HBCUs. From laudatory statutory language and ringing presidential endorsements to perennial congressional resolutions and statements of support, US lawmakers have often described HBCUs in glowing terms and frequently make clear their esteem for historically Black postsecondary institutions. In 2002, for example, lawmakers issued a report by the White House Initiative on Historically Black Colleges and Universities saying, "[t]he historically Black institutions of higher education are a national resource to be treasured, nurtured, and developed."[46]

Despite such glowing praise, government support for HBCUs pales in comparison to lawmakers' esteem. There has never been a formal line in the federal budget guaranteeing protection or financial assistance to historically Black colleges. Instead, these institutions have had to rely on infrequent legislative innovations, such as Title III of the Higher Education Act, which targeted government support to "developing institutions"; lobbying efforts geared toward obtaining financial support for individual institutions; presidential executive orders that generally establish White House initiatives or convene advisory boards focusing on HBCUs; and the indirect receipt of federal dollars by way of income from student financial aid.

From the mid-1970s through 1989, the percentage of government support that HBCUs received declined precipitously. This was especially
problematic for public HBCUs, given that aid from the federal and
state governments has comprised as much as 75 percent of the support
that they receive. Historically Black colleges operate with institutional
endowments that are, on average, one-eighth the size of their historically
White counterparts, which makes it difficult for them to provide institutional grants to their students, many of whom have significant financial
need.[47] Historically, Black colleges and universities have never received the
same level of support that their predominantly White counterparts have
enjoyed, and in recent decades, PWIs have been prioritized over HBCUs
when it comes to state allocations.[48] Many HBCUs have struggled to provide high-quality postsecondary services in the face of dwindling resources.

Although government financial support for HBCUs has been modest
and arguably inadequate, particularly when measured against its support
for other higher educational institutions, government and public policy
have affected Black colleges in a variety of ways. Perhaps most obvious is
the regime of legal segregation that necessitated the development of a dual
system of colleges and universities. Rather than ensure that Black students
would enjoy the same educational institutions as their White counterparts,
nineteenth-century lawmakers and their successors tasked with marshaling
public resources for the task of educating young citizens opted for a system
of separate educational accommodations for Black and White students.
The Morrill Land-Grant policies of the late nineteenth century were the
first major pieces of legislation that helped to institutionalize this decision.
After passage of the 1862 Morrill Land-Grant Act marked a bold commitment by the federal government to extend public support for the establishment of flagship colleges in every state, Black citizens' efforts to matriculate
into these institutions were met with resistance. Rather than affirming that
Black citizens would enjoy the use of public institutions that benefited
from their and others' contributions to the tax system, lawmakers passed a
second Morrill Land-Grant Act in 1890, which supported the creation of
separate Black colleges.

In the years since, federal and state governments have exerted additional influence on HBCUs. Government funding has supported the development of infrastructure and programming. Congressional and state
charters have formally incorporated HBCUs and other higher educational
institutions into their political territories, and state governments have had

a say in the governance of public HBCUs. Federal and state financial aid programs and in-state tuition rates have helped to make college afford-able. At the same time, the federal government has placed extra pressure on HBCUs when it has taken steps to limit race-based affirmative action programs that have been critical to providing traditionally underrepre-sented Black and Brown students with access to the full range of four-year higher educational institutions.

Whatever the nature of government's impact on HBCUs, there can be no doubt that their development and work have fostered important changes in the political landscape. As evidence presented in this volume illustrates, HBCUs have played a central role in cultivating highly engaged Black citizens, suggesting that government support for HBCUs has had important feedback effects that have helped shape and reshape the dy-namics of American political power. Government support for HBCUs has significantly altered the calculus of political participation for many Black Americans by providing them with a resource—educational attain-ment derived from an empowering institutional setting—that significantly increases the probability that they will engage in politics. Indeed, public policies that have enabled HBCUs to provide a unique pathway to higher education have had important implications for Black citizens' material well-being and their life opportunities and have reshaped the costs and benefits associated with engaging in politics.

Moreover, government policy affecting HBCUs may also convey messages that shape invested citizens' attitudes toward government and their inclination to participate in political activities. It is possible that some aspect of the education provided in HBCUs fosters feelings of confi-dence and efficacy that promote high levels of political engagement among graduates. Evidence suggests that by transmitting these resources and cog-nitive lessons to their students, HBCUs have played an important role in promoting higher levels of political engagement among Black Americans. And, in supporting their work, government has contributed to the feed-back effects that HBCUs have had, helping to shape their impact on the fight for American democracy.

Data and Research Design

To examine the role that HBCUs have played in American political de-velopment, I use a mixed methods research approach that draws upon analysis of qualitative and quantitative data. First, I use historical analysis to examine the development of HBCUs and their relationship with the state. Here, I pay particular attention to the extent to which federal and state government actors were involved in the founding and early development of Black colleges and the role that the government has played in supporting their mission of providing higher educational opportunity to African Americans. Primary documents from HBCU library archives, historical newspapers, memoirs and biographies, legislative statutes, government reports, and the *Congressional Record* provide valuable insights into the politics surrounding the origins of Black colleges during the nineteenth century and their subsequent development. In addition to historical documents and archived materials, I conducted in-depth interviews with lawmakers and HBCU administrators who offer unique insights into the changing nature of government interaction with Black colleges.

Second, I examine how HBCUs have helped to shape the distribution of political power in the United States. To gain insight into how HBCUs have expanded educational opportunity to Black Americans and the impact that their work has had on the political landscape, I draw upon original survey and interview data. I developed the College Experience Survey, a national web-based study fielded by Qualtrics LLC in February 2018. The study examined respondents' higher educational experiences at both HBCUs and non-HBCUs, as well as measures of political and civil engagement. The survey included a nationally representative sample of 2,000 Americans who have at least some college experience, with an oversample of 1,000 Black Americans, approximately 30 percent of whom attended HBCUs. It also included twenty-minute follow-up interviews with 100 volunteers who completed the survey. These interviews provided additional insight into the nature of respondents' higher educational experiences and their engagement with political and civic activities.

To delve deeper into the HBCU educational experience and its connection to political engagement, I developed a more extensive interview study that would focus particularly on HBCU alumni. During the summer of 2019, my research team and I conducted interviews with more than 100 HBCU alumni who attended Black colleges in as early as the 1940s and as late as 2019. Typically lasting between 30 minutes and one hour, these interviews provided valuable insight into the HBCU educational experience, helping to bring into greater focus our understanding of the role that these unique institutions have played in shaping political engagement and citizenship in the United States.

Finally, I conducted interviews with African American political elites to gain insight into how HBCU and non-HBCU higher educational experiences have shaped the development of Black political leaders. These interviews offer insight into how HBCU attendance and non-attendance have shaped the political socialization, efficacy, and interests of Black Americans wielding political power at the elite level. In addition to shedding light on personal background and the decision about where to pursue higher education, these interviews also focused on the nature of the college and/or early employment experience, motivation for seeking office, and respondents' work in politics and public policy.

This book tells the story of how HBCUs have helped to shape American democracy. I argue that by making powerful contributions to the development of Black citizens, Black leaders, and the nation's racial consciousness, HBCUs have helped to shape political discourse, political representation, and the legislative agenda. Moreover, HBCU campuses have offered generations of Black citizens an opportunity to learn without the racist micro- and macroaggressions that are all too common in other spaces. HBCUs have been important engines of citizenship and state building. As such, all Americans have a stake in this story and understanding the role that Black colleges have played in American political development.

In what follows, Chapter 1 considers the emergence of HBCUs during the nineteenth century, highlighting how their arrival presented a radical and important intervention into existing debates about race, education, and citizenship—debates that had previously been shaped by the institution of slavery. In a social, economic, and political landscape that was steeped in White supremacy, how did the proponents and opponents of Black education view the propriety of schooling for Black people, its purpose, and what it should look like? Chapter 2 traces the political development of HBCUs from Reconstruction through the early 1960s, shining a light on how the politics surrounding the establishment of Black colleges contributed to the development of unique institutional cultures strongly informed by a clear sense of political purpose. Not only did HBCUs work with the intention of empowering Black Americans to inhabit their roles as citizens, but these institutions also helped to set the stage for the civil rights movement of the mid-twentieth century by producing many of its leaders. These leaders, in turn, would help to set a new agenda for government and public policy. Chapter 3 examines the role that HBCU alumni, faculty, and students played in driving the US civil rights movement of the 1940s and 1950s, revealing the explosive impact that HBCUs with their valuable network of students and faculty and distinctive commitment to racial uplift would have on American democracy in the twentieth century.

Turning to an examination of HBCUs as unique educational organizations, Chapter 4 offers an in-depth look at how HBCUs offer their students distinctive postsecondary experiences that are conductive to both learning and personal development. This chapter also considers the forces that bring students to HBCUs—from family legacies, to finding refuge after negative K–12 experiences, and more. In Chapter 5, I examine the critical role that HBCU faculty have played in developing empowered citizens, considering the curriculum that they offer, their engagement with students in the classroom, and their approach to mentoring students as they work toward degrees. Chapter 6 describes how HBCU programming and student activities foster political and civic engagement. Do HBCUs offer programs and experiences that may be particularly empowering for the development of politically and civically engaged citizens? This chapter examines the intentional approach that HBCUs take to develop strong citizens and leaders.

Chapter 7 draws on in-depth interviews with a dozen Black political elites (including sitting members of Congress, state legislators, and former elected officials) to highlight the role that HBCUs have played in fostering the development of Black elected officials. HBCUs have educated 40 percent of Black members currently serving in the US Congress, and HBCU alumni are similarly well represented among Black elected officials at all levels of government, including state and local legislative offices and the courts. Do HBCUs provide educational experiences, programming, and networks that help inspire their students to embark on careers in public life?

The book's concluding chapter considers the lessons that HBCUs offer for the broad landscape of higher educational institutions, many of which are struggling to find purpose in the contemporary political and historical moment characterized by social unrest, declining political engagement, and increasingly acrimonious and polarized politics. At a time when the cultivation of actively engaged citizens is crucial for the health of American democracy, political leaders and the broad landscape of higher educational institutions can learn a great deal from how HBCUs have empowered generations of people.

I

An Act of Empowerment

Race, Democratic Citizenship, and the Creation of Black Educational Institutions in the Nineteenth Century

"Oh Lord, please send me back to Wilberforce."
—Hattie Quinn Brown (c. 1869), writing as a
Wilberforce University Student[1]

A YEAR AFTER ENROLLING AT Ohio's Wilberforce University, sixteen-year-old Hallie Quinn Brown found herself taking an unexpected leave from her studies. In 1869, at the end of her first year of college, a trip home to attend her sister's wedding turned into an extended stay when Hallie discovered that her mother was ill and that her family needed her help on their farm. The devoted daughter was happy to pause her education to help her family; nevertheless, she yearned to return to her beloved campus, often praying, "Oh Lord, please send me back to Wilberforce."[2] Their daughter's education was important to Hallie's parents, Thomas and Frances Brown. Born into slavery, they had gained their freedom before the Civil War and raised their children in a forward-thinking Christian household that viewed education as a pathway to self-sufficiency, respectability, and advancement. They invested equally in the education of their sons and daughters, and when Frances had recovered from her illness in 1870, they moved their entire family to Wilberforce, Ohio, so that Hallie could resume her studies and their youngest son could begin his first year at the university.[3]

In the decades after the Civil War and the end of slavery in the 1860s, for Hattie Quinn Brown and other Black Americans, the education that could be gained at colleges like Wilberforce offered a pathway toward economic opportunity, reputability, and racial uplift. Black colleges worked to provide educational experiences that were designed specifically for African Americans, with the goal of counteracting the web of racism, discrimination, and White supremacy that so sharply limited their life chances in the United States. In this way, Black colleges were important for unlocking greater opportunity for African Americans.[4] They helped Black students gain tools they could use to shape the society in which they were living—a society that had long been the beneficiary of so much Black sacrifice. By doing so, Black colleges had a powerful impact on the democratic landscape in the United States. As many scholars have noted, an educated citizenry is part and parcel of a well-functioning democracy.[5]

In a system of governance in which power ultimately rests with the people, it is imperative that citizens possess the knowledge, skills, and ability to participate in the process of collective discourse and decision-making. In that way, educational institutions—from elementary and middle schools, to secondary schools, to colleges and universities—do more than provide tools that can open the doors to economic opportunity and gainful employment. They also play an important role in the development of democratic citizens, given the strong correlation between educational attainment and the likelihood that people will engage in political activities like voting, contacting elected officials, volunteering for political organizations or candidates, contributing money to campaigns, and participating in protests.[6] Informed citizens are better able to navigate political institutions and to advocate for their rights. They are better prepared to select representatives to champion their interests in the halls of power and to engage directly in civil and political activities. Thus, it comes as little surprise that those who have more education are more likely to be tapped for participation by political parties and candidates.[7]

For these reasons, as African Americans gained new educational opportunities—and then used that education to engage in new forms of civic and political activity—the early history of Black education in the United States is tightly tied to a broader change in the democratic landscape of the nineteenth century. As this chapter explains, the federal government played an important role in shaping Black Americans' access to educational opportunities, as new changes in public policy at the federal level influenced the early creation of Black colleges. Critical Race Theory, which recognizes racism as a pervasive feature of life in the United States that is embedded in institutions and systems, offers valuable insights that help us understand the dynamics behind government actions related to HBCUs and its posture toward Black higher education from the period between the Civil War to the end of the end of Reconstruction.[8] On one hand, changing political dynamics gave politicians interested in wielding government power an incentive to support Black higher education and HBCUs to appeal to newly enfranchised and empowered Black citizens and elected officials. Rather than creating the comprehensive set of policies that would have been necessary to marshal newly emancipated Black citizens toward equal opportunity and stability, lawmakers delegated much of that work to the Black community and institutions like Black colleges that made targeted investments in Black Americans.

On the other hand, the support that government actors directed toward Black colleges failed to compensate for the simultaneous hardships that they inflicted on them and Black people aspiring to attain higher education during this period. Perhaps the most egregious government action was the exclusion of Black students from state-supported educational institutions that their tax dollars helped to finance. As Gloria Ladson-Billings and William F. Tate point out in their analysis of education using a Critical Race Theory lens, the right to exclude African Americans has long been used as a mechanism for sustaining Black subjugation in the United States. The wholesale denial of education to Black people followed by an insistence upon "separate but equal" educational institutions helped to embed inequality into American social, economic, and political life.[9] This willingness to create a "separate but equal" higher educational system also made it possible for government policymakers to institutionalize the practice of systematically providing Black colleges with fewer resources than they provided White educational institutions, thereby weaving disparity and inequity into the structure of US higher education.[10] While government has provided support for Black colleges and for Black Americans seeking education, this support has never been equitable.

Conventional wisdom holds that the federal government was largely "hands-off" when it came to intervening in education prior to the mid-twentieth century, yet the history of government interventions that directly shaped Black Americans' access to education belies that claim. When Congress created the Freedmen's Bureau in 1865 and the Morrill Land-Grant Act of 1890, for example, the federal government helped to expand educational opportunity for Black citizens. State-sanctioned slavery and anti-literacy laws, on the other hand, exemplify government interventions that placed severe restrictions on Black educational opportunity. Thus, the case of Black educational access shows that the range of policies that we think of as "education policy" extends beyond widely recognized programs like federal student loans and grants to also include a broader set of government interventions that expanded or restricted access to learning opportunities.

Education and Contested Citizenship for Black Americans

For much of US history, the institutionalization of racism in the country's political and governmental structures belied the boldly expressed belief in the "self-evident [truth] . . . that all men [*sic*] are created equal [and] that they are endowed by their Creator with certain unalienable Rights . . . [including] Life, Liberty, and the pursuit of Happiness."[11] Indeed, the history of US educational institutions—long characterized by concerted efforts to subject Black Americans to second-class citizenship and deep disparity in educational opportunity—directly contradicts the lofty values of equality and justice proclaimed in the nation's founding documents.

The distribution of educational opportunity has always been unequal in the United States (and in the Colonies), and this has been especially true for African Americans. When the nation was founded, delegates to the Constitutional Convention debated the prospect of including a provision for educational support in the US Constitution, but they ultimately declined the idea. Rather than defining education as a right for US citizens or otherwise institutionalizing a national commitment to it, the framers of the Constitution left education to state and local governments, which, they maintained, were best suited to determine the educational needs of local communities. Because education offers a pathway toward independence, self-determination, and the propensity to question—and potentially disrupt—the status quo, restricting or outright denying educational access has been a primary mechanism that proponents of White supremacy have used to restrict Black Americans' freedom. This delegation of control over education provided the foundation of long-standing regional disparities and has proven to be a resilient feature of the policyscape, as those with an interest in reaping the benefits of free or cheap labor, particularly in the South, fought to retain tight control over educational access.

During the colonial era, and then in the early years of the United States in the eighteenth and nineteenth centuries, the nation's earliest schools were launched and maintained through the support of churches, philanthropists, and individual families. Some support also came from states or local governments and property taxes.[12] However, as is often the case with federalism's division of labor, entrusting state and local governments with developing and administering their own education systems resulted in substantial unevenness—particularly in terms of educational access and quality.

Beginning in the 1830s, influential public school advocate Horace Mann, who served as secretary of the Massachusetts Board of Education and then as a member of the US House of Representatives, advocated for the creation of "Common Schools" throughout the United States. A system of tax-funded public education, Mann held, was necessary for effectively preparing young people for future labor opportunities and participation in democratic citizenship. Moreover, he argued, for public schools to be most effective, they needed to be made universally available to students from all backgrounds. In the thirty years before the start of the Civil War, reformers in the Common School movement succeeded in expanding the reach of public schools, particularly in the northeastern United States and in cities.[13] However, despite the egalitarian nature of the Common School movement, some of its advocates supported expanding education but objected to the notion of universal schooling because it could be interpreted to mean racially integrated schooling.[14]

After the Civil War, formerly enslaved people advocated for the creation of Common Schools in the South, but their efforts were limited by resistance from White planters whose interest in retaining a population of uneducated Black laborers trumped their interest in securing public education support for the region. As education scholar James D. Anderson notes, in 1876 "virulent racism" fueled a coalition between politically powerful White planters and small farmers that centered on halting the expansion of universal public education that would include Black children and pursuing a system of publicly supported schools that would funnel the funds that had been intended for Black students to White students.[15]

In addition to this active opposition from White farmers and politicians, Black Americans also faced challenges in their efforts to establish schools during the postwar period. They struggled to recruit and support qualified teachers to instruct Black students, and when communities were able to find teachers, they frequently found it difficult to secure the funds necessary to pay the teacher's salary. Moreover, the unwillingness of many

White property owners to sell or rent land to Black communities for the purpose of establishing schools made it difficult to start new schools.[16] White property owners recognized education's capacity to disrupt the nation's racialized power structure, and they were eager to undermine any Black communities' endeavors to create schools. Because of this pervasive legal and social discrimination, Black Americans had no access to equitable educational opportunities during the nation's early history, including advanced education.

In the two decades that followed the Civil War, policymakers interested in expanding educational opportunity focused on the need for Common Schools, paying little attention to the need for secondary schools and colleges.[17] Yet, it was during the antebellum period—around the time that education reformers launched calls to create Common Schools throughout the United States—that churches, religious leaders, and philanthropists founded the earliest Black colleges. A Quaker philanthropist founded Pennsylvania's Cheyney University in 1837; an educator and abolitionist founded the Normal School for Colored Girls (which became known as the University of the District of Columbia) in 1851; a Presbyterian minister established the Ashmun Institute (which would become known as Lincoln University) in Pennsylvania in 1854; and leaders in the African Methodist Episcopal (AME) Church and the Cincinnati Conference of the Methodist Episcopal Church established Ohio African University (which later became known as Wilberforce University) in 1856.

Severe restrictions on educational opportunity were integral to the larger system of racial oppression in the United States that sharply limited social advancement and precluded full participation in democratic citizenship for Black Americans. The five Black colleges created before the Civil War in Pennsylvania, Washington, DC, Ohio, and Missouri, and then the others that began to appear after the war, were among the few institutions in the early United States that were created with the express purpose of investing in and empowering Black citizens.[18] It is important to note, of course, that some of these institutions were established with the support of White government officials, industrialists, and philanthropists whose interest in steering Black education away from liberal arts and toward industrial education drove their interest in directly shaping their development. By supporting training in areas like carpentry, cooking, and other industrial and agricultural skills, they worked to promote education that would support the South's racial hierarchy, ensuring that Black workers would be available for agricultural, industrial, and domestic labor.[19] Nevertheless, by providing an unprecedented avenue toward education and advanced learning for Black Americans, early Black colleges stood to challenge the regime of White supremacy that had, since the nation's founding, degraded Black Americans' social status, severely limited their economic opportunity, and prevented them from fully participating in the exercise of political power. Unequal access to high-quality education represented one of the most crucial factors that sustained this regime, and the emergence of Black colleges in the nineteenth century represented a clear and present threat to White supremacy.

Public Policy and Historical Efforts Shaping Black Educational Opportunity

> In 1865 the United States Government appointed Major Gen. O.O. Howard to establish the Freedmen's Aid Society, and through it to open schools for the education of the Negroes in the South. The log cabins, the former slave pens, the hastily constructed frame buildings were inadequate for the masses who thronged to receive instructions. Eye witnesses inform us that the scenes were most pathetic: it being no uncommon sight to see the hoary-headed woman, bent with age and toil, but anxious to learn to read, in the school room, seated beside her daughter and granddaughter—all three poring [*sic*] over the same spelling book.
> —Hallie Quinn Brown (1925), writing as former president of the National Association of Colored Women[20]

From the earliest arrival of Africans in the American colonies, education represented a social and economic resource that could disrupt systems of racial oppression, and policymakers used government institutions to actively constrain Black freedom by restricting access to education. Tools like anti-literacy laws, school segregation, and withholding access to educational resources helped to subordinate Black people, to restrict their freedom, and to minimize their power.

Anti-literacy Laws

In the pre-Emancipation economic system that centered on the forced servitude of enslaved people and the legal subjugation of Black people (whether enslaved or free), literacy represented a powerful mechanism for achieving freedom and gaining protection from exploitation.[21] The system of racial stratification that existed in the United States in the eighteenth century relied on the subjugation of Black Americans through strict restrictions on their ability to build social and economic power. It was to this end that policymakers created anti-literacy laws making it illegal to teach enslaved Black people—and in some cases free Black people—to read or write. These laws were rooted in the recognition that literacy could pave the way to engagement with anti-slavery literature, communication between enslaved and free Black people, the ability to forge passes to move freely away from plantations, and escape to freedom.[22] Being able to read also helped to protect free Black people from fraud and exploitation in business.[23]

In 1740, South Carolina created the first anti-literacy law, and over the next century, six other slaveholding states followed suit. These policies were a direct response to fears of Black uprising. The publication of abolitionist David Walker's *Appeal to the Colored Citizens of the World* in 1829 sparked concern among slaveholders who feared that Black people would be influenced by the work's condemnation of slavery and its bold call for Black people to rise up to dismantle the system. Two years later, Nat Turner's slave rebellion in Virginia intensified concerns about the impact that anti-slavery ideas could have on inciting Black violence, encouraging White lawmakers to use anti-literacy laws as a means for suppressing Black resistance.[24] By one estimate, in their attempts to prevent Black people from uprising between the passage of the first anti-literacy law in 1740 through the conclusion of the Civil War, southern states successfully prevented 4 million Black people from learning to read and write.[25]

Creating Schools for Black Children

With enslavement and anti-literacy laws preventing Black Americans' access to education, the creation of Common Schools—or tax-funded public schools that would be accessible to all citizens—as a policy proposal had important implications for Black education. Many proponents of a national system of public schools argued that creating such a system and ensuring that it included all children and young people without regard to race or ethnicity was essential to the nation's vital democratic interests. However, some White people balked at the idea of helping to pay for Black children's education, and they worked to block government support for Black education.

The fate of Senator Henry Blair's (R-NH) proposed Blair Education Bill offers a powerful example of the difficulty of achieving education policy reform that would provide for the education of Black students. Introduced into Congress in December 1881, the Blair Bill outlined a permanent, tax-supported system of national public elementary schools that would include all children, no matter their racial group. Given the proposal's capacity to extend unprecedented federal support toward the endeavor of educating Black children, it was met with staunch opposition among congressional Democrats. Southern Democrats were outraged at the proposal's provision that the federal government would supervise Common Schools, finding the notion of inviting the federal government to monitor southern educational institutions unacceptable and fearing the potential impact that such a program could have on race relations in the region.[26] Despite numerous attempts to get the proposal passed, Congress repeatedly rejected the Blair Bill and its support for a federal system of Common Schools in the United States. The failed Blair Bill offers a powerful example of southern lawmakers' willingness to forgo federal programs that would provide valuable social benefits when they threatened to disrupt the South's racial hierarchy.

The Civil War and the Morrill Land-Grant Act of 1862

The founding of five Black colleges prior to the Civil War represented milestones in the effort to fight against the historic suppression of Black education in the United States. These early Black colleges set a powerful precedent and sparked subsequent efforts to expand Black Americans' access to educational opportunity. During the 1860s, several events took place that would help create the conditions for this expansion of Black educational institutions. The end of slavery and the Civil War transformed the country and the government, immediately altering the nature of Black Americans' relationship with the government and establishing the education and socioeconomic stability of recently emancipated Black citizens as critical responsibilities for the United States. Additionally, as discussed below, the passage of the 1862 Morrill Land-Grant Act marked the creation of pivotal legislation during this period that had important implications for the evolution of Black educational institutions.

From the nation's founding through the periods of expansion and reform that followed, state and local governments bore the preponderance of responsibility for education in the United States. The federal government did, however, use land grants to support education as early as the eighteenth century. The Land Ordinance of 1785 provided for the sale of western land to settlers. The land was organized into townships that were divided into sections, and the ordinance provided for the designation of at least one section that would be used to support public education for the local children. As a result, this policy helped to provide the foundation for what would eventually develop into a national system of public grade school education.[27]

During the Civil War, Republican congressman Justin Morrill (R-VT) succeeded in significantly expanding the federal government's activities in the area of education by spearheading the passage of the 1862 Morrill Land-Grant Act. The policy, which he had first proposed to the House of Representatives without success in 1856, provided federal land grants to each state to support the creation of at least one flagship university. Previous failures to pass the proposal were rooted in disputes over states' rights, as opponents—particularly those hailing from the South—argued that government intervention in education would be a violation of the Constitution and the limits it placed on the federal government.[28]

While Southern Democrats' objection to the notion of federal intervention in education thwarted Morrill's earlier attempts to pass the bill, changes to the political landscape that came with the Civil War precipitated a reversal of fortune in 1862. Principal among those changes was the secession of the Confederacy from the Union and the fact that many of the Southern Democrats who had objected to the Morrill land-grant bill were no longer serving in the Congress. Moreover, an increasing interest among politicians in providing support to farmers and other members of the agricultural community gave the proposal a fighting chance. The rapid industrialization and shift to manufacturing that were taking the American economy by storm raised questions about the stability of the agricultural economy.[29] Politicians like President Abraham Lincoln viewed the land-grant proposal as a valuable mechanism for demonstrating support for farmers who had been advocating for the creation of agricultural colleges that would deviate from the more theoretically grounded classical curriculum by centering pragmatic training in agriculture and mechanics.[30]

Yet, while the Morrill Land-Grant Act has been widely regarded as focusing particularly on agricultural and mechanical education, the bill that Justin Morrill saw passed on July 2, 1862 appealed to a wide range of interests, supporting agricultural and industrial education but also programs providing instruction in classical and scientific studies.[31] Indeed, Morrill's bill attracted the support of a broad coalition that included college presidents, educators, and political leaders. Organizations representing agricultural interests like the US Agricultural Society also lent their support to the proposal, recognizing its potential to bring new resources to colleges, the children of farm families, and eastern states that were witnessing booming development among their western counterparts.[32]

The 1862 Morrill Land-Grant Act brought the federal government into the business of offering support to higher education. Not only did it help expand educational opportunity in the United States, its support for the creation of three new Black colleges—Alcorn State University in Mississippi, Hampton University in Virginia, and Claflin University in South Carolina—set a precedent for federal institutional support via land grants. For its role in dramatically expanding the number of higher educational institutions in the United States and helping to expand access to college, historians have lauded the 1862 Morrill Land-Grant Act as "forward-looking legislation" that was passed in "the darkest hours of the Civil War."[33]

However, as a number of scholars have also noted, despite its longer-term impact on the creation of Black colleges, the program still highlighted and perpetuated many kinds of racial disparity in American education. Although the Act's statutory construction was race neutral, and despite the fact that it provided support to some Black colleges, most of its resources went to institutions that catered only to White students. Moreover, only about 10 percent of Black Americans living in the United States were free in 1862, and only an estimated 5–10 percent of enslaved Black Americans were literate before the Civil War.[34] Thus, the number of Black people who would have been candidates for enrollment in an advanced academic program during the early years of land-grant colleges was slim.[35] As Leedell Neyland notes, "4,000,000 blacks in America were in slavery, and since the approximately 250,000 'free Negroes' in these states were highly circumscribed in their social interaction with Whites, the early land-grant colleges became White bastions, barring blacks from admission by both custom and law."[36] Edward Danforth Eddy concurs with this observation, pointing out that during the postwar period as southern states were readmitted to the Union, with the exception of four states that allocated part of their endowment for Black colleges, Morrill Land-Grant funds went overwhelmingly to White colleges and their students.[37]

While the 1862 Morrill Land-Grant Act helped to democratize higher educational access by supporting the establishment of land-grant colleges throughout the nation, it had the inadvertent effect of causing states and land-grant college leaders to request more money to help them manage low enrollments, student attrition, overworked and underpaid faculty, and facilities that were in disrepair.[38] Moreover, while the law did not explicitly omit Black students from its benefits, the fact that it entrusted the states and their respective higher educational institutions with administering the land grants meant that African Americans were overwhelmingly excluded. Despite this exclusion, the use of federal grants to support institutions that were originally focused on Black education represented a larger political shift taking place at this time—one that marked an important step toward the use of land grants to support Black higher education in the coming years.

The Rise of Black Political Power and Resulting Educational Gains during Radical Reconstruction

In the aftermath of the Civil War, as the nation entered the Reconstruction era, there were substantial shifts in both state and federal political power structures, including heightened attention to the needs of Black people. With the passage of the federal Reconstruction Amendments between 1865 and 1870, and the activation of an unprecedented number of Black voters, the election and appointment of Black leaders into government offices at the local, state, and national levels helped to generate real change for Black Americans.[39]

Support for better educational opportunities for Black citizens loomed large as a tool for integrating those who were formerly enslaved into their roles as citizens. Along with support from Black communities, the Freedmen's Bureau, state governments, and philanthropic societies were the primary sources of funds to support Black education during this period.[40] While some emphasized the value of education for Black citizens in terms of its capacity to provide economic security, others pointed to the necessity of education for developing Black leadership that could spearhead efforts to uplift the race.

Some of the earliest support for Black education came from the Union army during the Civil War. For thousands of soldiers, schools created or maintained by the army provided their first educational opportunity, and by the end of the war an estimated 20,000 Black soldiers could read.[41] After the war, the Freedmen's Bureau was created to provide basic assistance to formerly enslaved people, including housing and legal assistance, and the Bureau drove the second major avenue of public investment in Black education. Historian Thavolia Glymph uncovers another surprising source of financial support for Black colleges. During the Civil War, the federal government established the "Freedmen's Fund," which was derived from Black workers' court fines as well as a special, additional tax on their wages. These funds were used to purchase clothes, medicine, and other supplies for the newly emancipated citizens. Once the war came to an end, the remains of the Freedmen's Fund were distributed to various higher educational institutions, including Howard University and other HBCUs, with Howard receiving the largest portion of the funds.[42]

Those interested in the development of newly emancipated Black citizens emphasized the importance of providing them with educational opportunity. In a social, economic, and political landscape that was steeped in White supremacy, proponents and opponents of Black education debated the propriety of schooling for Blacks, its purpose, and what it should look like. In lieu of providing formerly enslaved people with direct reparations to account for their previous situations and sacrifices, lawmakers targeted resources to educational institutions, enlisting them in the task of providing marginalized populations with the tools necessary for economic self sufficiency and democratic citizenship. Importantly, Black leaders were central figures in the fight for Black educational opportunity. In Tennessee, for example, fourteen Black state legislators fought to ensure that Black students had access to land-grant funds to pursue college degrees. While their appeals did not result in the desegregation of East Tennessee University (later renamed University of Tennessee in 1879), the state's flagship land-grant institution, they did succeed in securing "Morrill scholarships" to support the state's Black applicants seeking to attend private Black colleges.[43]

During the nineteenth century, Black colleges emerged as powerful mechanisms for transmitting social status, economic opportunity, and a sense of civic duty to Black people. By shouldering a disproportionate share of the work to habilitate some of the nation's most marginalized citizens, Black colleges took on important democracy and state-building tasks.

While government actors failed to offer comprehensive support to Black citizens after the Civil War, the Reconstruction era did see some government support for the establishment and cultivation of Black colleges and universities. The Freedmen's Bureau would prove central to the establishment of higher educational opportunities for Black people. The creation of Howard University, to be discussed in more detail in the next chapter, provides an important example of government support for emerging HBCUs. Although a private institution, Howard was founded through a US congressional act in 1867 because it was established in the District of Columbia.[44]

Although these new institutions helped set important precedents, they were still created in the context of a deeply racist and violent political environment. Thus, many Black citizens who had experienced poor treatment at the hands of institutions were deeply distrustful of government support, believing that it would be better to develop educational opportunities outside the structures of government. Indeed, newly freed Black citizens could not avoid experiences where their citizenship was devalued and disrespected by the society in which they were living. For example, when the Freedmen's Bank—another Reconstruction era institution, which had been established to give formerly enslaved people a secure place to deposit their money but was plagued by mismanagement, fraud, and overexpansion—collapsed in 1874, it undermined Black Americans' faith in institutions. Despite having set up the bank, the federal government did not intervene to prevent its clients from experiencing financial ruin, and the bank's failure severely undermined notions of institutional reliability for Black advancement.[45] In light of substantial mistrust of government institutions and rising frustration with the failure of politicians and political parties to represent the interests of Black citizens, some advocates for Black educational opportunities encouraged Black communities to take steps to establish their own independent colleges, without state support, to make a clear statement of their refusal to rely on government institutions to ensure Black advancement.[46]

During the 1870s and 1880s, alongside this unprecedented growth of Black political power and educational opportunity, there was a rising White supremacist backlash eager to suppress any Black empowerment. The violence and politics of this backlash led to a period of post-Reconstruction "Redemption," characterized by unabashed efforts in the southern states to promote White supremacy and to crush Black political power. Driven by this backlash to any expanding Black political and education opportunity, politicians from southern states successfully maneuvered in Congress to end Reconstruction. In 1876, the presidential election ended without a clear winner—to break the dispute, Democrats agreed to allow the

Republican candidate, Rutherford B. Hayes, to be named president, but only if Hayes agreed to withdraw federal troops from the South where they had been monitoring implementation of the Reconstruction amendments.

As a result of this agreement, known as the Great Compromise of 1876, and the subsequent withdrawal of federal troops, the period of Reconstruction with its unprecedented Black inclusion in democracy—characterized by active voter engagement and participation in mass and elite politics—was soon undone by violent voter suppression laws and a broader repressive backlash against the strides that Black people had made and an ushering-in of the Jim Crow regime.[47] Throughout the South, states implemented literacy tests and poll taxes to suppress the number of Black people eligible to vote.[48] In western Alabama, the fact that White voters were outnumbered at the polls sparked a substantial increase in the Ku Klux Klan's efforts to abuse and intimidate Black citizens during the late 1860s.[49] As Richard Valelly notes, "No major social group in Western history, other than African Americans, ever entered the electorate of an established democracy and then was extruded by nominally democratic means such as constitutional conventions and ballot referenda, forcing that group to start all over again."[50] In the face of this blatant hostility and discrimination that they encountered living in the South, many Black Americans decided to move to some of the new western states and territories, generating what became known as the "Exodus movement" whereby thousands of African Americans migrated to the West.[51]

There were also a number of decisions passed down by the Supreme Court that further contributed to the reversal of progress Black citizens had seen during Reconstruction. In a decision in 1873 in a case known as the *Slaughter-House Cases*, the Court held that the Fourteenth Amendment's privileges and immunities clause only protected rights pertaining to federal citizenship, but not state-level citizenship. Thus, Black Americans continued to be vulnerable to state-level denials of the civil rights outlined in the US Constitution. In the 1876 case *United States v. Cruikshank*, the Supreme Court held that—despite the equal protection clause of the Fourteenth Amendment—the Constitution's Bill of Rights only applied when a person's civil rights were violated by the federal government itself, but not if those rights were violated by state governments or private actors.

The Court further decimated Black civil rights with the Civil Rights Cases of 1883. In their decision on a set of five cases, the Supreme Court nullified Congress's Civil Rights Act of 1875, which had outlawed race-based discrimination in public spaces. The 1883 decision, however, held that Congress overreached in its interpretation of the Thirteenth and Fourteenth Amendments in passing the Act and that Congress could not outlaw private acts of discrimination. Finally, the Court's 1896 decision in *Plessy v. Ferguson* upheld racial segregation, asserting that separate-but-equal facilities were constitutional.[52]

Together, these decisions by the Supreme Court contributed to an increase in violence against Black citizens and deprived them of even minimal protections before the law. As Lucius Barker, Mack Jones, and Katherine Tate note, "by 1883 the Supreme Court had nullified the principal sections of the civil rights laws designed to protect black rights and to shield them from intimidation and terror. Consequently, black political participation as voters and officeholders was severely constrained, and blacks were rapidly reduced to a state of penury and powerlessness."[53] During the Jim Crow era, which began in 1878 and continued into the mid-twentieth century, the legal racial segregation that these Supreme Court cases enabled resulted in vastly unequal educational experiences among Black and White students, as Black students were forced to attend separate schools that did not receive comparable resources to those allocated toward schools that White students attended.

Moreover, suppressing Black educational opportunity was a prominent tactic in efforts to disrupt Black advancement. As political scientist Kimberley Johnson notes, "segregated and unequal education was designed to visibly reflect and maintain the subordinated status of African Americans."[54] Historian Leedell Neyland further affirms this idea: "With most blacks becoming disfranchised and increasingly powerless in the south, and with the re-establishment of home rule in most states, many white officials and leaders began to speak openly against higher education for blacks."[55] The steep decline in Black political power hindered Black Americans' efforts to address racial disparity in access to educational opportunity, while also making vulnerable the progress they had achieved in expanding learning opportunities that had been made in recent decades, including access to higher educational opportunities that the Morrill Land-Grant Act's support for Black colleges had helped to create. Efforts to erase the progress that Black people had made during the postwar era illustrated the powerful connection between political power and education.

*The Morrill Land-Grant Act of 1890: Landmark Legislation
for Black Education*

Despite the regression in civil rights for Black citizens in the post-Reconstruction era, the passage in 1890 of the Second Morrill Land-Grant Act—which represents perhaps the most noteworthy eighteenth-century education policy development—would help propel a significant new expansion of Black educational access.[56] In a follow-up to the 1862 legislation, Justin Morrill—who was by then a US senator—crafted a bill that would extend additional federal support to the land-grant institutions in each state on an annual basis. This extension of additional support provided vital resources to the land-grant colleges that struggled in the face of modest enrollments, with many students engaged in remedial coursework; high levels of student attrition; underpaid and overworked faculty; and strained institutional facilities.[57]

Complex political dynamics shaped the creation of the Second Morrill Land-Grant Act.[58] Justin Morrill had made a dozen unsuccessful attempts to pass legislation to follow his 1862 Act before finally succeeding. One of the most controversial aspects of his new bill was the fact that it provided for the support of both public Common Schools and land-grant colleges. The battle over whether the federal government should support Common Schools was a racially charged one, with opponents of national intervention in local and state education at the grade school level taking issue with the possibility that the federal government would actively monitor southern grade schools and potentially force racial integration or otherwise shift resources to Black students.[59]

As had been the case in the years leading up to the Civil War, agricultural interests represented a substantial force in national politics. In the South, groups like the National Grange of the Order of Patrons of Husbandry—also known as "the Grange"—emerged to promote community among farmers and to advocate on behalf of their interests in the public sphere.[60] Farmers had been assured that the First Morrill Land-Grant Act would provide unprecedented support for agricultural and mechanical education and directly benefit the young people of their region, but many felt that the legislation had failed to live up to its promise to target benefits to the agricultural community.[61]

As calls to reinforce the 1862 Morrill Land-Grant Act with additional legislation increased, members of the Grange worked hard to ensure that agricultural interests would be effectively represented if follow-up legislation were created, while at the same time, challenging the creation of any legislation that failed to do so.[62] This new political context in which both agricultural organizations and the colleges that were supported by the First Morrill Land-Grant Act actively advocated for a Second Morrill Land-Grant Act that would win more support for land-grant colleges enhanced Justin Morrill's ability to gain the support of his colleagues in the Senate and the House.[63]

Some of the people who supported the bill did so despite not supporting Black education. White populists, for example, who had fought for abolition and worked to build political coalitions with newly emancipated Black citizens, favored the proposal because of the addition of an amendment guaranteeing agricultural instruction remained a central feature of the teaching done in land-grant colleges and universities. Despite appearing to have more progressive views on race and educational opportunity, however, their support fell short of embracing publicly funded, racially integrated schools or funding for schools that would serve Black students.[64] Some White Populists even worked to limit Black Americans' access to public higher education. As education historian Scott Gelber notes, "most white Populists remained reluctant to share political power or patronage with potential African-American allies."[65] In Alabama, for example, they worked to take funds away from Black schools to give to White schools instead.[66] Nevertheless, their willingness to vote for the law to enable passage of the amendment guaranteeing agricultural instruction helped pass the legislation.

One of the most prominent questions that shaped discourse around establishing follow-up legislation to support land-grant colleges was whether and how Black college students should be treated under the policy. Southern states were particularly concerned about this, and calls for additional clarity on this question prompted lawmakers to address it directly in the 1890 legislation. In the text of the law, they inserted a stipulation that the program benefit White and Black Americans but also that in states that operated racially segregated colleges, racial segregation was permissible as long as the state provided "a just and equitable division" of funds to Black and White schools.[67] This meant that rather than directing funds to one school that accommodated all students, some states would divide resources between institutions to preserve racial separation.

While this stipulation had the effect of institutionalizing a separate-but-equal approach to higher education—six years before *Plessy v. Ferguson* institutionalized race-based segregation in public accommodations—the passage of the 1890 Morrill Land-Grant Act was nevertheless landmark legislation that would lead to the creation of new Black colleges. And in the decades ahead, these colleges would, as the next chapters discuss in detail, serve to educate and empower a generation of Black leaders and citizens whose ideas and activism would, in the twentieth century, help transform the meaning of American democracy.

The Long-Term Impact of Black Colleges and the Power of Black Education

> Said a Spartan father to his son who complained that his sword was too short—
>
> "Add a step to it!"
>
> Women, step forward! Grasp your opportunity, grapple at short range and the victory is yours.
>
> —Hallie Quinn Brown (1925), writing as former president of the National Association of Colored Women[68]

The land-grant legislation that helped spur the creation of Black colleges during the late nineteenth and early twentieth centuries played an important role in the nation's movement toward becoming a more inclusive, multiracial democracy. Although the long struggle to create Black colleges and other educational institutions to support Black people illustrates how profoundly anti-democratic the United States was, the Black colleges that were established during this period would go on to educate key figures in US history, while also helping to invigorate a political and racial consciousness that would fuel long-term political engagement among Black citizens. Particularly noteworthy is the fact that Black women—whose intersecting marginalized identities made them particularly vulnerable to the effects of racism and discrimination—were included in Black colleges' efforts to empower Black Americans through education.

The life and work of figures such as Hallie Quinn Brown bring into powerful view how Black colleges and universities provided a key political lever for Black citizens—and Black women in particular—to drive important change in American democratic institutions. Shortly after graduation from Wilberforce University (formerly named Ohio African University, established in 1856), Brown joined the thousands of northern missionaries going South to teach Black children and adults, moving to Mississippi and South Carolina.[69] In 1885, she became dean of South Carolina's Allen University, which was affiliated with the AME Church; she then taught for four years in public schools in Dayton, Ohio, before joining Booker T. Washington at the Tuskegee Institute in Alabama where she served as the dean of women. Finally, she returned to Wilberforce in 1893 where she served for a decade as a professor of elocution while also lecturing and engaging in political and civic work.[70]

The elocution and public speaking training that Brown received at Wilberforce helped her become a celebrated and influential figure in both the United States and Europe. Critics described her as "magnetic," "eloquent," and "unquestioningly brilliant."[71] She used her fame to fight for causes like women's rights, education, desegregation, temperance, and antilynching. She went places that few American women—let alone Black American women—had gone before. In 1899, she represented the United States at the International Congress of Women in London; she lectured before Britain's Queen Victoria on multiple occasions and was even invited to join the queen for tea one summer; and she was named a member of the Royal Geographical Society in Edinburgh. Brown was also a pioneer in the movement to establish Black women's clubs in the United States. From 1905 to 1912, she served as president of the Ohio State Federation of Colored Women's Clubs; and in 1920 she began a four-year term of service as president of the National Association of Colored Women.[72]

In 1923, she penned a fiery essay to protest efforts by the Daughters of the Confederacy to erect a statue commemorating the southern "Black Mammy" at the US Capitol. "If they wish to slave their conscience and make amends for the wrongs heaped upon the black mammy," she wrote, "let them begin to change the conditions in this fair Southland. Let them see that adequate wage—living wage—is given the laborer on the farm and in the home. Let them see that decent accommodations are provided for the negro traveler. . . . Let them visit the shacks they call schools in the rural districts, where little black children, half-fed, half-clad play a farce game of going to school and trying to learn."[73]

Education was a central focus of Brown's leadership in the NACW. In a letter to the members of the national organization in 1926, she launched a campaign to raise $50,000 to support a new scholarship fund, writing,

One of the most promising auguries for the future prosperity and harmony of this country is the establishment of the various institutions—such as Oberlin, Howard, Fiske, Wilberforce and others for the advancement of higher education and the diffusion of useful knowledge, the knowledge which is derived from instruction and education. . . .

The women of our group are in no way inferior to those of other races. Although deprived, as a whole, of the blessed boon of liberty and education; humiliated and ostracized, she suffers not by comparison with the most highly favored of the land. No organization is better fitted to carry on a great educational movement than the National Association of Colored Women. We believe in education and we intend to support it. There must be an awakened sense of responsibility. The public should know the significance of education. Therefore, as your president, I send forth this program with the assurance that our earnest, staunch women will support this cause for the sake of themselves and their daughters, the future womanhood of the race.[74]

Just two years before, Hallie Quinn Brown had participated in the Republican Party convention in Cleveland, Ohio, where she spoke on behalf of civil rights and in support of Warren G. Harding's campaign for president. She also held the distinction of being one of the first women to speak on his front porch campaign. In 1926, she published *Homespun Heroines and Other Women of Distinction*, an edited volume showcasing the valiant strides and valuable contributions that Black women have made to American history. Finally, Brown used her influence and talents as a lecturer to raise funds for both Wilberforce and the effort to preserve Frederick Douglass's home in Washington, DC.[75]

Hattie Quinn Brown was a trailblazer whose extraordinary contributions to American civic and political life made her a pioneer. Yet, at its core, her story is not unique. Like hundreds of thousands of Black Americans who were empowered by the education that they received at Black colleges, Brown drew upon the knowledge and skills, confidence, and community-mindedness that she cultivated at Wilberforce University to help drive profound political change in the United States. Her story, like those discussed in subsequent chapters, illustrates the legacy of Black colleges and the significance of federal higher education policy interventions like the Morrill Land-Grant Acts, which helped set the stage for Black colleges—and their faculty, staff, students, and alumni—to influence the democratic landscape in remarkable ways.

The Power of Black Education

The education of Black people in the British colonies and subsequently in the United States has always been a political matter. In a nation built on the cheap or entirely uncompensated labor and un(der)acknowledged sacrifices of Black people, from as far back as the seventeenth century, efforts to generate and sustain tight control over Black energy, output, and personhood have been part and parcel of the nation's institutional foundation.

The effort to prevent the education of Black Americans is a powerful example of this. As Christopher Span and Brenda N. Sanya note, the education of enslaved people "was a direct challenge to the societies and people that sanctioned African enslavement and persecution and systematically denied them the right to learn and attend school and become full-fledged citizens."[76] Years of mass complicity in sustaining slavery in the United States relied on the careful cultivation of Black hardship and the proliferation of racist ideas intended to justify the brutal enslavement of human beings. White academics participated in the creation and maintenance of this system of oppression by using supposed science to bolster ideas of Black inferiority and sub-humanity. These ideas were used to justify a system where supposed Black fecklessness and incompetence required the denial of their freedom and self-determination. Thus, the notion of Black intelligence was an important battleground in the struggle between efforts to oppress Black people and the movement toward Black liberation.

Although today figures like Hattie Quinn Brown, Rosa Parks, the Reverend Dr. Martin Luther King Jr., and so many others call to mind the central role that HBCUs have played in cultivating Black leaders and promoting the civic and political inclusion of Black Americans, it is easy to forget the deeply engrained and centuries-long structural oppression of Black people in the United States that made the emergence of these institutions highly unlikely. The violence, racist oppression, and contentious political discourse surrounding efforts to promote Black advancement, including the creation of Common Schools and land-grant colleges, underscores the formidable barriers that Black Americans faced in their efforts to transform the democratic landscape.

In the face of sharp efforts to suppress Black education and Black civil rights during the nineteenth century, the establishment of Cheyney

University in 1837 was more than the provision of educational opportunity for Black people; it was a political act—as was the creation of every Black college thereafter—because Black colleges represented a set of institutions that were dedicated to the life of the Black mind and to cultivating, celebrating, and perpetuating Black excellence. They actively undermined efforts to cast Black people as unqualified for the rights and responsibilities of democratic citizenship. Moreover, they worked to develop Black citizens who were both inclined and well equipped to assume leadership positions in their families, in their communities, and in public life.

As new Black colleges emerged around the turn of the century, a central question facing Black Americans was what education should look like. A primary debate centered on whether to focus on vocational/industrial curriculum or to emphasize a classical liberal arts education. The former, which was prescribed by thinkers like Booker T. Washington, emphasized imparting knowledge and skills for agricultural and mechanical work and training students to work in trades. The latter, on the other hand, was most closely associated with advocates like W. E. B. Du Bois, who supported education in the liberal arts, which they viewed as a critical prerequisite for wielding the civic and political power necessary for true freedom and racial uplift. As Christopher Span and Brenda Sanya note in describing this perspective, students trained in the liberal arts

> would emerge with the knowledge, skills, and confidence necessary to challenge a nation that firmly believed African Americans to be genetically and culturally inferior to whites, that regarded them as second-class citizens undeserving of such constitutional protected liberties as the right to vote and equal protections and treatment under the law, and that established laws and cultural practices that segregated and disparaged African Americans in all aspects of public life.[77]

A liberal arts education had the capacity to cultivate advanced leadership skills in Black citizens and to prepare them for the demands of public service. Arguments for an educational philosophy that would cultivate leadership and political skills for Black Americans were supported by the impact that Black Americans were already having as they engaged in civic and political activities during the nineteenth century. For example, starting in the 1830s, African American leaders in the various states participated in "colored conventions" where they organized to discuss the most challenging problems facing Black people, including slavery and emancipation, voting rights, lynching, and economic opportunity.

In the wake of the Civil War and during the twelve years of Reconstruction, the federal government intervened to ensure that southern states complied with the newly ratified Thirteenth, Fourteenth, and Fifteenth amendments to the Constitution, which respectively abolished slavery, conferred the rights of citizenship to those born in the United States, and ensured the right to vote for Black citizens. During this time, which lasted from 1865 to 1877, Black Americans enjoyed an unprecedented level of political influence.[78]

For Black Americans who answered the call to public service after the Civil War, previous experience as ministers and teachers provided a dominant pathway to politics. By one estimate, approximately seventy Black state legislators during Reconstruction were teachers by profession.[79] Indeed, Black citizens took active roles in their local communities through churches and other civic organizations, and they were elected and appointed to a range of government bodies including city councils, state legislatures, and the U.S. House of Representatives and Senate.[80] As Millington Bergeson-Lockwood notes, Black citizens "understood citizenship to be worthless without the ability to assert political power and, through electoral organizing, made claims on the power of the political party system."[81] The creation of Black colleges at this time and the incorporation of a liberal arts curriculum built on these traditions of Black leadership.

As Black Americans took an active role in politics, the quest to attract Black votes made politicians and political parties more attuned than ever before to Black interests, a shift that intersected with the rise of Black colleges.[82] In addition to the impact that the Reconstruction Amendments had on boldly articulating and affirming Black citizenship, the service of Black soldiers during the Civil War was also regarded as powerful justification for Black Americans' claims to full and equal participation and protection in civic and political life.[83]

Education was a top priority for Black citizens during this period, and Black lawmakers actively advocated for federal, state, and local efforts that would expand educational opportunities for African Americans. For example, at an 1889 convention in Illinois, participants argued in support of school desegregation, enhanced teacher quality, and greater educational and workplace opportunities for Black people.[84]

The emergence of HBCUs had a powerful impact on Black political power during the nineteenth century as their alumni moved into elected and appointed offices during Reconstruction.[85] As Kimberley Johnson notes, "for many African American leaders who had been stripped of political power during the long ascendancy of the Jim Crow order, [Black colleges] provided an important organizational and intellectual base to retreat to and regroup."[86] Government action during these decades, despite failing Black Americans in so many ways, was a key factor in the emergence of Black colleges, and the history of Black college creation and development illustrates how public policy can generate changes in the political landscape.

As they emerged during the nineteenth century, Black colleges worked to bridge the gaps created by a racist policy regime, and they did so in a political context that teemed with efforts to marginalize Black people. They offered critical educational opportunities for Black Americans in ways that would help reshape the political landscape, create new generations of Black leaders, fight harmful stereotypes about Black people, and invest in Black excellence.

2

Setting a Foundation for Change

The Political Mission of Black Colleges (1870s–1964)

BEFORE 1965, BLACK COLLEGES WERE widely viewed not as a connected set of higher educational institutions but as separate, individual schools existing within the broad landscape of American colleges and universities. The Higher Education Act (HEA) that President Lyndon B. Johnson signed into law that year helped to shape our appreciation of Black colleges as a united set of institutions and a clearly defined target of public policy. The landmark legislation also established the term "HBCU" as a politically powerful category and symbol of Black higher education. Title III of the HEA provided federal funds to HBCUs, specifically supporting the work of postsecondary institutions founded prior to 1964 with the purpose of educating African Americans. By historicizing Black colleges and emphasizing their shared mission of promoting Black advancement through education, the HEA has played an important role in shaping how we think of Black colleges and their relationship with government.

The HEA, with its new federal support for and formal definition of Black colleges, emerged at a political moment characterized by social unrest, youth political activism, and demands for Black civil rights. This was not the first time that Black colleges' relationship with government and the political landscape was on sharp display. As this chapter will show, politics and policy have contributed to the development of Black colleges since their beginnings in the eighteenth century. Indeed, the work that HBCUs have done to promote equal opportunity and racial uplift through education has been directly related to—and immensely consequential to—policy decisions and the nation's political landscape.

Among educational institutions, HBCUs are distinctive because an inherently political mission of empowering African Americans has been central to their development from the very beginning. Since the nineteenth century, these organizations have supported educational, social, political, and cultural advancement for citizens who were often excluded from mainstream institutions and relegated to the margins of society.[1] Scholars have even described HBCUs as representing a "social contract" between Black Americans and the state—promoting full citizenship by way of opportunity, as a way of correcting for the historical injustices and disparities wrought by slavery and segregation.[2] For some, HBCUs represent the nearest thing to reparations provided in the wake of slavery.[3]

Furthermore, Black colleges exhibited a keen awareness of the political environment as they engaged in efforts to empower Black Americans in ways that could disrupt the racial dynamics of the nation's power structure. During the nineteenth century, this awareness was apparent in how university founders and leaders articulated their missions, in the mottos they embraced, in whom they recruited to serve as their leaders and faculty, in their approach to educating their students, and in their posture toward the community and the broader political landscape.

HBCUs have a long tradition of acting as a center for African American political activity.[4] Black communities in states across the growing republic came together and organized with the purpose of raising the substantial funds necessary to establish a university that could offer members of their race a high-quality liberal arts education. As these communities struggled to stay afloat with limited financial resources, many prioritized supporting Black colleges, making sacrifices that were seen as crucial to achieving freedom and racial advancement. Black colleges were actively engaged in raising support, often thinking outside of the box when working to secure financial stability. For example, in 1871 the Fisk Jubilee Singers, a prestigious choral ensemble consisting of Fisk University students, began traveling the United States and Europe giving concerts to raise funds to support their university.[5] Early Black college alumni hosted bazaars and fairs across the country to raise money for their beloved campuses.

Black college faculty and administrators were major players in the political landscape during the nineteenth century. Black faculty occupied a prominent role as thought leaders who helped to shape a new discourse on race, equality, and citizenship in the United States. Black colleges produced, supported, and sustained many of the Black intellectuals who have shaped the nation's thinking on critical issues like race, equity, citizenship, and democracy.[6] They provided institutional bases for intellectuals at the vanguard of the US civil rights movement as they fought for full citizenship for African Americans and the dismantling of legal racial apartheid in the United States. As their faculty and students fought for racial justice, HBCUs stood at the forefront of important battles over academic freedom and intellectual activism. Black faculty members and administrators were also powerful advocates for their universities and other issues critical to Black people. It comes as little surprise that Black college leaders and faculty members were often seen as strong candidates for political leadership during the Reconstruction era.

This chapter considers three of the earliest Black colleges—the Institute for Colored Youth (later named Cheyney University), Wilberforce University, and Howard University—to show in more detail how, despite formidable resistance to Black education, the earliest Black colleges helped establish a tradition of educational excellence and political impact that other HBCUs would build upon in the decades to come.

Building an Army of Teachers: The Institute for Colored Youth/Cheyney University

The creation of Cheyney University—the nation's first Black college—in 1837 was a direct response to the oppressive political and policy landscape that sustained slavery and the marginalization of African Americans in the United States. Originally called the African Institute, it became known as the Institute for Colored Youth in 1842 and finally became Cheyney University of Pennsylvania in the early 1880s. Its founder, Philadelphia philanthropist Richard Humphreys, who was a member of the Religious Society of Friends (also known as Quakers), hailed from the British West Indies where his family owned slaves and earned its fortune through coffee and sugar plantations.[7]

In 1764, Humphreys moved to Philadelphia where he lived and worked for more than seventy-five years as a silversmith and merchant of china and crockery. Over that time, he noticed the web of forces that oppressed Black people and resulted in chronic economic hardship.[8] Despite the fact that the idea of educating African Americans was "very unpopular," as the *American Journal of Education* noted during the late nineteenth century,

Humphreys decided to contribute to educational structures that could help remove these barriers and promote economic opportunity among Philadelphia's growing Black population.[9] Upon his death in 1832, he left $10,000—a full tenth of his estate—for the purpose of establishing "[a] benevolent society or institution . . . having for its object the benevolent design of instructing the descendants of the African race in school learning, the various branches of the mechanic arts and trades, and in agriculture, in order to prepare and fit and qualify them to act as teachers in such of those branches of useful business as in the judgment of the said society they may appear best qualified for."[10] In the trust that he established to support the school, he institutionalized a board of thirteen members of the Religious Society of Friends who would ensure that the funds were used for this purpose.

The Institute for Colored Youth taught its first seven students on a 133-acre farm located in Bristol Township, a rural part of Philadelphia county. Over the following year, members of the board raised additional funds for the institution, and in 1842 it received a charter from Pennsylvania.[11] The earliest days of the Institute for Colored Youth were not without challenges. Perhaps the most noteworthy was students' frustration with a policy requiring that they spend four hours each school day doing manual labor, compared to three and a half hours doing academic coursework. This arrangement, which essentially rendered them indentured servants, invited defiance, with some students running away and one even setting the barn on fire.[12]

In 1848, the Institute moved to a more urban location on Philadelphia's Lombard Street, where it became an evening school for apprentices and then a trailblazing high school offering unprecedented educational opportunity to Black students.[13] By 1852, it had a total of thirty-one students—fifteen men and boys and sixteen women and girls. Its building housed a preparatory program and a high school program, each with separate departments for male and female students. The preparatory program worked to address any gaps in primary (the equivalent of elementary school) education and to prepare students to take the examination for advancing to the high school. The high school curriculum was organized into introductory, junior, and senior classes, each involving eighteen months of study, and training included coursework in English, mathematics, history, and classics.[14] The program was particularly focused on preparing men and women to be teachers.[15] The institute was noted for its all-Black faculty, its free tuition and textbook access, and its publicly accessible library, which was added in 1852.[16] With its reading room and collection of approximately 1,300 books, the library was considered a jewel of both the institute and the community.[17]

The Institute for Colored Youth was devoted to empowering its students and the broader Black community by offering unprecedented educational and intellectual opportunities. It brought Black guest speakers like Frederick Douglass, William Catto, and John B. Reeve, who delivered public lectures open to campus, alumni, and broader community audiences on subjects like the state of Black people in the United States, how Black Americans should think about—and engage with—the then-ongoing Civil War, and the significance of education in society.[18] The institute also had a debating society that invited prominent guests to deliver lectures on the topic of race, including talks titled "The Negro and His Condition" and "What Is Most Helpful to the Negro Race, Money for Education?"[19]

The work of providing high-quality educational opportunity for Black students—children and adults—was inherently political, and like other institutions devoted to the education of African Americans, the Institute for Colored Youth worked to counter notions of Black intellectual inferiority that had been cultivated to justify slavery and racial oppression and to undo generations of forced ignorance. In 1853, the Pennsylvania Society for promoting the Abolition of Slavery commissioned Benjamin C. Bacon to generate a report on the status of education for African Americans in the state, and he took particular note of the effort that Black citizens exerted to overcome illiteracy. He wrote several memos to this effect:

> "The wife Sarah has learned to read tolerably well since she was 40 years old—never received any instruction worth mentioning."

> "Pretty good scholar—went to school only two months—slave-born."

> "Though a slave for 50 years, she began, when about 65 years of age, to attend Sunday school, with crutch and staff, (being very lame,) and got so as to read tolerably well in the bible—is now 80, and goes to Sunday school and Church, when able."[20]

Black Americans' faith in education as a mechanism for improving their life chances was well founded. As the *American Journal of Education* noted in the late nineteenth century, education permitted Black Philadelphians to progress "more and more from the condition of mere day laborers into that of skillful and industrious artisans and tradesmen."[21]

Given the central role that intellectual deprivation played in efforts to degrade African Americans and to limit their access to power, teachers were, without question, important political actors during the nineteenth century. The teachers at the Institute for Colored Youth were at the vanguard of this powerful social impact. By working to empower Black people through education, the faculty and alumni of early Black colleges like the Institute for Colored Youth, Wilberforce University, and Howard University disrupted society's dominant, heavily racialized power structure. Moreover, Black educators served as powerful symbols of Black excellence, embodying not only the ability of Black people to become accomplished thinkers and learners but also their potential to spread knowledge and skills broadly among their students.

Inevitably, these pioneering Black teachers faced constant condescension and controversy over whether they were suited to teach Black students. This comes as little surprise when we consider the implications of their existence for the racial power structure in the United States. Despite the threats they faced, Black teachers and advocates pushed back hard against it. For example, Caroline LeCount—an 1863 graduate of the Institute for Colored Youth who went on to teach in Ohio, Kentucky, and Pennsylvania—advocated for job opportunities for Black teachers, disputing notions that Black teachers were unsuited to teach Black students.[22]

This questioning of the suitability of Black teachers ultimately highlights the impact that an influx of African American educators had for increasing competition within the previously all-White teaching profession. The Institute for Black Youth's pioneering work hiring and training Black teachers at a time when teachers working in government-funded public schools were predominantly White was a direct political claim—one that, in its commitment to the education and empowerment of Black citizens in the United States, has reverberated for centuries.[23]

Moreover, in a society where the racial order relied on views of Black inferiority and White superiority, the cultivation and deployment of a cadre of Black teachers who could bring examples of the intellectual capacity and achievements of Black Americans to communities across the nation—and to people who might not have fathomed its existence—could be revolutionary. As a report from *The American Freedman*, a publication of the Freedmen and Union Commission, noted, the Institute for Colored

Youth "furnished ocular proof to thousands of skeptical whites of the capacity and educational susceptibility of the colored people."[24] The Institute was intentional in its efforts to showcase Black excellence. For example, each spring it held public examinations for their students. According to *The American Freedman*, these displays "elicited strong expressions of admiration even from prejudiced opponents."[25]

The Institute for Colored Youth's impact spread as its students began to graduate, many of whom also began to teach, thus furthering the school's impact beyond the campus and among subsequent generations. In 1865, twenty-eight years after its founding, more than half of those who had graduated from the Institute for Colored Youth were working as teachers.[26] By 1880, that proportion had increased to 70 percent.[27] By specializing in the production of Black teachers, the Institute for Colored Youth played a crucial role in preparing men and women who would operate on the frontlines of the post–Civil War fight for democracy. Its teachers and graduates would help pave the broader path to Black empowerment, working to educate Black people, waging war against their oppression in classrooms throughout the North and the South, and providing a new professional opportunity that belied stereotypes of Black people as simpleminded, feckless, and lazy.

The movement of Black men and women into the teaching profession also marked an important shift in the range of vocational options available to them as well as activation of new opportunities for competition between Black and White people in the labor force. In 1862, for example, John Quincy Allen, an alumnus of the Institute for Colored Youth and a pioneer among the city's Black educators, was selected as one of Philadelphia's public school teachers, breaking the color barrier for public school teachers in the city while besting a pool consisting of thirty White candidates. His selection confirmed that high-quality educational opportunities could position Black professionals to be highly competitive in the job market while also empowering Black Americans to move into areas of American life that had previously been off-limits.[28] Given the redistribution of power that education—and by delivering it, teachers—could generate, it comes as little surprise that efforts to extend education to newly freed Black citizens were met with disdain and, in many cases, violence in the form of Ku Klux Klan attacks, teacher kidnappings, and the burning of schoolhouses.[29]

Black educators also took on a new prominence as members of the political landscape. Professor Edward A. Bouchet, one of the first African

American graduates of Yale University who was a faculty member at the Institute for Colored Youth for twenty-six years, was featured alongside other prominent Black Philadelphians in a newspaper article conveying their thoughts on what the election of Democrat Grover Cleveland as president of the United States meant for Black Americans. In the feature, he expressed the view that Cleveland's election could be a failure to Black people and that, if it was, the Republican Party would be "in some degree responsible." But, he offered a hint of optimism, adding that if Cleveland did end up failing Black Americans, it could potentially push the Republican Party to "arouse from its state of semi-indifference and demonstrate its worth again as of old."[30] Indeed, Black educators became leaders within the community and were sought-after lecturers whose thoughts on a range of social and political issues helped to shape the contemporaneous political discourse.[31]

Some also rotated in and out of public service and political roles. For example, Institute for Colored Youth principal Ebenezer D. Bassett went on to become the first African American diplomat, serving as minister to Haiti.[32] Other figures like Fanny M. Jackson-Coppin—a woman who had been born into slavery and who, after taking over in 1869 became the nation's first female African American principal, would lead the school for more than three decades—were esteemed members of the African American community who were recognized for their intellectual contributions to the elevation of the race.

Jackson-Coppin led a movement to raise funds for an industrial school for Black students, bringing the Institute for Colored Youth's students into the work of fundraising for the worthy cause.[33] In June 1885, at a community meeting on the educational interests of African Americans hosted at Philadelphia's Twelfth Street meeting house, she was a featured speaker and advocated for the development of teachers who would help spread education to Black people in the South. She also emphasized the importance of providing more industrial educational opportunities for students in the North where racial discrimination was a formidable barrier to opportunity for Black people in the region. *The Christian Recorder* relayed her thoughts, saying,

> In the Southern States, during the days of slavery, the degradation attaching to all kinds of work led to colored people becoming artisans, and having indeed, most of the skilled manual labor in handicrafts left

to them. But it is not so in the North. Here it is impossible for colored young men to become apprentices to learn blacksmithing, carpenter work, or that of any similar vocation. Hence when they grow up, however well taught in the learning of the schools, those not adapted to teaching are in danger of enforced idleness. No one can guarantee the future of any who are so circumstanced.[34]

Jackson-Coppin would go on to become one of the most influential African American educators and educational advocates of her time. This prominence is particularly noteworthy because it points to the significance of the teaching profession and early Black educational institutions like the Institute for Colored Youth for providing a pathway to influence for both Black women and men during the nineteenth century.

As the first institution dedicated to the advanced education of Black students in the United States, the Institute for Colored Youth played a key role in setting many precedents for Black education and for demonstrating the efficacy of Black education generally and to federal and state lawmakers, in particular. Although the institute's work would blaze a path for the eventual federal support of new Black colleges in the second half of the nineteenth century, the federal government's involvement with the Institute for Colored Youth was noticeably thin. As J. Henry Bartlett noted in articles for the Quaker publication *The Friend*, "That nearly forty years of freedom should have passed without any adequate arrangement for training Negro teachers is surely a reproach for our country." He went on to note the contrast with the US government's efforts to help produce teachers elsewhere:

The first effort in making Cuba fit for freedom was to bring a very large number of her teachers at no expense to themselves for special training at Harvard University. This first effort has been followed by others both for Cuba and the Philippines, but if one were to agitate a like movement for Colored teachers, he would likely himself be relegated to a "Jim Crow car!"[35]

At the start of the new century, the Institute for Colored Youth had a closer relationship with state policymakers and continued to lean into its work of developing teachers. In 1904, the Institute for Colored Youth moved to Cheyney, Pennsylvania and became the state's newest teachers college. Each year, the Commonwealth of Pennsylvania contributed $25 per student to the college, raising the amount to $200 per student in 1911, and continuing to increase the amount in subsequent years.[36] In 1919, Pennsylvania elected William C. Sproul as governor. A Quaker and an advocate for education, Sproul helped to increase the state government's support for the school, leading to its designation as one of fourteen state normal schools specializing in teacher education. From 1951 through the early 1960s, the institution was known as Cheyney State Teachers College and then, from 1960 on, Cheyney State College. By 1962, the school's enrollment had reached more than 850 students, both Black and White.[37]

The close interconnection between educational opportunity and politics that characterized the founding and development of the Institute for Colored Youth—the first Black college—set a precedent that would endure as additional colleges for African Americans appeared on the educational landscape. Moreover, as frontline activists, Black teachers spearheaded efforts to expand Black Americans' access to the knowledge and skills that would not only enable them to seek gainful employment and economic opportunity but also equip them to lean into their roles as democratic citizens.

A Monument for Black Freedom, Equality of Mind, and Intellectual Power: Wilberforce University

The few institutions of higher learning that existed for Black students in the decades leading up to the Civil War faced extreme resistance and modest public financial support. But through acts of extraordinary courage and dedication, Black leaders and activists continued to build new colleges for Black Americans, and their eventual success in these efforts helped lay the foundation for the long-term impact that HBCUs would, as this book discusses, have on American democracy in the century ahead.

One of the three Black colleges established before the Civil War whose impact is today widely celebrated was Wilberforce University. Wilberforce was founded in Xenia, Ohio, in 1855 by the Conference of the Methodist Episcopal Church of Cincinnati, Ohio. Named for the English abolitionist William Wilberforce who helped to abolish the slave trade in the British empire, many viewed Wilberforce as "the colored people's University," noting its emphasis on self-sufficiency, service, and the responsibility of each person to contribute to the betterment of society.[38]

By all accounts, Wilberforce's campus was a place of pride, noted for its beauty and described as a property that had been "previously fitted up as a fashionable watering place, at a cost of some $50,000. This property consisted of 52 acres of land, in a beautiful and healthy region, upon which there had been erected a large edifice with numerous rooms, well adapted to the purposes of a collegiate institution."[39] After the strain of the Civil War forced the conference to suspend the university's activities in the summer of 1862, the African Methodist Episcopal (AME) Church under the leadership of Rev. Dr. Daniel A. Payne purchased the university for $10,000 in March 1863.[40] Wilberforce was the first college to be owned and operated by Black Americans and, along with Pennsylvania's Lincoln University, it was one of the first institutions to offer Black students post-secondary training and bachelor's degrees.

Embracing the motto *suo marte*—by one's own toil, effort, and courage—Wilberforce specialized in the development of leaders who would help to reshape society. Before the Emancipation, it was a stop on the Underground Railroad and known for educating students who went on to work as abolitionists, taking an active role in working to dismantle slavery.

It was at Wilberforce that Hallie Quinn Brown found her voice—a voice that would make her a powerful force in the fight for racial uplift and, in particular, the rights of African American women. During college, Hallie gained formal training in elocution and the art of expression, and she would use these skills throughout her illustrious career as an educator, missionary, activist, and renowned public speaker. When Hallie graduated from Wilberforce with a bachelor's degree in 1873, she became one of the first Black women to earn a college degree in the United States. She also put her speech training to work as the salutatorian of her class, delivering a speech titled "Be Careful How You Make History."[41]

Among the students educated at Wilberforce were the mixed-race children of numerous southern planters. The university also attracted the attention of powerful political figures, such as US senator from Texas and former Texas Supreme Court justice John Hemphill, who brought his mixed-race daughters, Theodora and Henrietta, to Wilberforce in the fall of 1859.[42] As W. S. Bailey, the editor of the African American newspaper *The Free South*, wrote when traveling through Ohio in 1858:

At the Wilberforce University, a beautiful place, situated about three miles northeast of Xenia, Ohio, are about one hundred pupils, mainly the children of Southern slaveholders. It is somewhat strange to see that slaveholders are in the main anxious to extend Slavery over free territory, and yet are glad to send their children into free States to be educated. (To save them this trouble, they should pass a law for all the children of slaveholders to have free access to the public or private schools in the Southern States.). The children, however, are not to blame for their condition, and we are proud to see the sweeping progress they are making in learning under the superintendence of Professor [and University President] R.S. Rust, a most amiable, gentleman, of Manchester, NH. May his philanthropy and devotion to the equality of mind receive the approbation of co-operation of all good people.[43]

Wilberforce persevered through institutional and national crises. The onset of the Civil War shook the nation and challenged even the most robust institutions. Black Union soldiers played an important role in protecting Ohio from Confederate soldiers, and they were especially interested in Wilberforce's safety. In October 1863, J. H. Welch, a Black soldier from the 55th Massachusetts Regiment, wrote to the *Christian Recorder* remarking on his interest in the paper's coverage of wartime happenings at the University and concern that the University might be destroyed, "I rejoice that the white man has not had much of a hand in the matter. Thank God for that. They have been working hard to obtain that fine place; but they had their largest guns elevated too high; consequently missed the University."[44]

Wilberforce's president, Rev. Dr. Richard S. Rust, fought to keep the university open despite the challenges of war. As the *Christian Recorder* noted just two months into the Civil War, "the present national conflict came near crushing the enterprise" of educating the young men and women at Wilberforce but credited President Rust for maintaining operations. It went on to assert that "the cause of humanity, the elevation of the colored man, the best interests of our race call on us to rally around our University in the present crisis and by our prayers, our sympathies, our efforts to place it on a permanent foundation so that in the future it may be a source of moral and intellectual power, while from its halls shall go forth those who shall be pioneers in the great work of emancipation, and educators of the rising generation."[45]

Historical evidence suggests that Black colleges like Wilberforce University were viewed as providing valuable service to the Black community, and their success was as a matter of shared interest for African

Americans. By the fall of 1863, university leaders and advocates focused squarely on securing Wilberforce's long-term stability by actively recruiting young men and women to attend the school and working to ensure the University's financial stability. University leaders and advocates prioritized repaying the University's $8,000 debt, viewing it as the most important first step to ensuring Wilberforce's long-term sustainability and impact.

Black newspapers broadcasted appeals for support across the nation, homing in not just on the value of supporting education in the abstract, but on the political significance of such support in the face of the history of the enslavement and racial oppression of African Americans in the United States. As a writer for the *Christian Recorder* noted in 1863:

> Friends of Education, friends of the oppressed, it is to you we now appeal for aid. We make this appeal in behalf of your OWN SONS AND DAUGHTERS; in behalf of our oppressed race, and in behalf of generations yet unborn. For what purpose are our Colored Soldiers now marching in the field of battle? To purchase at the price of their own blood and lives, FREEDOM for our oppressed race; freedom for generations in far-off periods of the coming future. Now, shall we not unite with them for the consummation of this GREAT AND GLORIOUS WORK? Will we not labor, toil, and make sacrifices to educate, qualify, and prepare our children, and the oppressed, who are just stepping forth from the midnight darkness of Slavery, to enjoy Freedom in all its fulness, and to fill with honor and manliness, every position to which they may be called during life. Let the emphatic response from every direction be AY!
>
> Let it be recorded on the brightest page of American History that on the first Anniversary of Freedom's birth-day in the United States, we founded a GRAND UNIVERSITY, one from which living streams of light and knowledge shall continually flow, making glad the hearts of millions and in attestation of the fact, may the Institution stand as an everlasting monument.[46]

In late 1863, Wilberforce's new president, Bishop Daniel A. Payne, a pioneer in the AME church and one of the earliest Black college presidents in the United States, launched a fundraising campaign that attracted the support of a broad array of supporters throughout the Midwest and southern states. Different geographically anchored conferences within the

AME church pledged to raise thousands of dollars to support Wilberforce by hosting bazaars and festivals during the holiday season. In addition to appeals for financial contributions, leaders and supporters encouraged parents to send their children to the university as another way to support its work.[47]

By November 1864, the university's debt had been reduced to $5,000 and supporters continued their energetic appeals for funds. In a letter to the editor of *The Christian Recorder* on November 4, 1864, R. H. Cain of Brooklyn, New York, wrote a powerful appeal for support, underscoring the need for higher educational institutions that were committed to Black excellence in the liberal arts and all academic areas:

> We have felt that if one or two of our race need a liberal education through the *backdoor of some college*, and have been "dubbed" Doctor or Professor, and turned out to *wait on some literary society of whites, we were exalted thereby*. No, it is not enough. We must have an institution where we can have a *faculty of distinguished colored gentlemen*, teaching all the sciences, and elaborating systems, and theories of scientific investigation, producing something new, improving by research on old systems. We need a class of refined men and women, who will change the moral status of our people, we need educated daughters, that we may have educated wives and mothers, that our children may be taught, by the fireside, the great duties of life. Then we need this college, because there are thousands of our people who will now need it, who never could get it before. Then we will need it because there is so much prejudice in other institutions, that it is crucifixion to our children to send them to them, in consequence of the Negrophobia, which is rampant in nearly every institution of learning in this land.[48]

Broad commitment to Wilberforce's mission of fostering Black excellence inspired broad and steadfast support, and the university managed to successfully attract students and financial assistance through the Civil War period.

By the end of the war, Wilberforce was well on its way to paying its remaining debt and attracting students from across the country. Soon after the war came to a close in April 1865, however, tragedy struck. On April 9, less than a week after Confederate generals surrendered at Appomattox Court House—and also the same evening that President Abraham Lincoln was assassinated at Ford's Theater in Washington, DC—Wilberforce University burned to the ground. The university was insured for only $8,000, whereas the *New York Times* estimated that the fire resulted in $50,000 of damage.[49] While there has long been uncertainty whether the fire was a matter of arson or accident, Bishop Payne's communication to the Society for the Promotion of Collegiate and Theological Education at the West recalled "a day forever memorable in American history [when] incendiary hands set fire to our college edifice."[50]

The university would not close down, however, and efforts would soon be made to rebuild the campus buildings, underscoring the commitment among its community toward its work. As the university worked to rebuild after the fire, supporters were clear-eyed about the magnitude of the challenge but also about the necessity of fighting for equal educational opportunity for Black people during the postwar era. Members of the university's extended community, as well as Congress and the state legislature, contributed to the effort to rebuild after the fire.[51] As one member of the Wilberforce community wrote in April 1866:

If there ever was a time when an effort should be made to educate our children it is now. Our relation to this country has materially changed. God has brought us through the Red Sea, and we believe He will take us across Jordan into the land of *equal rights before the law*. We shall be called upon to fill offices of trust, profit and honor as fast as we are qualified for them. There is a bright future before us. Let us then make every effort in our power to make Wilberforce University, by God's sanction, a blessing to mankind.[52]

By the time of the fire, Wilberforce already had an impressive legacy, and many of the university's graduates were by then prominent civic, political, and educational leaders in the United States, actively shaping the country's racial dynamics of power and leadership. Yet some questioned whether the level of support the University received matched the magnitude of its significance to the work of Black advancement. They also pointed out the disparity between the support Wilberforce received and the amount of support allocated to other institutions. In a letter to *The Christian Recorder* in 1868, one writer asked whether support for Wilberforce would ever approach the same level that Princeton University enjoyed.[53]

Although it was hardly enough compared to the amount of loss, the federal government, via the Freedmen's Bureau, sent $3,000 to Wilberforce to help rebuild the university. The costs were clearly much more (as one supporter noted: "Without at all showing ingratitude for the 3,000 granted . . . Wilberforce ought to have received 10,000 instead of not a third that sum from the hands of the generous hero [General O. O. Howard], who dispensed the nation's gifts."[54])—nevertheless, the federal government's support for Wilberforce at the time of the fire highlights an important early example of the federal support for Black higher educational institutions and their democracy enhancing work.

At the time of the fire, there were only about a dozen other Black colleges, and in general, those institutions had been established and sustained through private resources. But the federal government's support for the rebuilding of Wilberforce University helped sustain its powerful work to empower Black Americans and set a precedent of government participation in efforts to support Black higher educational institutions.

Promoting Black Excellence in the Nation's Capital: Howard University

The story of Howard University offers perhaps the most powerful example of the way that the relationship between the federal government and Black colleges during the nineteenth and early twentieth centuries would help shape American democracy. Founded in Washington, DC, in 1867, Howard was situated on fifty acres of land in the nation's capital. The campus sat atop a range of hills that offered views of the city and the Potomac River and was conveniently located near the 7th Street railroad.[55] Howard was established as a private institution with the purpose of providing higher education without regard to race, sex, or color. It was also founded with a distinctly political purpose. As one writer recalled in an 1874 statement describing the university's roots:

> Situated in the Capital of the nation, Howard University is designed to put into practice those great principles of civil rights, of liberty, of equality and fraternity toward whose realization the nation is slowly struggling today. Its conductors are laboring to prove that civil rights are not a philanthropist's dream, beautiful in theory, but impossible in reality, but a real and practical good, capable of doing more than any one thing to elevate and purify the American people. Its objects and aim are

national, not sectional, and the good which it seeks to do, will not be limited by nationality, religious opinion, complexion, or sex.[56]

The New York Evening Post concurred, noting Howard's democratic purpose:

The great argument against conceding to [the African American citizen] the right to suffrage has been his ignorance. He must remove that objection, or he will be in constant danger of either being directly oppressed by laws which have a partial operation, or made the tool of cunning men, who have their own selfish ends to serve at his expense. The object of those who have established the Howard University is to give him an opportunity of fitting himself to sustain the part now assigned him in our political organization.[57]

From the first, the university was connected with the federal government. The university's location in the nation's capital, for example, made it necessary to secure a charter from the US Congress.[58] This represented a significant hurdle given the dynamics of the national political landscape at the time and President Andrew Johnson's frequent opposition to the efforts of Radical Republicans in Congress and their allies who worked to offer much-needed support to formerly enslaved Black Americans after the Civil War.[59] Nevertheless, the charter was successfully passed, and Howard University was established.

In addition to its founding charter, Howard University's graduates were often closely connected to the federal government. For example, each of the ten students in Howard's graduating law class in 1869 worked in jobs related to the government—specifically, as clerks in the Freedmen's Bureau and the Register of Deeds's Office, and as officers with the Capitol Police.[60] The University was named for Civil War hero General O. O. Howard, who was then leading the Freedmen's Bureau as its commissioner. Howard would serve in that role until 1874, and he would also serve as the president of Howard University from 1869 through 1874. The editor of *The Standard* commented on Howard's conviction in supporting the university, saying that he "sees the necessity of securing to the 'colored' race equal civil and political rights."[61] The president of the Board of Trustees was Rev. Dr. Charles B. Boynton, who was also the chaplain of the US House of Representatives.[62]

Many viewed Howard's success as part and parcel of the nation's responsibility for supporting Black people in the wake of slavery. In 1871, Senator Samuel C. Pomeroy contributed $10,000 to help establish a female professorship at the Howard University School of Medicine.[63] New York congressman Gerritt Smith donated $1,000 to Howard, noting in a letter that "I do not forget that Howard University needs money. . . . If we would save this guilty nation, we must educate the deeply wronged colored people. Heaven help Howard University, its students and teachers."[64]

Francis Louis Cardozo, secretary of state of South Carolina and the first African American to be elected to statewide office in the United States, resigned from his position in the South Carolina government to accept a professorship at Howard.[65] As Secretary Cardozo wrote in a report to the state's legislature in 1871: "I resigned my office on the 31st of October to accept a Professorship in Howard University. I did this under a profound conviction that I can be of more service in the great work of reconstruction in the South by occupying such a position, where I can prepare the rising generation, of my own race especially, for the honorable discharge of the important duties resting upon them as American citizens."[66]

Howard University was closely associated with the Freedmen's Bureau and its commissioner General O. O. Howard who was the University's third president. As Professor Silas Loomis, Howard University's dean of faculty, noted in an address marking the start of the Medical Department's second term in 1869, "[the Freedmen's Bureau] received the bitter opposition. And anathemas of all opposed to the progress of humanity thus carrying this institution into every political contest. All the acts of this branch of the Government have, therefore, been particularly subjected to the fiercest criticism that the most bitter, cruel, and malignant enemy could invent, and Howard University being the most prominent institution aided by the Bureau has received the fiercest attacks."[67]

Due to opposition from Southern states, the Freedmen's Bureau would close in 1872, only five years after beginning operation. Nevertheless, the Bureau's early support for Howard University was essential in building the school's foundation and setting up its longer-term impact. Despite the loss of funding after the closure of the Freedmen's Bureau, a combination of private funding and loans helped sustain the university between 1873 and 1878; and beginning in 1879, Howard received annual federal appropriations from Congress.[68]

This support helped Howard University to alter the democratic land-scape through its boldly egalitarian approach to higher education—an approach rooted in a firm commitment to investing in and empowering students while providing broad access to the benefits of first-rate educa-tion. A decade after its founding, Howard had fifty-seven students and seven faculty members and had grown to include a normal school and legal, medical, and theological departments.[69]

A solid commitment to gender egalitarianism was woven into the university's culture. In a powerful example of this posture, during an event launching a new academic term in the fall of 1869, Howard Medical Department professor Dr. Silas Loomis concluded his remarks by saying: "I close with a single remark to the ladies. All departments of the University are open to you, and we welcome you not only to the medical profession, but to any and every professional pursuit that you may choose to enter and compete for honorable distinction."[70]

The faculty and leadership of Howard Law School were keenly aware of the challenges that their students faced—and would continue to face—as they worked to promote justice for Black people. They paid direct atten-tion in their teaching to issues of race and democracy, and they consistently wove them into the school's curriculum and programming.

In a lecture to Howard's law students during the early 1870s, Professor A. G. Riddle offered a clear-eyed account of the stakes for the students' suc-cess: "Gentlemen, you cannot afford to fail, not any of you; and the failure of one is the failure of all in the wise world's judgement. You must not only equal the average of your white competitors; you must surpass them. The world has already decided that a colored man who is no better than a white man is nobody at all."[71] He went on to emphasize his students' contested birthright, noting that "I deem it of importance that you should under-stand that your right to bear your part in the government of our common country rests upon an older and better foundation than a mere statutory grant, and that the mere repeal of a law cannot divest you of the right; and that your present enjoyment of it is only the new exercise of a very old right."[72]

Similarly, in his February 1871 commencement address to Howard University Law School students titled "Duty of the Young Colored Lawyer," prominent US Senator Charles Sumner noted the unparalleled barriers facing emerging Black attorneys and the Black community. He entreated students "in the sacred cause of Justice" to be "faithful, constant, brave." He continued:

> No matter who is the offender—whether crime be attempted by political party, by Congress, or by President—wherever it shows itself, whether on the continent or on an island in the sea, you must be ready at all times to stand forth, careless of consequences and vindicate the Right. So doing, you will uphold your own race in its unexampled trials.[73]

In an 1878 speech at Howard, Frederick Douglass also commented on the challenges facing the Black community and the necessity of perseverance and hard work for achieving change, saying, "If one can't get up, he will be helped down. They have a fair chance to get up. They are on the way to Congress, and if the negro can stand Congress, Congress ought to stand the negro. The colored men have been forced up by abnormal conditions, but they are coming up gradually by their own exertions."[74]

Howard University administrators and faculty members were not only prominent in higher education, they were also prominent players in the political landscape. In 1872, Howard professors petitioned Congress to intervene to halt discrimination against Black medical professionals by the Medical Society of the District of Columbia.[75] John Mercer Langston, a legendary law professor and founding dean of the Howard Law School, was a noted advocate for civil, political, and educational rights for Black Americans. Langston had personal experience with discrimination and barriers limiting access to legal study.

After being denied admission to law school as a young man and discouraged from pursuing legal study by his friends who feared the toll that chronic discrimination would likely take on him, Langston studied law as an apprentice under an abolitionist attorney in Ohio and was admitted to the bar in Ohio. Prior to joining the faculty at Howard Law School as dean in 1868, he had worked as an abolitionist and then became one of the first Black Americans elected to political office in the United States after winning a race for town clerk in Ohio. Langston's colleagues described him as "one who had undergone many hardships, who had made many self-sacrifices for the benefit of his once down-trodden race, and at a time when it cost something to acknowledge or advocate the rights of the Negro."[76]

Professor Langston served as acting president of the University in 1872 and was widely considered as a contender for permanent appointment in the role. Of his work as acting president, Will Thomas wrote in the *Christian Recorder*: "As an early visit to Howard University brought us face to face with my old friend, Professor Langston, who is the acting President in the absence of General Howard, and it is pretty well understood that the several departments this fall will open under more favorable auspices than ever before. Mr. Langston is determined that neither expense nor pains shall be spared to render this school abreast of the most advanced wants of the educating community."[77] The editor at the *Christian Recorder* concurred, noting that "Professor Langston has inaugurated the strictest economy and the highest order of discipline in all its departments. He has brought the College out of an enormous debt, and put it at once in a position of independence with prospects of making it one among the first and wealthiest Institutions in the country."[78]

John Mercer Langston was also actively engaged in policymaking during his time as a faculty member and administrator at Howard Law School, helping to craft the Civil Rights Act that Charles Sumner successfully marshaled through Congress in 1875. After leaving his post at Howard, Langston began a new career in diplomatic service, serving as US minister to Haiti and then the Dominican Republic. He then moved to Virginia and accepted the Virginia state legislature's appointment as the first president of Virginia Normal and Collegiate Institute, a new Black college (which later became known as Virginia State University). Then, he became the first Black American to represent Virginia in Congress when he won election to the House of Representatives in 1890.

Growing recognition of Howard University's contributions to the advancement of Black people, its significance to the District of Columbia, and the efforts of university leaders who advocated for public support prompted Howard's movement toward greater financial stability during the late nineteenth century. In March 1879, Congress began making annual allocations of funds to Howard University, in the first year providing $10,000 from a general appropriations bill that could be used for "maintenance."[79] This direct congressional funding would continue on an annual basis into the twentieth century.

As higher education faced widespread hardship during the 1920s and 1930s, support from the federal government remained crucial for Howard's ability to continue providing transformative education to its students. Mordecai Johnson, Howard University's first African American president, lobbied Congress for funds to support institutional development and

succeeded in attaining valuable resources that enabled the university to expand student housing, add a library, and enhance classroom and research
spaces. In 1928, Congress passed the Cramton Bill, which provided federal funding to Howard University on an annual basis. Between 1930 and
1960, thanks in large part to President Johnson's advocacy on Capitol Hill,
Howard received more than $30 million from Congress.[80]

Federal support for Howard University, like the Black colleges and
universities that gained crucial support from the Morrill Land-Grant
Acts in the 1860s and 1890s, played an important role in the creation
and early development of the university. This early funding and the
broader interconnections between Howard faculty, administration, and
graduates brings into view how federal policy intersected with the extensive and expansive private efforts that Black educators, political leaders,
and philanthropists undertook to bring Howard University and other
forerunners of Black higher education into existence. Moreover, the close
and long-standing relationship between Howard University and the federal government illustrates how federal education policy intervention and
funding can help drive broader social and political change.

Unlike higher educational institutions that take an ivory tower approach to engaging with the world, retreating from the turbulence of politics, Black colleges have been closely associated with and engaged in the
political landscape from their inception. As the political development of
Cheyney University, Howard University, and Wilberforce University illustrate, HBCUs played an important role in helping to cultivate generations
of leaders who would help drive the fight for American democracy during
the late nineteenth and early twentieth centuries. For Black Americans in
the nineteenth century, the call to teach was as crucial as the call to take up
arms in the Civil War. Black faculty and college leaders played an important role on the political landscape and were actively engaged in efforts to
dismantle racial oppression. Indeed, in their very existence on the political
landscape, Black colleges and universities served as important monuments
to and symbols of black excellence—with all of the political implications
that doing so entailed.

3

Higher Education as a Movement
HBCUs and the Fight for Civil Rights

We [the students of Clarke, Morehouse, Morris Brown, and Spelman Colleges, Atlanta University, and the Interdenominational Theological Center] do not intend to wait placidly for those rights which are already legally and morally ours to be meted out to us one at a time. Today's youth will not sit by submissively, while being denied all of the rights, privileges, and joys of life. . . . We must say in all candor that we plan to use every legal and non-violent means at our disposal to secure full citizenship rights as members of this great Democracy of ours.

—Atlanta University Center Student Leaders,
"An Appeal for Human Rights," 1960[1]

DURING THE MID-TWENTIETH CENTURY, HBCUS were powerful players in the fight for civil rights. Their campuses offered intellectual fortresses for grappling with questions of race, equality, and justice, and they were hubs for strategizing how to dismantle the entrenched system of racial hierarchy that traditionally subjugated Black people in the United States.[2] Their faculty members were thought leaders who grappled with big questions regarding race, justice, and democratic citizenship, actively contesting centuries of received wisdom forged in an academy that historically excluded and marginalized Black thinkers and questioned the very notion of Black excellence. Pioneering Black scholars who were taught in and employed by HBCUs crafted the legal and political strategies that would help to reshape the bounds of citizenship and substantially alter the relationship between Black Americans and the government.

In addition to the role that Black colleges played in providing thought leadership that inspired and provided the foundation for the movement for Black freedom, they cultivated a generation of graduates who would serve as generals in the fight for civil rights. These leaders brought close familiarity—and in some cases, firsthand experience—with the horrors of slavery and racial oppression to their efforts to compel the nation to make good on its promise of equality and justice for all. Moreover, during the 1950s and 1960s, HBCU students were bold and energetic frontline participants in the movement for Black freedom whose courage and discipline were essential to the fight for legal and political change.[3] Their youthful idealism and impatience with the hypocrisy of pervasive racial discrimination despite the nation's purported egalitarian values translated into stalwart political organizing and intrepid defiance of the Jim Crow order.

The role that Black colleges played in the movement for Black freedom and the fight against racial segregation during the mid-twentieth century highlights the sustained role that Black colleges have played in promoting political change and fighting for an inclusive, multiracial democracy. Segregation policies had restricted generations of Black citizens, and as civil rights leaders launched a full-fledged social movement focused on dismantling them, HBCUs emerged as central hubs for the movement. Indeed, Black colleges were pivotal to the eventual dismantling of segregation—an impact that helped transform American education and the broader democratic landscape.

Given the prominence of education as a battleground where many civil rights battles were fought, it comes as little surprise that Black colleges, their faculty members, their students, and their alumni played a prominent role in the movement for Black civil rights. Many of them had close encounters with the tradition of racial discrimination that was tightly woven into the educational landscape in the United States, for example, as some southern states avoided desegregating their higher educational institutions by offering scholarships to Black students to attend out-of-state undergraduate, graduate, and professional programs. Such practices were the subject of multiple court cases that the NAACP Legal Defense Fund took on during those decades.[4] Similarly, Black leaders worked to address the unequal treatment of Black colleges and historically White colleges by state lawmakers who systematically funneled more funding and support to predominantly White institutions and limited support to traditionally Black schools.[5]

Racial segregation also shaped Black students' experiences with other landmark higher education programs, particularly those offering financial assistance to college students. The Servicemen's Readjustment Act of 1944 (popularly known as the "G.I. Bill"), for example, is heralded as having helped to make college and vocational training affordable for the generation of men who had served in World War II. Yet racial segregation in higher education and government failure to invest in HBCUs in the same way that it had invested in traditionally White colleges and universities restricted the extent to which Black veterans would be able to use their G.I. Bill benefits for educational programs.[6]

Before the passage of the 1964 Civil Rights Act, segregation played a powerful role in shaping Black Americans' educational choices; their experiences on campus and in the communities they called home; and their engagement in democratic citizenship. HBCUs offered Black Americans valuable educational opportunities that proved central for the nation's fight for democracy during the civil rights movement. Moreover, Black colleges served as institutional hubs for the Black students, faculty, and community members on the frontlines of the Black freedom movement of the mid-twentieth century, providing intellectual and geographical bases from which efforts leading to the Supreme Court's 1954 *Brown v. Board of Education* decision, the 1964 Civil Rights Act, and the 1965 Voting Rights Act would emerge. As this chapter discusses, Black colleges were central to the civil rights movement and helped to transform the educational and democratic landscape in the United States.

HBCUs and the Intellectual Foundation for the Civil Rights Movement

If Black churches were the heart and soul of the civil rights movement during the 1950s and 1960s, Black colleges were arguably its mind and body. Before 1964, approximately 90 percent of all Black college students in the United States attended HBCUs, which were uniquely suited to connecting scholars doing pioneering work on race and the Black experience with students and broader communities interested in fighting for social justice. Central to HBCUs' significance in the fight for democracy was their status as bastions of Black excellence, committed to the cultivation of knowledge and skills to equip their students for a life of independence, stability, and—most important—the ability to contribute to racial uplift. Those offering a liberal arts education were committed to scientific inquiry, the study of classics and the humanities, critical thinking, and fostering intellectual discourse with the dual goals of achieving greater understanding of the world and cultivating the development of future leaders.

The very notion of Black excellence was political, and the scholars who embodied it and worked to nurture it in their students recognized the importance of adding Black Americans' perspectives to the intellectual discourse on race. Black colleges educated and employed prominent Black intellectuals like Anna Julia Cooper, W. E. B. Du Bois, Alain Locke, Booker T. Washington, Ida B. Wells, and Carter G. Woodson, who defied stereotypes of Black inferiority to become recognized leaders in their fields. Their work as pioneers in the study of race, Black history, and Black political thought created the intellectual foundation upon which the movement for Black freedom would take shape. Black college faculty members tackled a range of complex issues, such as segregation and racial discrimination, race relations, and Black Americans' contributions to American culture.

Among the most prominent Black intellectuals during the late nineteenth and early twentieth centuries who helped set the terms of discourse on issues like race, citizenship, and Black education were W. E. B. Du Bois and Booker T. Washington. Du Bois had attended Fisk University and later taught at Wilberforce University and at Atlanta University, and he was a prominent sociologist, historian, and civil rights advocate. He was also the editor of the NAACP's quarterly journal, *The Crisis*. Washington was also an HBCU graduate, having attended Hampton Normal and Agricultural Institute (which later became Hampton University) and Wayland Seminary (which later became Virginia Union University), and he was the founder and first president of the Tuskegee Normal and Industrial Institute (which became Tuskegee University) in Alabama.

Washington and Du Bois offered differing views on how higher education could best promote racial uplift for Black Americans, and their contrasting perspectives were apparent in the multiple approaches embraced in early Black college curricula. While Du Bois was an outspoken advocate for a liberal arts approach to Black higher education, which he viewed as necessary to the development of leaders prepared for robust political participation and full civic engagement, Washington believed that progress for Black Americans would be best served by a focus on practical, industrial education and entrepreneurship. In 1895, Washington offered a clear articulation of his perspective in a speech to a multiracial audience at the Atlanta Cotton States and International Exposition world's fair:

> The wisest among my race understand that the agitation of questions of social equality is the extremest folly, and that progress in the enjoyment of all the privileges that will come to us must be the result of severe and constant struggle rather than of artificial forcing. No race that had anything to contribute to the markets of the world is long in any degree ostracized. It is important and right all privileges of the law be ours, but it is vastly more important that we be prepared for the exercises of these privileges. The opportunity to earn a dollar in a factory just now is worth infinitely more than the opportunity to spend a dollar in an opera house.[7]

As Washington expressed in what became known as his "Atlanta Compromise" speech, he believed that the quest for democratic citizenship for Black people was not as pressing as the need for economic opportunity. This need, his argument held, would be best served by institutions like Alabama's Tuskegee Institute, which focused on providing instruction in teaching and practical skills like farming and vocational trade work.

Du Bois fervently disagreed with the idea that democratic citizenship was less urgent than accessing economic opportunity for Black Americans, and he responded to Washington's assertions in a 1903 collection of essays titled *The Souls of Black Folk*. In it, he described Washington's views as reminiscent of "the old attitude of adjustment and submission" among Black people that he saw as out of step with the interests of Black citizens.[8] To the contrary, he viewed the fight for civil and political rights to be a top priority for Black people and considered a broad-ranging education to be crucial for racial uplift. From this perspective, providing Black people with rigorous advanced education in the form of liberal arts training was critical to the cultivation of Black leaders who would be essential to the project of racial progress.

Washington's and Du Bois's dramatically different visions of Black education shed light on the nature of policymakers' efforts related to Black colleges. Given the occupational limitations that structured Black economic opportunity during the late nineteenth and early twentieth centuries, Washington advocated an industrial approach to education that focused on instruction in trades and domestic skills that would prove economically useful.

For Black colleges like Booker T. Washington's alma mater, Hampton Normal and Agricultural Institute, instruction in trades like printing, farming, janitorial services, and painting was intended to provide students with the skills necessary to find economic stability while taking part in this rebuilding. As William L. Allen notes, "Hampton's industrial education curriculum was intended to be apolitical," as Samuel Chapman Armstrong, its white founder and a mentor to Booker T. Washington, "believed 'Blacks should abstain from politics and civil rights.' "[9] Washington's emphasis on industrial education as a pathway toward helping Black people to build economic stability for themselves and wealth for the rebuilding society resonated with members of the White elite, and he was able to raise considerable financial support for this type of education through public and private sources.[10] It was in this vein that policymakers devised a "separate but equal" system of Black higher education that did not threaten to disrupt the racial order of Black subjugation to Whites.[11]

Du Bois viewed the government's failure to ensure that Black Americans enjoyed equal access to liberal arts higher education as a concerted effort to inhibit Black Americans' ability to achieve true self-determination and advancement.[12] A major source of frustration for Du Bois was the realization that Washington's emphasis on industrial education and the support that it garnered for institutions like his Tuskegee Institute took resources away from colleges that would provide Black students with education in the liberal arts.[13]

While Du Bois and Washington grappled with the appropriate approach to Black advancement during the late nineteenth and early twentieth centuries, other thought leaders weighed in on how best to support and empower Black people, and HBCUs offered fertile intellectual environments for their pioneering scholarship. During this period, Black colleges supported prominent Black women scholars who offered early examples of intersectional analysis.[14] For example, Anna Julia Cooper—the first African American woman to earn a doctoral degree in the United States—asserted that the Black woman was "surely the greatest sufferer from the strain and stress attendant upon the economic conditions noted among our people."[15] The onetime Wilberforce College faculty member who would become known as the "Mother of Black Feminism" raised important questions about the rights of Black women who had long been relegated to the margins of economic, social, and political life in the United States.

Cooper's contemporary and fellow Wilberforce faculty member, Mary Church Terrell, also brought analysis of the status and experiences of Black women into prominent intellectual spaces, publishing in noteworthy venues like *The Crisis*, the *Journal of Negro History*, and the *North American Review*. Terrell was one of the first African American women to earn a college degree, and she became a well-regarded advocate for civil rights and women's suffrage. In a 1910 article, Terrell highlighted the important but underappreciated role that Black women played in society, asserting that "[T]he colored women of this country are contributing as much to the country by good citizenship as their more favored sisters. . . . 'Judging by the depths from which they have come rather than the heights colored women need not hang their heads in shame.'"

For Terrell, a high-quality education was part and parcel of good citizenship. Reflecting on her frustration with people who failed to recognize the necessity of educational training for young people, she emphasized that formidable social and economic competition made education a necessity rather than an option:

> Remember that good citizenship means a good, thorough education. I think I am a very pleasant person at times, but if you want to see me fully aroused, you just let me hear some older person trying to persuade young people that they do not need an education. They tell of Billy Jones who never went to school a day in his life. . . . But the times have changed and the people change with the times. What could be done thirty or forty years ago cannot be done now. Competition is growing keener and keener every day.[16]

Terrell's assertion that a solid education was part and parcel of good citizenship underscored a foundational thread in Black political thought recognizing education as more than simply a means to employment opportunities. From this perspective, which is reflected in the values embraced by many Black college educators, HBCUs' work to empower Black citizens reflects a democratic imperative.

Indeed, prominent Black thinkers educated in and working at HBCUs devoted considerable time and intellectual space to questions of citizenship and democratic inclusion. As Black Americans navigated a society riddled with race-based disparity, unequal access to publicly supported institutions and accommodations, and a legal system that routinely failed to protect Black people from exploitation and violence, these thought leaders brought previously muted Black perspectives to conversations about racial justice. Journalist, civil rights leader, and NAACP cofounder Ida B. Wells was a bold participant in these conversations. Wells was the product of three HBCUs—Mississippi's Rust College, Fisk University, and Lemoyne-Owen College in Memphis, Tennessee—and she spent her life advocating for equality and the fair treatment of Black people. Writing in 1913, the outspoken opponent of lynching offered a bold reproach of the chronic violence leveled against Black Americans in a country that claimed to be a democracy:

> Our democracy asserts that the people are fighting for the time when all men shall be brothers and the liberty of each shall be the concern of all. If this is true, the stragglers are bound to take in the Negro. We cannot remain silent when the lives of men and women who are black are lawlessly taken, without imperiling the foundations of our government. Civilization cannot burn human beings alive or justify others who do so; neither can it refuse a trial by jury for black men accused of crime, without making a mockery of the respect for law which is the safeguard of the liberties of white men. The nation cannot profess Christianity, which makes the golden rule its foundation stone, and continue to deny equal opportunity for life, liberty and the pursuit of happiness to the black race.[17]

Wells's critique of the hypocrisy apparent in how Black people were treated in the United States during the Jim Crow era placed a spotlight on issues that were often ignored in the dominant White scholarly discourse about democratic citizenship. It also represented a bold form of civic engagement by a Black woman of considerable influence who actively used her writing as a platform to advocate for racial justice during the early twentieth century.

In addition to Black intellectuals who used HBCUs as perches from which to weigh in on issues like racial justice and racial advancement during the early twentieth century, others used them to contemplate the ways in which American culture failed Black people. Carter G. Woodson, for example—who was known as the "Father of Black History" and who was a pioneering historian on the faculty of Howard University and then West Virginia State University—challenged the American education system's approach to teaching about the Black experience in schools.

In his 1933 book *The Mis-education of the American Negro*, Woodson offered a bold assessment of historical efforts to oppress Black people that noted the significance of both physical and intellectual domination as tools that kept Black people in bondage:

> Starting out after the Civil War, the opponents of freedom and social justice decided to work out a program which would enslave the Negroes' mind inasmuch as the freedom of body had to be conceded. It was well understood that if by teaching of history the white man could be further assured of his superiority and the Negro could be made to feel that he had always been a failure and that the subjection of his will to some other race is necessary, the freedman, then, would still be a slave. If you can control a man's thinking you do not have to worry about his action.[18]

Woodson commented particularly on what he described as the intentional "neglect" of political education for Black people during the post–Civil War period, as illustrated by efforts to limit Black students' access to printed copies of the US Constitution:

> Not long ago a measure was introduced in a certain State Legislature to have the Constitution of the United States thus printed in school histories, but when the bill was about the pass it was killed by some one who made the point that it would never do to have Negroes study the Constitution of the United States. If the Negroes were granted the opportunity to peruse this document, they might learn to contend for the rights therein guaranteed.[19]

Woodson was an outspoken critic of dominant renderings of American history that failed to accurately reflect the Black experience, and he actively fought to expand the discourse on Black people's contributions to the nation and world.

One of his most enduring contributions was successfully launching Negro History Week—the precursor to Black History Month—in February 1926. Woodson's HBCU-based work covered a range of topics, including the consideration of Black citizenship and democracy in the face of racial

inequality, but his contributions to the study of Black history were especially consequential for paving the way for widespread resistance against
segregation and racial discrimination that would take place during the
mid-twentieth century.

Like Woodson, philosopher Alain Locke, who was on the faculty of
Howard University between 1912 and 1925, revolutionized how the academy
engaged with Black culture. Locke taught one of the first courses on race
relations at Howard University and was a leading figure in the scholarly
discourse on race and culture. In 1935, he outlined his thoughts on racial
segregation, offering ideas that would reemerge nearly three decades later
as activists worked to desegregate schools:

> Negroes . . . should and must resort to the courts to secure any consid-
> erable or wholesale improvement of the [segregation] situation. This
> becomes more imperative when you realize that separation and a parity
> of standards and facilities are naturally antagonistic and rarely if ever
> co-exist. Without assessing the psychological damages to the minority
> and the impairment of the basic social democracy of the community, it
> actually turns out that only in a minimum of cases is there any approach
> to equality of opportunity under a dual school system.[20]

Locke's views on the negative impact that segregation had on citizens were
in opposition to dominant perspectives that took for granted that racially
separated accommodations were an acceptable arrangement. In addition
to contesting the received wisdom of "separate but equal," Locke and other
Black intellectuals ignited conversations that would grow over time and
eventually contribute to the emergence of the Black freedom movement.
As centers of Black excellence and amplifiers of Black voices and ideas, Black
colleges represented a powerful threat to White supremacy. As Albritton
notes, HBCUs have historically been "one of the few places where Black
people could (and can) come to have their voices heard and affirmed."[21]
This was certainly the case during the late nineteenth and early twentieth
centuries as HBCUs empowered a vanguard of Black intellectuals who set
a strong intellectual foundation for the fight for Black civil rights.

Throughout the Jim Crow era, Black intellectuals working in and educated by HBCUs actively engaged in broad-reaching political discourse
while also providing students at their home institutions with intellectual environments that placed the concerns of Black Americans front

and center. They contested conventional notions of race, citizenship, and democracy, questioning dominant perspectives by calling attention to the contradictions that were so apparent in the Black American's experience. Black intellectuals working at HBCUs also provided counsel to policymakers interested in addressing the needs of Black Americans. During the Great Depression, for example, newly elected president Franklin Delano Roosevelt turned to Black sociologists as he worked to address the needs of the struggling Black community.[22]

Not surprisingly, Black scholars' intellectual freedom was constantly at risk during the Jim Crow era as southern lawmakers aimed to restrict Black intellectuals' voices and to ensure that they did not disrupt the long-standing system of racial stratification. Efforts to threaten the standing of Black scholars and the solvency of the Black colleges that provided their intellectual and professional bases by sustaining sharp disparities between Black and predominantly White colleges was a central strategy for achieving that end.[23]

Nevertheless, HBCUs succeeded in empowering a generation of Black intellectuals who were democratic gadflies, questioning conventional notions of democracy and citizenship and boldly casting light on hypocrisies that demanded correction in a nation that proclaimed a commitment to equality and justice for all. Moreover, HBCUs were in the business of Black excellence—grappling with it, cultivating it, and showcasing it in a focused and unabashed way. Their work—and, indeed, their very existence—was political, and by carving out space for Black perspectives and empowering intellectual inquiry and discourse among Black thinkers, they were clear and present threats to White supremacy and the marginalization of Black Americans in the polity.

Developing the Architects and Generals of the Civil Rights Movement

The disruptive intellectual culture that grew out of HBCUs during the Jim Crow era fueled the development of many of the key strategies that were integral to the success of the civil rights movement of the 1950s and 1960s. Howard Law School professor and vice dean Charles Hamilton Houston and law students Thurgood Marshall and Pauli Murray were among the most influential architects of the legal strategy that would help to dismantle segregation in the United States. As the leader of Howard Law School during the 1920s and 1930s, Houston worked to build a program of legal education that would specialize in generating excellent Black civil rights attorneys.

For many of the Black faculty and students teaching and studying law during this era, personal experience with racial discrimination offered a powerful impetus for working within the nation's legal institutions to achieve social change. In Houston's case, his experiences during World War I made him acutely aware of the injustice that many Black veterans felt after fighting to defend US democracy abroad only to be denied equal rights and fair treatment upon returning home. It was this awareness and resulting disappointment in the exclusion of Black Americans from full democratic citizenship that led him to devote his life to the cause of civil rights. Viewing lawyers as social engineers who could help transform society, Houston embarked on a distinguished career as a legal practitioner and educator.

Houston's greatest contribution to the civil rights movement that would take shape during the 1950s was his work during the late 1920s and 1930s to transform Howard Law School from an unaccredited institution that was one of the few to admit Black students for legal study into a respected and accredited powerhouse of legal education. Known for his stern and demanding attitude toward students, Houston was determined to shape Howard Law School into the "West Point of Negro leadership."[24] As Juan Williams notes, when Houston addressed students on the first day of classes during the fall of 1930, it was strictly business: "He didn't bother to welcome them. He bluntly announced that Howard was no longer for students who did not want to give their full attention to the study of law. He warned them that their success in college meant nothing to him, and it would give him great pleasure to flunk out Phi Beta Kappas."[25] Houston had no patience for students who were not serious about their studies. But those who rose to his lofty expectations were treated to extraordinary learning opportunities, including access to influential visiting professors and guest speakers and immersive engagement with the local justice system that included visits to courts, police precincts, and jails.[26]

In addition to his work as a professor and school administrator, Houston was a renowned civil rights attorney who guided the NAACP through a series of court cases that challenged segregation and established crucial legal precedents that set the stage for watershed legal change during the mid-1950s. He gave his most accomplished students unique opportunities to engage in this work and to have an impact on the civil rights landscape.

Houston's efforts to transform Howard Law School into a leading institution for legal education were successful, and by the 1930s the school was steadily graduating excellent lawyers who would go on to challenge racial discrimination across the country. Moreover, its faculty and enrolled students were directly engaged in the fight for Black civil rights through legal research and active legal practice.

During the early 1930s, Thurgood Marshall—a graduate of Lincoln University—was one of Houston's top law students at Howard Law School. Marshall worked closely with the demanding Houston, whose mentorship inspired extraordinary contributions to the cause of civil rights and racial justice. He was on the team of lawyers who crafted the legal strategy that would successfully overturn the landmark *Plessy v. Ferguson* decision that had upheld race-based segregation in 1896. In 1954, a decade after graduating from Howard Law School, Marshall would argue the landmark *Brown v. Board of Education* case before the US Supreme Court, which ruled school segregation to be unconstitutional. Thirteen years later, he would go on to become the nation's first Black Supreme Court justice.

Pauli Murray was another Howard Law school graduate whose pathbreaking career as a civil rights lawyer and scholar contributed to the dismantling of Jim Crow segregation during the 1950s. Murray—who had been the only woman in their law school class and its top-ranked graduate—pioneered arguments that would play a central role in the successful challenge of racial segregation through the courts.

Describing their law school experience at Howard, Murray recalled that the school "provided excellent training for anyone devoted to the struggle to enforce civil rights. We had a small student body, and students and faculty shared a camaraderie born of our mutual commitment to the battle against racial discrimination."[27] The faculty that Murray described included prominent attorneys who had successfully argued before the Supreme Court during the 1940s and 1950s, and as Murray noted, "[m]any of the briefs in key cases before the Supreme Court were prepared in our law library, and exceptionally able students were rewarded for excellence by being permitted to do research on a brief under the supervision of a professor."[28]

Murray also recalled the unique training that Howard Law School professors offered students who would almost surely pursue careers geared toward enhancing Black civil rights: "Our training included not only learning the law and how to think on our feet but also how to conduct ourselves in hostile situations. Many of the students planned to practice in the South, where it was still rare to see a Negro attorney in a courtroom."

One of Murray's Howard Law professors, Dr. Leon R. Ransom, was especially well regarded for his legal achievements, his intellectual acumen, and his devotion to preparing students for the challenges that lay ahead as legal practitioners. Murray remembered his being clear-eyed about the fact that "Negro lawyers must be able to endure public humiliation, even physical danger, when challenging deeply entrenched racial customs." Recalling his focus on preparing his students for the challenges that faced Black attorneys who dared attempt to disrupt the Jim Crow racial order, Murray noted, "He was determined that his students would be tough enough to survive in no-holds-barred legal combat."[29] The pioneering work that Howard Law School faculty members like Charles Hamilton Houston and Leon Ransom did to train legal practitioners who could boldly challenge Jim Crow helped to generate foundational legal precedents during the 1930s and 1940s that paved the way for watershed legal decisions and policy changes in the subsequent decades that would prove crucial to the civil rights movement.

Black colleges' commitment to equality and expanding opportunity for the traditionally marginalized was apparent in their gender-egalitarian approach to student admissions. While most traditionally White colleges and universities limited women's access to their programs, HBCUs were among the first to admit women during the nineteenth century.[30] By accepting women into their student bodies, HBCUs created a pathway for women's democratic engagement that would contribute to women's active participation in the civil rights movement of the mid-twentieth century.

Yet this gender egalitarian approach to admissions did not mean that women students were treated as full and equal citizens on campus, particularly in the male-dominated environment of Howard Law School during the 1930s and 1940s. For Pauli Murray, Howard Law School was the first all-male environment that they had ever experienced, and they felt patently marginalized as a member of the student community. Murray recalled instances where faculty members would make insensitive remarks questioning women's decision to attend law school, and intense frustration when faculty repeatedly ignored their attempts to participate in class by refusing to call on them when they raised their hand to speak. Murray's experience of sexism during law school inspired them to create the term "Jane Crow," which described the intersectional discrimination that emanated from the combination of layered racism and sexism.[31]

Despite the challenges that Murray experienced as a woman pursuing a law degree, they actively engaged in activism and intellectual efforts to promote civil rights during law school. They participated in nonviolent protests against segregation in Washington, DC, restaurants, pioneering student activism tactics that would become more widespread in subsequent decades. They also published an article titled "Negro Youth's Dilemma," which raised bold questions about the mismatch between Black veterans' participation in World War I and their exclusion from full democratic citizenship at home.

Murray's most pathbreaking intellectual contributions included bringing intersectional analysis to conversations about racial discrimination and civil rights, building on their notion of "Jane Crow" to highlight the multiple identities that exist within marginalized communities, which are often overlooked in reform efforts. Murray's senior paper, "Should the Civil Rights Cases and *Plessy v. Ferguson* Be Overturned?," made the bold argument that, rather than focusing on whether or the extent to which "separate but equal" facilities and accommodations were equal, civil rights claims would be more powerful if they emphasized the unconstitutionality of segregation based on the Thirteenth and Fourteenth Amendments. Although Murray's argument was initially met with laughter from their fellow law school classmates, Thurgood Marshall would draw upon Murray's bold argument a decade later to successfully challenge race-based segregation in the landmark *Brown v. Board of Education* case.[32]

Howard Law School was central to the pathbreaking work that Charles Hamilton Houston, Thurgood Marshall, Pauli Murray, and other legal architects did to devise the legal strategy that would eventually dismantle Jim Crow. Moreover, in cultivating and empowering thought leaders in fields from history to political science to philosophy, and beyond, HBCUs generated the intellectual foundation upon which the successful twentieth-century movement for Black civil rights was built.

HBCUs and the Generals of the Civil Rights Movement

In addition to fostering the work of the intellectual architects of the civil rights movement, HBCUs were also essential to the movement for Black freedom because they cultivated the leaders who would become frontline generals translating bold calls for democracy and equality into a social movement that gripped the nation. Perhaps the most well-known general was the Reverend Dr. Martin Luther King Jr., who graduated from Morehouse College in 1948 at the age of nineteen with a bachelor's degree in sociology. Writing decades after graduating from college, King remembered Morehouse as a site of racial awakening and recalled with appreciation how the HBCU environment fostered open discussion about race:

> There was a free atmosphere at Morehouse, and it was there that I had my first frank discussion on race. The professors were not caught up in the clutches of state funds and could teach what they wanted with academic freedom. They encouraged us in a positive quest for a solution to racial ills. I realized that nobody there was afraid. Important people came in to discuss the race problem rationally with us.[33]

After completing his studies at Morehouse College, King went on to become the cofounder and first president of the Southern Christian Leadership Conference (SCLC), where his activism centered on building a broad effort to pursue social change through nonviolent protest strategies such as peaceful disruption and civil disobedience. A leader in the Baptist church, King and his colleagues in the SCLC actively organized the religious community in the fight for Black freedom, and he actively drew on the ideas and lessons that he learned as a Morehouse student in his work as one of the nation's foremost civil rights leaders.

While Martin Luther King embodied civil rights leadership in its most centralized form, Ella Baker—another HBCU graduate and prominent civil rights leader—offers a prominent example of a leader who took a more decentralized approach to political organizing. In 1960, as student sit-ins were starting to command the nation's attention, the Shaw University alumna gathered approximately 200 students at Shaw University and began an organizing effort that would grow into the Student Nonviolent Coordinating Committee (SNCC). Baker's own experience as a student at Shaw during the 1920s influenced her interest in social justice and her grassroots approach to political organizing. During college, she was a serious student who immersed herself in the work of great moral philosophers like Aristotle, Socrates, and Kant, as well as the work of pioneering Black historian Carter G. Woodson.[34]

Baker's engagement in campus activism at Shaw offered some of her earliest experiences challenging institutional authority and protesting rules and practices that she found unfair. Like many students at Black colleges during the 1920s, Baker sometimes found herself frustrated by Shaw's strict culture of rules, regulations, and closely held authority on the part of administrators, which reflected a trend of conservatism on many of the South's Black college campuses. On one occasion, for example, Baker defied campus leaders when Shaw's president invited Baker and other students to perform spirituals for White guests who were visiting from the North. Staunchly refusing to perform on the grounds that such performances were demeaning, Baker defied the wishes of campus leaders.[35] While her defiance likely tarnished her reputation with campus authority figures, it offered an early indication of the willingness to dissent that would fuel her pathbreaking civil rights activism.

After graduating from Shaw, Baker engaged in numerous efforts to promote civil rights for Black Americans. Her work to empower a broad base of young leaders was central to SNCC's emergence as a major force for organizing young people around efforts to promote voter registration and to fight segregation and racial discrimination through sit-ins, boycotts, freedom rides, voter registration, and voter mobilization.[36]

Organizing Black college students was central to Baker's approach to fighting for civil rights. In an oral history interview, she recalled the central role that college students played in igniting the youth activism that was central to the movement's progress and ultimate success during the late 1950s and early 1960s. Disputing notions that the movement was primarily a top-down affair, Baker emphasized that

> [Students] sat-in, and history will record that it spread like wildfire. I think it spread, to such an extent, because of, you know, just the young enthusiasm. . . . There was a great deal of dissatisfaction among the young that hadn't been articulated with the older leadership. Part of the spread was that my sister would call her brother at a given college and ask why aren't you doing it? So, I saw it taking place.[37]

Recognizing the opportunity to foster connection between various student efforts emerging in her home state of North Carolina, Baker decided to try to build partnerships among students at the state's Black colleges. As a first step toward strengthening communication and cooperation among groups, she helped to launch an introductory planning meeting:

> First, I wired A&T College and Bennett College. I was thinking of these as sites for the meeting. I found out I couldn't have it there for reasons. I know Bennett College had something coming up that they couldn't displace the use of their building for, couldn't change. So, I went to Raleigh and got an agreement with the student leadership there in Raleigh for having this meeting, and then getting Shaw University to agree to permit it to be held there, and worked out with the officials down there the basis on which we would come. [The Southern Christian Leadership Council] was to pay for the food of those who came. The original concept was a leadership of 100 or 125.[38]

Far exceeding Baker's estimation, the meeting attracted enthusiastic interest from students in colleges and universities in both the North and the South, and nearly 300 people attended the meeting.

Ella Baker's unique brand of other-oriented support for young grassroots activists was crucial to the effectiveness of the student movement. In contrast to the top-down approach of other "adults" in the movement who engaged with student activists, students viewed Baker's involvement as uniquely honest, respectful, and empowering.[39] Former Fisk University student and SNCC leader Diane Nash recalled that "Ella Baker was very important to giving direction to the student movement." She continued:

> And, not giving direction in a way of her making decisions as to what the students ought to do, but in terms of really seeing how important it was to recognize the fact that the students should set the goals and directions and maintain control of the student movement. So, she was there in terms of offering rich experience of her own, and advice, and helping patch things up when they needed to be patched up.[40]

Many student activists embraced Baker's leadership style, which contrasted with the strong leader-centered model that many older activists employed. Student leader and Morehouse College alumnus Julian Bond echoed Nash's recollection of Baker's approach to organizing, recalling the contrast between Baker's approach and that of other older leaders: "Ella Baker used to say, 'Strong people don't need strong leaders, because they themselves are strong. They don't need somebody saying 'Follow me,' or 'Do this' or something.' So that put us at odds with the SCLC because they had the strong leader, Martin Luther King." According to Bond, "Miss Baker," as the students respectfully called her, had a no-nonsense attitude and commitment to democracy and expected democratic principles to permeate all aspects of civil rights organizing. Her serious and intentional approach to organizing inspired awe, confidence, and admiration among student activists:

> [She] was not somebody you joked or laughed around with. She was right on the edge of being stern. But she was never harsh. She always searched for consensus. She never said, "Do this." But she always was able to pose questions to you that made you think about alternative ways to end up with a solution that involved some kind of democratic process involving everybody. . . . She wouldn't tolerate someone coming in and saying, "Okay, here's what we're going to do." It had to be talked out among us all. It took us forever to make decisions. But when we made them, you had the feeling that everyone had had their say. It might not be the decision you wanted, but at least you got to say something about it, to argue your point of view and that was the way we thought it best to operate. That you couldn't fight for democracy without being democratic. Your method and your goals had to be the same.[41]

Ella Baker, Martin Luther King, and other generals in the fight for Black freedom and democracy embraced a variety of approaches, but their close engagement with Black colleges was a noteworthy feature that they shared in common. As the products of Black colleges, they were familiar with institutional environments centered on the cultivation, recognition, and defense of Black excellence. For these figures, racist notions of Black inferiority were in direct opposition to their lived experiences at HBCUs.

Moreover, the humiliation that Black people experienced in the United States during the Jim Crow era, particularly in the segregated South, contrasted sharply with the oasis that Black college campuses provided, offering refuge from the indignities of Jim Crow segregation. For these leaders, their HBCU college experience influenced how they approached their work to transform the legal and political landscape.

Black College Students on the Frontlines of the Civil Rights Movement

As early as the late 1800s, students at Black colleges engaged in activities aimed at reforming campus culture and dismantling systems they viewed as oppressive on their college campuses.[42] Many students studying at Black colleges were subject to conservative campus cultures characterized by close scrutiny of students' dress, behavior, and movement on and off campus. Students at a Talladega College, Oakwood College, and other HBCUs raised objections to mistreatment on campus at the hands of White faculty and administrators. They also protested the dearth of Black faculty and the failure of many institutions to appoint any Black presidents.[43] Students, thus, demanded campus reforms that would ensure that they were treated with respect and dignity on campus and changes to campus leadership that would better reflect the student body.

When Black students embarking on their lives as young adults arrived on southern college campuses in the midst of Jim Crow, they often brought with them firsthand knowledge of the injustice and humiliation of racism. These experiences reflected Black Americans' second-class status throughout society and particularly in the South. In his powerful description of the lived experiences of many southern Black Americans, historian Bobby Lovett recalls that Black people could spend their money in White stores but could not use public facilities like restaurants, restrooms, or water fountains. Black Americans were subject to violence in the form of assaults, racial slurs, and mistreatment at the hands of law enforcement officers and others.[44]

During the 1930s and 1940s, student activism at Black colleges became more outward facing, turning from a focus on campus dynamics and leadership to problems in the communities that surrounded them. During the spring of 1943, for example, Howard University students participated in marches to protest segregated restaurants in the Washington, DC, area.[45] During that same decade, students at Georgia's Savannah State College were arrested for their efforts to desegregate Savannah's bus system.[46]

One factor that contributed to the growing trend of student civic and political activism was the fact that students' engagement in their campus communities and, particularly, in campus governance often stood in stark contrast with their marginalized status in society and in the polity. HBCU campuses offered young Black Americans a measure of freedom within— and protection from—the broader Jim Crow social and political landscape.

As educational historian Joy Ann Williamson notes, "At black colleges, students found themselves in the paradoxical situation in which they could run for office and vote in campus elections but not local, state, and national ones."[47] In this way, Black colleges offered their students experiences as campus citizens that contrasted sharply with the nature of their citizenship in the broader United States.

By the late 1950s and early 1960s, many HBCU students were ready and willing to engage in frontline battles for civil rights, courageously taking part in sit-ins, freedom rides, marches, and other organized efforts aimed at forcing legal change to dismantle Jim Crow. HBCUs provided energizing environments that catalyzed students' advocacy work. They offered unique opportunities to engage with prominent Black thinkers who expanded students' perspectives on questions of citizenship, justice, and democracy and sharpened their interest in pushing back against racist oppression.

Julian Bond, a Morehouse College alumnus and one of the founders of SNCC, grew up in HBCU communities. His father, Horace Bond, had served as an HBCU president, first at Georgia's Fort Valley State College and later at Pennsylvania's Lincoln College. Recalling the distinctive HBCU environments in which he grew up, Bond noted that "[During the 1940s and 1950s,] almost every prominent black person who made speeches or went around would come to a place like Lincoln University. They wouldn't go to the University of Pennsylvania or Penn State. Nobody would invite them there. So they came to Lincoln. They came to Black colleges." Having access to a veritable "who's who" of prominent Black America had a profound impact on the young people studying at HBCUs during their formative years. As Bond recalled, "Being on [an HBCU] campus opened my world up and exposed me to people and to things and events, all kinds of things that I never would've seen."[48]

Like Bond, John Lewis—who would go on to serve as the chair of SNCC and later as a member of the US Congress—recalled the important impact that Nashville's Fisk University had on his development as a civil rights activist. During his sophomore year at Fisk, civil rights was in the air throughout campus. He recalled, "in the dorms, in the dining room, wherever you went, it seemed, the talk was of the [civil rights] movement. 'Free by '63'—you heard that slogan everywhere."

He also remembered the extraordinary roster of speakers who regularly visited the campus. "There were so many," Lewis recalled: "Fred Shuttlesworth; Daddy King, Dr. King's father; Roy Wilkins; Thurgood

Marshall. One day [my friend] Harold [Cox] and I were walking across the Fisk campus when W. E. B. Du Bois strolled right past us. I was awed, dumbstruck—but not so paralyzed that I couldn't backtrack, introduce myself and shake that man's historic hand."[49]

In addition to enjoying access to Black luminaries on campus, HBCU students also had the opportunity to work closely with some of the movement's key leaders in the classroom. As a student at Morehouse College, Julian Bond counted Dr. Martin Luther King Jr. as a professor. Not long after, King would become the most widely recognized leader of the fight for Black civil rights. Describing the experience of learning under the guidance of the civil rights icon, Bond recalls that

> [F]rankly, at the time, we didn't think there was anything about it. He was a famous person, but he was nowhere near the famous person he is now. . . . He was very easy and informal. So we'd come once a week. The class was a team-taught class. He and the fellow who had been his philosophy professor when he had been a Morehouse student. The two of them would sit in the front of the room, six students in the class, and we'd talk about philosophy. Most of the time we talked about the civil rights movement, the Montgomery Bus Boycott.[50]

This unique combination of experience pushing boundaries on campus, studying in campus environments that offered a taste of citizenship that sharply contrasted with the blatantly second-class treatment that they encountered from the broader society, access to prominent Black thinkers and leaders on campus, and early civil rights protest experience paved the way for the emergence of a powerful student movement during the late 1950s and early 1960s.

Haunted by the brutal 1955 murder of Emmett Till and other examples of the inhumane treatment that Black people experienced under Jim Crow, students studying at North Carolina A&T University in Greensboro organized the first of what would become a series of lunch counter protests.[51] In February 1960, four North Carolina A&T students—Ezell Blair Jr., Franklin McCain, Joseph McNeil, and David Richmond—occupied seats at the lunch counter of a local Greensboro, North Carolina, Woolworth's Department Store, which only served White customers. When asked to leave, the students refused and remained seated until the store closed. The next day, the student protesters returned, this time with more activists in tow, including students from Bennett College, another Greensboro HBCU.[52]

Their peaceful protest attracted nationwide attention and sparked a series of subsequent protests by college students across the country, including their counterparts studying in Atlanta's cluster of Black colleges. Julian Bond recalled the impact that the Greensboro sit-ins had on the student community in Atlanta: "I was in this café one morning, and [fellow Morehouse student Lonnie King] came up to me with this newspaper that talked about the Greensboro sit-ins. He engaged me in going around the café, talking to other students, about doing the same thing in Atlanta. Our circle got larger and larger and larger and larger."[53]

After gathering a growing number of student supporters over the course of a few days, Lonnie King and Julian Bond decided to approach local Black academic leaders for support. As Bond described, "We went to the president." He continued:

> There were Morehouse, Spelman, Clark, Morris Brown colleges, the Interdenominational Theological Center, a seminary, and Atlanta University, a graduate school. So here are four colleges, two graduate schools—six schools of 4,000 students. So we made sure we had somebody from each school and picked on the student body presidents particularly because they were leadership figures and other people would follow them and formed this group and then we began the sit-ins.[54]

The Atlanta students formed a group called the Committee on Appeal for Human Rights, and in March of 1960 Bond, King, and a Spelman student named Hershelle Sullivan took the lead in crafting "An Appeal for Human Rights." In this manifesto, which was initially published in Atlanta's major newspapers and eventually in the *New York Times* and the *Congressional Record* as well, HBCU student leaders proclaimed:

> [We] have joined our hearts, minds, and bodies in the cause of gaining those rights which are inherently ours as members of the human race and as citizens of these United States. . . . We want to state clearly and unequivocally that we cannot tolerate in a nation professing democracy and among people professing democracy, and among people professing Christianity, the discriminatory conditions under which the Negro is

living today in Atlanta, Georgia—supposedly one of the most progressive cities in the South.[55]

The students went on to enumerate examples of the injustices that Black Atlantans faced in education, employment, health care, and access to public facilities and accommodations. They also denounced efforts to restrict Black people's voting rights, asserting that, "Contrary to statements made in Congress by several Southern Senators, we know that in many counties in Georgia and other southern states, Negro college graduates are declared unqualified to vote and are not to register."[56] As this example illustrates, a robust HBCU network facilitated collaboration among Black college students.

The wave of activism that began in Greensboro soon swept the southern states, and HBCUs were key conduits of student energy. In March 1961, nine students studying at Jackson, Mississippi's Tougaloo College who were members of their school's NAACP chapter launched sit-ins at their local public library. The "Tougaloo Nine," as they became known, inspired other Black college students to fight for Black freedom and to push back on segregation in Mississippi.[57]

Like North Carolina and Mississippi, Tennessee also had a vibrant student movement during the early 1960s. When Chicago native Diane Nash arrived in Nashville in 1959 to begin studies at Fisk University, she was disturbed by the humiliating segregation that she encountered in her college city. Nash recalled that, like many Black northerners stunned by the harsh reality of life in the Jim Crow South, she "keenly resented segregation and not being allowed to do basic kinds of things like eating at restaurants, in the ten-cent stores even" and feeling "stifled" and "shut in very unfairly."[58] Although she hailed from a family where activism and protest were not the norm, Nash's encounters with segregation nevertheless evoked a need to fight back against the injustice that she observed and experienced. A conversation with a fellow student led her to nonviolent protest workshops organized by civil rights activist Rev. James Lawson, which took place near Fisk's campus at Clark Memorial United Methodist Church. For Nash and a number of her classmates, engagement with Lawson's teaching sparked a bold turn to activism.

In his recollections of student engagement in Lawson's weekly workshops, John Lewis recalled the increasing momentum as local college students began to join in movement efforts. "When school began that fall semester of '59, it became clear that word of our Tuesday night gatherings had spread. A year earlier we rarely had ten people in that room. Now there were often more than twenty, black and white alike, women as well as men, students from Fisk and Vanderbilt, Tennessee State, Meharry Medical School and ABT."[59]

By 1960, Diane Nash and John Lewis were among the central organizers of the Nashville student movement, which focused on desegregating lunch counters at stores throughout the city. Black colleges were important landmarks and tributaries in the landscape of student protest activity, and they provided a hub for Black student activism. Describing the strategies that student activists employed, Nash noted the prominent role that Tennessee's network of HBCUs played in the movement:

> The students met on Tennessee A&I's campus, and we marched, I think, three abreast. We were very organized. One of the things that we made it a point to do was that whenever there was a demonstration, we were to be overly dressed. The men generally wore suits and ties, and the women— we looked like we were dressing up for Sunday. And anyway, we marched quietly. We were met later by students at Fisk. We passed Fisk's campus. And other students, other schools had points where they joined in to the march. There were many thousands of people that marched that day. We marched silently, really. And the long line of students must have continued for many, many blocks. Miles, maybe. And we marched to the mayor's office.[60]

HBCUs were central to the power of the Black student movement because they provided a network of young people and mentors to spark and support social movement organizing. HBCUs also provided the young activists with a crucial and politically empowering status—that of college students, a group that tends to be associated with positive characteristics like hard work, responsibility, and self-improvement. Student activists emphasized their status as college students, proudly displaying indicators of their student status while protesting. For example, quiet studying was the pastime of choice for students protesting lunch counter segregation. John Lewis describes the careful training that student activists received before they descended on downtown stores to sit at segregated lunch counters:

> No aggression. No retaliation. No loud conversation, no talking of any kind with anyone other than ourselves. Dress nicely. Bring books,

schoolwork, letter-writing materials. Be prepared to sit for hours. Study, read, write. Don't slouch. No napping. No getting up, except to go to the bathroom, and then be sure there is a backup to fill your seat while you're away. Be prepared for arrest. Be prepared to be taken to jail.[61]

Lewis noted that the stores in which students were protesting began to mount "counterattacks," directing their staff "to stack goods—wastebaskets, blankets, lampshades, pots and pans—on the lunch counters to keep us from studying." Such efforts to retaliate against Black college student activists had direct consequences for their academic lives.

In May 1963, inspired by protest activities in Greensboro, Nashville, and Atlanta, hundreds of Black teenagers and children marched for civil rights in Birmingham, Alabama. Their nonviolent protest was met with brutal repression by Birmingham law enforcement commissioner Bull Connor, whose officers arrested and jailed the young activists. When the students persisted, showing up to protest again the following day, Connor unleashed dogs and water hoses on them, to the horror of a national audience watching violent footage of the event on television. John Lewis recalled the horrifying images:

> I . . . was absolutely stunned by what I saw. Snarling German shepherds loosed on teenaged boys and girls, the animals' teeth tearing at slacks and skirts. Jet streams of water strong enough to peel the bark off a tree, aimed at twelve-year-old kids, sending their bodies hurtling down the street like rag dolls in a windstorm. It was absolutely unbelievable. It looked like battle footage from a war.[62]

Given the geographic diversity of HBCU student bodies and their interconnectedness as a network, students around the country watched with horror the violence and brutal repression that their peers were experiencing in Birmingham. As Lewis recalled, "A lot of those kids being blasted by Bull Connor's fire hoses were students at Birmingham's largest black high school, Parker High. A lot of the kids attending Fisk and Tennessee State were *from* Parker. A lot of them *knew* some of the young men and women they saw being bitten by dogs on the TV news. It was all very, very immediate. It hit very, very close to home."[63]

Black college students' civil rights activism came at great cost for many. Joy Ann Williamson asserts that students' activism represented a form of sacrifice, as students had to finesse balancing their social movement work with academic responsibilities. As Williamson notes, "participation in demonstrations meant absence from class, which could incur harsh penalties because of the strict demerit system at many of the colleges and the attitudes of conservative administrators, faculty, and trustees who frowned on student involvement."[64] Not surprisingly, many students risked academic hardship, loss of scholarships, and even expulsion when engaging in civil rights activism.

Diane Nash recalled the challenge of juggling activism and academic responsibilities and the lengths students would go to in order to do so: "the students managed to move so fast . . . we would have meetings at six in the morning, before class, for those of us that had eight o'clock classes. And then we'd meet again in the afternoon."[65] For a number of students, their engagement in movement activities competed with their studies. John Lewis described his engagement with Jim Lawson's workshops as becoming "the focus of my life, more important even than my classes. I'd finally found the setting and the subject that spoke to everything that had been stirring in my soul for so long. This was stronger than school, stronger than church."[66] The sacrifices that students made to engage wholeheartedly in the movement included interrupting or completely discontinuing their studies.[67]

Nash also recalled that students shouldered the emotional toll of engaging in the movement while juggling academic demands: "People used to tickle me, talking about how brave I was sitting-in and marching and what have you because I was so scared. All the time," she said.

> It was like wall-to-wall terrified. I can remember sitting in class, many times, before demonstrations, and I knew, like, we were going to have a demonstration that afternoon. And the palms of my hands would be so sweaty, and I would be so tense and tight inside. I was really afraid.[68]

Julian Bond similarly recalls the dangers that he and other student activists encountered, noting the constant threat of violence and terrorism that the students encountered: "There were a couple of occasions. I remember we were picketing a grocery store once, and some guy threw battery acid at Lonnie King, in his face. It could have blinded him . . . [T]he Klan was counter picketing. Those people are terrorists. You don't know what they'll do. So there was an air of tension in the air."[69] Students were right to feel anxious. For most, a willingness to fight for racial justice came with the risk of compromising their own safety and well-being. Nevertheless, this generation of young activists forged ahead despite facing intense opposition from powerful adversaries, which included a number of southern state legislatures. HBCU students remained stalwartly committed to the advancement of African Americans and played a central role in the fight for racial justice.

HBCU Faculty and Administrator Support for Civil Rights and Student Activists

For many HBCUs and their leaders, efforts to empower Black students and their broader communities were met with forceful resistance from proponents of White supremacy. During the Jim Crow era, public Black colleges throughout the South contended with state lawmakers' expectations that they suppress campus protests and other attempts to counteract or otherwise disrupt the region's racial order.[70] In South Carolina, for example, political leaders demanded that the state's Black colleges "be purged of 'subversive' influences."[71] Similar efforts to suppress civil rights activism occurred in Alabama, Florida, Mississippi, Texas, and Georgia.[72]

Student activists faced opposition from law enforcement, which at times required intervention from HBCU leaders. While some Black college administrators, particularly those leading publicly funded state institutions, worked to minimize their institutions' involvement in protest activities that could invoke the ire of conservative state legislators, others—especially those leading private universities that were free from state governmental oversight—offered support that was integral to students' success.

John Lewis recalls an instance during his time at Fisk University when he and other students were arrested for protesting segregation in Nashville and the university's president intervened on the students' behalf:

> At eleven that night, after about six hours behind bars, we were released into the custody of the president of Fisk, Dr. Stephen J. Wright. With him were reporters and about two hundred cheering students. We were exultant. Those six hours had been an act of baptism for all involved. We felt as if we'd won a huge victory. We felt that way the next day when we saw newspapers trumpeting the violence and arrests with huge headlines. A rally was staged late that morning, Sunday morning, with more than a thousand students from across the city jammed into Fisk Memorial

Chapel to hear President Wright wholeheartedly endorse what we were doing. This was a big step. Up to that point Dr. Wright had been cautious, as anyone in his position might be. He had to answer to a board of trustees. He had parents calling from all over the country complaining about the trouble their sons and daughters were getting into, children they had trusted him to take care of. Not just racial lines were being drawn here. There were also generational lines *within* our race—lines that separated the older, conservative blacks from their offspring.[73]

In his support for the Tennessee student activists, President Wright demonstrated an important form of activism that came out of HBCUs. His willingness to offer unequivocal support to the students and to deal with any pushback that came from other university leaders, parents, and other stakeholders revealed his bold willingness to invoke the weight of HBCU institutional support behind the movement for Black freedom. Having President Wright's support was also valuable to students' morale, as it sent a clear message that, as they challenged formidable institutional structures, they had the formidable institution of Fisk University in their corner.

As President Wright's support for Nashville's student protestors illustrates, faculty members and administrators at Black colleges played an important role in the civil rights movement. Some faculty members engaged directly in activism. Others encouraged or otherwise supported their students' engagement in different ways. As Joy Ann Williamson notes, "Many black faculty did not participate in demonstrations or sit-ins but supported the movement by donating money to political organizations, allowing students to use the classroom to discuss movement issues, and refusing to punish students for their involvement. Others believed their role in the movement was to keep the college open."[74]

While some faculty members' engagement in civil rights activism was supported by their institutions, others found that their desire to participate in the movement for Black freedom was met with opposition. One of the biggest threats to faculty engagement was the specter of being labeled a communist, which was a common charge leveled against those who worked to dismantle racial discrimination in the South.[75] In Williamson's analysis of the complexities of faculty engagement in the civil rights movement, she notes that "like off-campus activists, faculty faced sanctions by the white power structure in the form of police, banks, merchants, and others that could negatively influence anyone who dared challenge the racial order. The overwhelming possibility of punishment made structural protections pivotal."[76] Chief among such structural protections were tenure and the promise of academic freedom. Moreover, for faculty working at public institutions, the possibility of retribution from state lawmakers created an additional tension between their interest in participating in the civil rights movement and their interest in sustaining their professional lives.

The 1963 March on Washington and Landmark Policy Change

The 1963 March on Washington was the culmination of decades of work by civil rights movement leaders including Martin Luther King (Morehouse), Bayard Rustin (Wilberforce and Cheyney College), A. Philip Randolph, Ella Baker (Shaw), and the young John Lewis (Fisk). These leaders who helped to develop the strategy that would contribute to landmark legislative changes in the form of the 1964 Civil Rights Act and the 1965 Voting Rights Act were acute observers of the complex political landscape in which they operated, and they were skilled at integrating that knowledge into their strategy.

For example, these leaders exercised the utmost care in navigating the rocky political terrain that surrounded the March on Washington. When an advance copy of SNCC chair John Lewis's speech evoked objections from the White House and religious leaders, senior activists beseeched Lewis to alter his remarks. The original draft of Lewis's speech offered a strong statement of activists' determination to achieve racial justice, including a militant indictment of racial discrimination and a bold call for a more disruptive approach, if necessary, to achieve change. He wrote:

> The revolution is at hand, and we must free ourselves of the chains of political and economic slavery. The nonviolent revolution is saying, "We will not wait for the courts to act, for we have been waiting for hundreds of years. We will not wait for the President, the Justice Department, nor Congress, but we will take matters into our own hands and create a source of power, outside of any national structure, that could and would assure us a victory."
>
> To those who have said, "Be patient and wait," we must say that "patience" is a dirty and nasty word. We cannot be patient, we do not want to be free gradually. We want our freedom, and we want it *now*. We cannot depend on any political party, for both the Democrats and

the Republicans have betrayed the basic principles of the Declaration of Independence. . . .

The time will come when we will not confine our marching to Washington. We will march through the South, through the heart of Dixie, the way Sherman did. We shall pursue our own "scorched earth" policy and burn Jim Crow to the ground—nonviolently. We shall fragment the South into a thousand pieces and put them back together in the image of democracy. We will make the action of the past few months look petty. And I say to you, WAKE UP AMERICA![77]

Political and religious leaders who saw an advance copy of the speech balked at what they considered incendiary language, and the movement's most senior leaders beseeched Lewis to soften his words. While Lewis complied, his sentiments offered an apt portrayal of the impatience that many Black college students felt for the slow pace of progress and their sense that President Kennedy, Congress, and other political actors could do more to ensure human rights for Black people. Julian Bond remembered the frustration that many students felt with political leaders and their wariness of political posturing in his description of efforts to convince Lewis to alter his speech:

> It just seemed to be typical of the desire of these older and more conservative civil rights organizations to sugarcoat the messages that were being delivered from the platform. We believed very strongly in what John was going to say. . . . We believed very strongly in our position that the Kennedy civil rights bill was not adequate, that it was weak and that the Democratic and Republican parties were too much alike and neither one of them as strong for civil rights as they should have been. We were fearful that the march would turn into sort of a campaign rally for John F. Kennedy's reelection and didn't want it to have that kind of political overtone.[78]

Lewis agreed to tone down his rhetoric when he delivered his speech on the steps of the Lincoln Memorial during that memorable event on August 28, 1963, but he and his fellow student activists held fast to the bold ideas that he had originally expressed.

The March on Washington was a powerful moment for the civil rights movement, with approximately 250,000 people from across the country gathering on the National Mall to demand racial equality. In addition to John Lewis's powerful remarks, Martin Luther King delivered his iconic "I Have a Dream" speech, an eloquent statement of the movement's purpose and vision. The following year, due in no small part to the crucial contributions of HBCUs, their students, their faculty, and their alumni, President Lyndon B. Johnson signed the 1964 Civil Rights Act, which outlawed segregation in public places as well as racial discrimination in employment. In 1965, Congress passed the Voting Rights Act, prohibiting discriminatory voting practices that had been established in the South to restrict Black people's ability to participate in political and civic life.

During the 1950s and 1960s, Black colleges provided a vast, interconnected web of institutional bases for student activists throughout the South. This network of Black college campuses generated essential energy for the movement by bringing students together, fostering serious grappling with questions of racial justice and citizenship, and creating pathways for activism. Moreover, Black colleges offered young activists the politically valuable identity of "college student," emphasizing their status as examples of Black excellence and juxtaposing this with the students' demands for fair treatment and human rights. This was essential to the powerful impact that their nonviolent organizing had on the movement.

The long history of historically Black colleges and universities has demonstrated the active role that higher educational institutions can play in social movements and social change. Not only did HBCUs produce intellectual pioneers who contested notions of White supremacy, advocated for economic, social, and political equality for Black Americans, and developed the legal strategy that helped to bring about the creation of landmark legislation like the Civil Rights Act of 1964 and the Voting Rights Act of 1965, they also generated leaders who mobilized mass-level engagement in the fight for Black civil rights. Their students brought courage, energy, and conviction to the frontlines of the movement. As such, HBCUs played an important role in helping to achieve a seismic shift in civil rights for Black Americans and a redistribution of political power during the 1960s.

4

"A Different World"

Why the Unique HBCU Experience Matters

WHEN ETHAN DAVIS NEARED HIGH school graduation in 2008, he was certain that his next educational chapter would unfold at an HBCU. Growing up in Encino, California, he hailed from a family that he described as financially "comfortable," attended a predominantly White high school, and had been actively engaged in sports. Ethan's decision to attend an HBCU seemed surprising to some, given the distance of most HBCUs from California—the nearest HBCU campus was located in Texas—and the fact that no other student from his high school graduating class went on to attend an HBCU. But Ethan recalls that "I only wanted to go to an HBCU. I didn't apply to any PWIs [Predominantly White Institutions] or anything of that nature. I was just really pretty much sold on the HBCU experience."

Like many students deciding where to attend college, Ethan paid particular attention to input from his parents. His father, an alumnus of Tennessee State University, was actively engaged in his alumni and fraternity networks. "Honestly, my dad pushed HBCUs so hard," says Ethan, recalling his father's encouragement to attend an HBCU. Given the transformative impact that his father's HBCU experience had on his life and the lives of their family members, Ethan gave his dad's perspective particular weight:

My dad was a first-generation college student, and I just looked at how much the HBCU he went to, Tennessee State, impacted his life, and that impacted my life. So, you kind of see this cycle like the second generation, that kids will have the same outlook that I have and they might go to an HBCU. I always wanted to. . . . It just changed my life so much. I can't even say. It just made me have so much more compassion for others and maybe really see how fortunate I was growing up and how blessed I am. I was fortunate, but I was even more blessed to go to Howard and just be at an HBCU for four years.

When asked to describe his time at Howard, the 2013 graduate said simply that it was "the best experience of my life."

In the years since the landmark 1964 Civil Rights Act prohibited racial discrimination in college admissions and opened the doors of predominantly White colleges for Black students, some have questioned the relevance of HBCUs in an increasingly diverse higher educational landscape.[1] In states like Georgia and Louisiana, proposals to enhance the efficiency of state education expenditures by merging public HBCUs with PWIs have evoked protest from HBCU advocates. HBCUs, they argue, are distinctive institutions that offer a unique and contemporaneously valuable higher educational experience. For that reason, they should remain intact.[2]

Do historically Black colleges and universities offer unique higher educational environments? Are there aspects of the HBCU experience that are particularly valuable for fostering learning and personal growth among students? This chapter uses a combination of quantitative and qualitative data to examine the culture and traditions of HBCUs and the type of educational experience that they provide. I begin by examining the factors that influence students' decisions about whether to attend an HBCU, in the first place. Then, I explore the HBCU campus experience with an eye toward aspects that may be unique to Black colleges. Finally, I consider the impact that the HBCU experience has on students' personal growth.

Given HBCUs' rich histories, it seems plausible that they provide a powerful and distinctive backdrop for campus life—one that constantly reminds students that their pursuit of higher learning and their work to exemplify Black excellence are part of an enduring legacy. Their campuses serve as living monuments to the triumphs that HBCUs and generations of HBCU students have achieved despite living in a broader society that, more often than not, fought to deny, suppress, or simply ignore

Black excellence. In terms of educational experience, institutions organized around a mission of cultivating and celebrating Black excellence seem uniquely positioned to foster academic success and personal growth among Black college students. As this chapter discusses, HBCUs offer uniquely empowering spaces that contribute to Black students' developing sense of identity, imparting lessons about their value as individuals and the opportunities and responsibilities that they possess as members of both the Black community and the broader society.

Data and Methods

To gain insight into how college experiences shape persistence to degree and provide a foundation for future personal, professional, and civic endeavors, this chapter and the three that follow examine African Americans' experiences at HBCUs and PWIs. The analysis draws on data from my 2018 College Experience Study, a national web-based survey fielded by Qualtrics in February of that year.[3] This nationally representative sample of 2,000 Americans who have at least some college experience includes an oversample of 1,000 Black respondents to ensure that it can shed light on the experiences of Black Americans. Approximately 30 percent of these Black respondents attended an HBCU for undergraduate study.

The College Experience Study provides insight into Black Americans' experiences in college (e.g., academic experience, engagement with faculty, participation in politically relevant activities) at HBCUs and PWIs, as well as their ultimate educational attainment, political attitudes, and political and civic engagement during and after college. Additionally, 100 respondents volunteered to participate in 20–30-minute follow-up interviews to offer further insight into the topics covered in the survey. This analysis also draws on qualitative data from 78 of the follow-up interviews that provided qualitative data from Black College Experience Study survey participants. With a team of student research assistants, I conducted these interviews over a three-week period during the summer of 2018. These interviews lasted approximately 20 minutes and were conducted via telephone. Interviewees received compensation in the form of a Qualtrics e-Rewards credit valued at $20.

Chapters 4 through 6 draw on a subset of data from the College Experience Study that focuses on responses of the 1,140 African Americans who completed the survey. Of these respondents, 32.3 percent attended an HBCU (see Table A.4.2 for descriptive statistics). Fifty-two percent are women, and the average respondent is forty-seven years old (born in 1971) and hails from a self described socioeconomic background that is "below average" to "average."[4] Sixty-three percent of African American respondents were first-generation college students, meaning that neither of their parents had completed a four-year degree (see Figure 4.1).[5]

To analyze these data, I draw on a combination of descriptive statistics and multivariate analysis. Given that HBCU attendees (32 percent) are somewhat overrepresented in these data, compared to their representation in the general population (approximately 20 percent), we must take caution in generalizing the results of this analysis. Nevertheless, the robust representation of HBCU attendees in this sample makes it possible to make useful comparisons between respondents in this pool. While my data and these techniques do not permit me to make causal claims, they do enable me to examine patterns related to the college experiences of this pool of African Americans.

To enhance my ability to gain insight into the HBCU educational experience, these chapters also draw on qualitative data from my 2019 HBCU Alumni Study. The HBCU Alumni Study consists of in-depth interviews with more than 100 HBCU alumni from around the country. A team of student research assistants and I conducted these interviews by telephone during the summer of 2019. Respondents' birth years ranged from the 1930s through the 1990s, and they attended public and private HBCUs. On

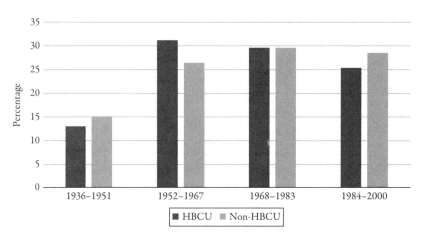

FIGURE 4.1   HBCU and non-HBCU attendance by age cohort.
Note: These differences are not statistically significant.
Source: The College Experience Study—Black Respondents.

average, these interviews were approximately 30 minutes in length. These data offer valuable insight into the HBCU educational experience and how it contributes to the development of democratically engaged citizens.

The Value of HBCU and PWI Higher Educational Experiences

As many students and families make substantial sacrifices to pay for college degrees, one of the most pressing questions shaping the discourse around higher education in the United States is whether college is worth it. How do Black Americans who attended HBCUs and those who attended PWIs perceive the value of their higher educational experience? Table 4.1

TABLE 4.1 Perceived Value of College Experience

"My college or university prepared me well for life outside of college."[A]

	Disagree Strongly	Disagree Somewhat	Agree Somewhat	Agree Strongly	
HBCU Attendees	5%	14	42	39	=100%
Non-HBCU Attendees	8%	19	47	26	=100%

"I am satisfied that the education I invested in with my student loans(s) was worth the investment for career opportunities."[B]

	Disagree	Agree	
HBCU Attendees	35%	65	=100%
Non-HBCU Attendees	44%	56	=100%

"I am satisfied that the education I invested in with my student loans(s) was worth the investment for personal growth."[B]

	Disagree	Agree	
HBCU Attendees	27%	73	=100%
Non-HBCU Attendees	36%	64	=100%

Notes: [A] Difference in mean responses is statistically significant at α = .001. [B] Difference in mean responses is statistically significant at α = .01.
Source: The College Experience Study—African Americans.

shows respondents' answers to three questions gauging their satisfaction with their higher educational investment. When asked about the extent to which they agree with the statement "My college or university prepared me well for life outside of college," 39 percent of respondents who attended an HBCU agree strongly, compared to 26 percent of those who did not attend an HBCU.

The second question asks respondents whether they agree or disagree with the statement "I am satisfied with the education I invested in with my student loan(s) was worth the investment for career opportunities." While 65 percent of HBCU attendees agreed with this statement, a more modest 56 percent of Non-HBCU attendees did. A similar question asked respondents whether they agree or disagree with the statement "I am satisfied that the education I invested in with my student loans(s) was worth the investment for personal growth." A full 64 percent of respondents who did not attend an HBCU agreed with this statement, compared to a whopping 73 percent of those who attended an HBCU. These responses suggest that respondents who attended an HBCU tend to place a particularly high value on the education that they acquired there. Qualitative data from in-depth interviews with Black Americans who attended HBCUs and PWIs can help us gain insight into why.

The Path to an HBCU Degree

Deciding where to attend college is one of the most consequential decisions that many young people make. For some, the transition to college provides an opportunity to build on interests and activities that proved rewarding during high school. For others, it offers an opportunity for reinvention— a chance to explore new interests and develop new connections while moving toward personal and professional goals. Whatever the student's mindset, the college that she, he, or they select will determine not only the environment in which their educational journey takes place, but also the type of college experience that they have. What factors shape students' decision to attend HBCUs?

Segregation Policy and Racial Consciousness

For Black Americans who attended college before the 1964 Civil Rights Act outlawed race-based discrimination in college admissions, racial segregation substantially narrowed their options. For most Black prospective college students during that period, the question was not whether to attend a Black college, but which Black college to attend. As Maxine, who attended Tennessee State University during the late 1960s, notes of that period, "this was during the time when some of the Black schools were the only options that some of us had."[6] Ronald, who attended Southern University in Louisiana during the 1970s also recalled:

> I was born here in Baton Rouge, Louisiana, and Southern University was the only one we could go to at the time. You know, we couldn't go to Louisiana State University because there was segregation. So, by the time I got to it, it was still at least a little bit [segregated]. . . . African Americans really were required to go to Southern University instead of Louisiana State University until all these athletes come along and they started recruiting African Americans in athletic departments. And, that's how LSU bust open.

Bennett College alumna Jean also recalled the limits that segregation placed on Black Americans' educational options when she was coming of age, offering the example of her older sister who also attended Bennett College: "When she graduated from Bennett, she could not attend the University of Mississippi, so the state had to pay for her to go to grad school someplace else. So, she went to the University of Wisconsin."

For Black Americans exploring college options during the mid-twentieth century, the media and awareness of major political events often played a role in shaping their thinking about higher educational possibilities. Jean, who began her studies at Bennett College during the late 1950s, noted that the popular media influenced her familiarity with HBCUs: "Long ago, when there was print media, all you heard about was Black HBCUs and then we were more exposed to . . . the *Pittsburgh Courier*, the *Chicago Defender*, the other prominent Black newspapers that really don't exist anymore."

For younger cohorts of Black college students, television shows like the popular American sitcom *A Different World*, which debuted in 1987, offered a look at college life at HBCUs. Justin, who attended Fayetteville State University and North Carolina Central University, noted that, aside from knowing about an uncle who had attended an HBCU in South Carolina, the media shaped his awareness and perception of Black colleges: "I didn't know anything else about HBCUs other than what I had seen on television, like Hillman [the fictional HBCU portrayed on *A Different World*], while growing up watching TV shows, stuff like that. I didn't have any other reference." For many Black college students like Justin, media portrayals of HBCUs played a role in shaping interest in pursuing higher education and in attending an HBCU.

Kenneth, who attended Talladega College during the early 1960s, highlighted the significance of political events for shaping higher educational access for Black college students: "Things didn't really open up in terms of White institutions being aware that they needed to do more [to attract Black students] until after the assassination of Martin Luther King in 1968; and I think it's not coincidental that Washington University in St. Louis was eager to have me as a doctoral student in 1969." For Kenneth, the close association that he perceived between HBCUs and racial uplift figured prominently in his thinking about higher education and his developing identity as a young adult. "The historical figures that formed my notions of what it meant to be Black in America, they and their leaders played a defining role in terms of my own self-conception—particularly places like Morehouse, because I came of age in the latter half of the 1950s, first few years or so of the 1960s, my college years," he said. "So, the Montgomery bus boycott was happening in Alabama, the sit-ins in Greensboro, North Carolina A&T, those were major events very much on my radar screen."

While the force of legal segregation played a prominent role in decisions about where to pursue higher education for more senior cohorts of Black Americans, the opportunity to live and learn in a college environment that centered and celebrated Black students was a theme that emerged across cohorts. For some HBCU attendees, experiences with racial segregation and discrimination led them to retreat to Black colleges after high school. Rhonda, for example, who attended high school in the late 1960s, remembers the transition to integrated schools as a difficult one: "I did not enjoy my high school years that much because it seemed like they did not want us involved in a lot of activities. Therefore, it was no doubt that I would go to an HBCU school." For Rhonda, the nation's clumsy attempts at school integration, which offered little assurance that newly integrated schools would provide inclusive learning environments, made attending Bennett College particularly appealing.

Vickey, who, like Rhoda, attended Bennett College during the 1970s, was drawn to HBCUs because of the experience that she had growing up in the midst of Jim Crow. "So, I'm a country girl. I grew up in a small, small town where minorities were treated as such. I grew up [with] colored only water fountains, segregated elementary and middle schools. It wasn't until a White school in my area burned down that we [integrated]." For Vickey, attending Bennett College offered "an opportunity for me to develop my own Black woman identity because I didn't feel I had one up until that point. And to be around women who looked like me, who had the same aspirations as I did—that was important to me, having grown up in rural North Carolina in the '60s and '70s."

For students like Tyrone, who graduated from Florida A&M University in 1994, HBCUs were the only institutions that they would consider for their postsecondary education. Describing his approach to selecting a college, Tyrone explained, "My considerations were the environment, [selecting a] place where I felt I would be comfortable in getting a higher education." Betty, who attended the Hampton Institute during the 1940s, similarly noted the importance of the educational environment at her HBCU. When asked what aspect of her college experience made the greatest impression on her, she replied simply, "Respect for my race." This sentiment was echoed by Tiffany, who attended Clark Atlanta University more than six decades later:

Around 10th grade when it started to become time for me to choose colleges I was interested in, I wanted to create an experience for myself that affirmed my blackness and my identity. So, the deciding and driving force for me picking an HBCU was the fact that HBCUs support and are created by Black people for Black people. I wanted to not have to explain to my roommate why I had my hair wrapped up at night. So, those are the types of things I was thinking through in terms of getting the Black experience.

For Black Americans like Kevin, who attended Jackson State University during the early 1980s, "Just seeing people of color achieve their educational and career goals" and "being able to foster relationships with people that serve as role models" in a program with an Afro-centric focus was central to the appeal of HBCUs.

The Influence of Family and Community Ties, Teachers, and Mentors

In addition to the powerful role that experiences with racial segregation and discrimination played for shaping the education decisions of generations of Black college students and the attraction of spaces that were designed with Black students in mind, the influence of family and community members, high school teachers and counselors, and other mentors have also played a central role in shaping decisions about where to go to college. Data from the College Experience Study suggest that African Americans who come from backgrounds that promote high levels of racial awareness may find HBCUs particularly attractive. Survey respondents were asked about the extent to which they agree with the statement, "My parents taught me what it means to be Black." As Figure 4.2 illustrates, while solid majorities of HBCU and non-HBCU attendees agreed either "somewhat" or "strongly" with the statement, 53.4 percent of respondents who attended an HBCU indicated strong agreement with the statement, compared to 44.7 percent of those who did not attend an HBCU.

As data from the College Experience Study illustrate, family ties have a powerful influence on Black Americans' decision about where to enroll for college, and this is especially true when parents or other family

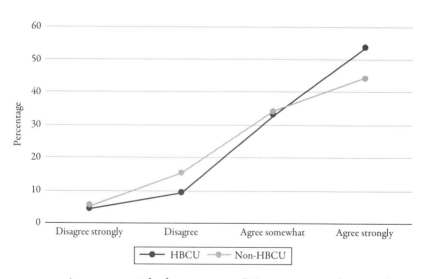

FIGURE 4.2 Agreement with the statement "My parents taught me what it means to be Black."

Note: Difference in mean responses is statistically significant at $\alpha = .01$.

Source: The College Experience Study—Black Respondents.

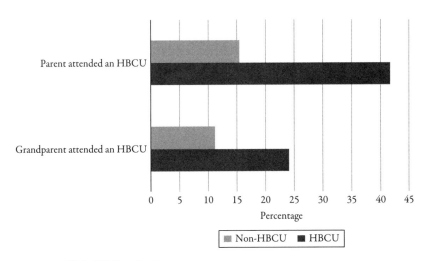

FIGURE 4.3 HBCU family ties.

Note: These differences are statistically significant at α = .001.

Source: The College Experience Study—Black Respondents.

members are members of a school's alumni network. Survey respondents who attended HBCUs were significantly more likely to have parents or grandparents who attended an HBCU than those who attended PWIs (see Figure 4.3). A full 41.6 percent of respondents who attended an HBCU also had a parent who did so, compared to only 15.4 percent of respondents who did not attend an HBCU. Similarly, 24.2 percent of respondents who attended an HBCU had at least one grandparent who also attended an HBCU, compared to only 11.3 percent of their counterparts who did not attend an HBCU.

While people who attended HBCUs and PWIs similarly emphasized the important influence that parents, family members, and high school counselors played in shaping their decisions about where to attend college, strong encouragement from trusted adults was a particularly salient influence for those who decided to attend HBCUs. For some, joining parents, grandparents, and other family members in the ranks of HBCU alumni made the decision to attend an HBCU an easy one. "I'm a multigenerational product of HBCUs," said Candice, who graduated from Spelman College in the early aughts. She continued:

I'm a fourth-generation college student. My great-grandmothers both attended college—I believe one of them went to what used to be called

Selma University in Alabama. It's no longer in existence. The other would have gone to whatever Alabama A&M used to be called. . . . My grandmother is a graduate of Alabama State, and my grandfather attended Tennessee State University. And, my parents of course—my dad went to Claflin University; my mother attended Elizabeth City State University in North Carolina. And, so I always knew that I would attend an HBCU. In a lot of ways, my parents were just like, "We're only paying for an HBCU," so I didn't even look at majority institutions when I considered going to college.

For others, parents played an even more direct role in shaping their decision about where to attend college. Crystal, the daughter of divorced parents, spent academic terms in California and summers and holidays in Nashville with her dad. One summer, she was surprised when her parents gave her a one-way ticket to Tennessee. "My sister and I didn't have a ticket to go back to LA, and so my dad said, 'Oh yeah, you're moving to Nashville because you need to get in-state status.' And, I was like 'in-state status' for what? And he was like, 'Oh, you're going to be going to Tennessee State.'" Despite her initial protest that she was planning to attend UCLA, Crystal's mother agreed with her father that an HBCU experience would be good for their daughter. Crystal agreed to give Tennessee State a try and to transfer to another college if she found that it was not a good fit. She recalls: "So, I really didn't have a choice, but I don't regret anything."

Interview data reveal more variation in the nature and value of adult guidance that Black students who attended PWIs received when deciding where to attend college. On one hand, PWI attendees like Michael, who studied at the University of Michigan, pointed to the same powerful influence of family legacy that emerged from conversations with HBCU attendees: "I grew up a fan of the [University of Michigan football] team. It was somewhere that people in my family had attended, like uncles and my grandmother." As his comments demonstrate, knowing family members or other connections who had attended a college can increase students' familiarity with the institution.

Yet, PWI students offered much thinner accounts of the role that their families played in directing them to a particular school or type of school than HBCU attendees did. In fact, beyond comments suggesting that they received relatively limited guidance on where to attend college when compared to their HBCU counterparts, PWI attendees also shared instances in which advisors proved less than helpful as they made this crucial decision. For example, Vanessa, who attended the University of California–Berkeley, described a particularly negative experience exploring college options: "My high school counselor told me that I was not college material, and she was not gonna help me get to school because I wasn't worth her time." These data suggest that the media, the broader social and political context, family members, and other personal connections can influence Black students' decisions about where to pursue college degrees. Strong HBCU ties through family connections emerge as particularly important influences in respondents' accounts of why they chose to attend HBCUs.

Paying for College and Financial Responsibility

With the rising cost of college, socioeconomic background and the availability of financial resources to fund higher education represent important factors shaping ultimate educational attainment. How do College Experience Study survey respondents who attended HBCUs and PWIs compare when it comes to socioeconomic background? Those who attended HBCUs report coming from more advantaged socioeconomic backgrounds than those who attended non-HBCUs. As Figure 4.4

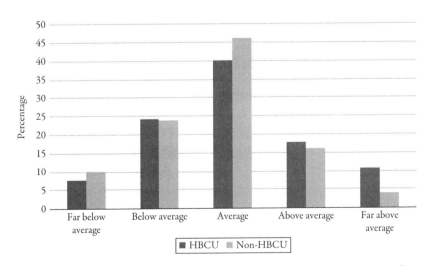

FIGURE 4.4 Youth socioeconomic status of HBCU and non-HBCU attendees.

Note: Difference in mean responses is statistically significant at $\alpha = .05$.

Source: The College Experience Study—Black Respondents.

illustrates, 10.6 percent of respondents who attended an HBCU report youth socioeconomic status that was "far above" their peers, compared to 3.9 percent of their counterparts who attended non-HBCUs. Moreover, 10 percent of respondents who did not attend an HBCU report having had a youth socioeconomic status that was "far below average," while 7.6 percent of their counterparts who attended HBCUs did so. While the backgrounds of Black PWI attendees and HBCU attendees represent the full range of the socioeconomic continuum, respondents who attended an HBCU are somewhat more likely to report hailing from more privileged backgrounds.

How do survey respondents meet the cost of college? Figure 4.5 compares the rates at which HBCU attendees and non-HBCU attendees benefited from various sources of financial assistance during their college years. For all respondents, regardless of the type of institution they attended, substantial proportions indicate having made use of the full range of financial resources available to fund their education: federal financial aid, parental and family support, private aid, and earnings from work during college. HBCU attendees are significantly more likely to perceive government financial aid as having contributed to their ability to attend college (see

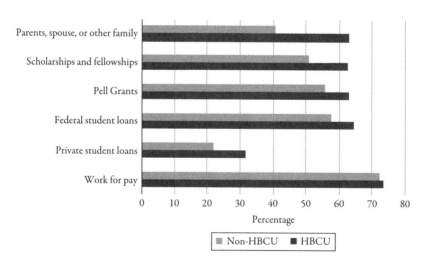

FIGURE 4.5 How respondents met the cost of college.

Note: Differences for "Parents, spouse, or other family," "Scholarships and fellowships," and "Private student loans" are statistically significant at $\alpha = .001$. Differences for "Pell Grants" and "Federal student loans" are statistically significant at $\alpha = .05$.

Source: The College Experience Study—Black Respondents.

Table A.4.3). The government's movement away from an emphasis on providing need-based grants toward an emphasis on student loans raises important questions about the implications of relying on government support to fund higher education. Vickey, for example, who attended Bennett College during the 1970s, recalls the significance of receiving federal financial aid to her ability to pay for college:

> My family situation wasn't the best. My father was ill at the time that I started college, and my mother was working as a domestic, so we didn't have a lot of money saved for college, and it was important for me to be able to receive financial aid. I attended college on work study, on a Basic Educational Opportunity Grant—they would be BEOGs. And, those were the types of things that allowed me to attend school because my family contribution was very minimal.

Just as HBCU attendees indicate that government student aid has made strong contributions to their ability to attend college, they are significantly more likely to indicate that student loans have burdened them with debts that have been difficult to repay.

It is also worth noting that HBCU attendees indicate that they have benefited from various forms of financial aid—support from federal financial aid, parental and family support, private aid, and earnings from work during college—at higher rates than non-HBCU attendees. A full 62.7 percent of respondents who attended an HBCU received financial support from their parents, spouse, or other family members, while 40.6 percent of those who did not attend an HBCU received support from these sources. This is perhaps unsurprising given the aforementioned data from Figure 4.4 demonstrating that HBCU attendees report coming from more privileged socioeconomic backgrounds at higher rates than those who did not attend an HBCU. Perhaps the families of students attending HBCUs are more likely to possess financial resources that they can extend to support higher education.

An important factor shaping students' persistence toward college degrees is the extent to which they carry substantial financial responsibilities in addition to their academic ones.[7] Survey respondents who attended HBCUs and non-HBCUs reported working for pay during college at virtually similar rates: a full 73.4 percent of respondents who attended an HBCU worked during college, as did 72.4 percent of those who did not attend an HBCU. For many, meeting the cost of tuition, fees, books, and living expenses drove the need to work during college. For others, the need to help support parents, siblings, or other family members made it necessary to balance their studies with part-time or full-time work.

Figure 4.6 illustrates survey participants' responses to the statement "How often did you send money to support parents or other family members while you were in college?" The majority of respondents indicate that they "never" did so: 65.7 percent of Black respondents who did not attend an HBCU indicated that they never sent money to support parents or family members during college, compared to 58.7 percent of HBCU attendees. On the other hand, a full 11.7 percent of respondents who attended an HBCU indicated that they "very often" sent money to support their parents or other family members during college, compared to only 6.9 percent of respondents who did not attend an HBCU. These data suggest that respondents who attended HBCUs represent both ends of the socioeconomic continuum: they may be more likely to hail from privileged backgrounds and have access to parental or family support to meet the cost of college; and at the same time, a substantial proportion of HBCU attendees may come from lower-income backgrounds that make

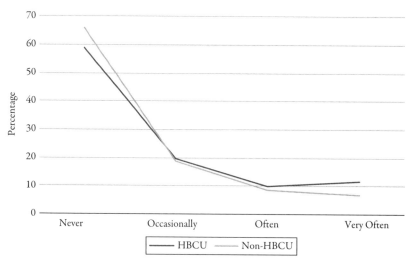

FIGURE 4.6 Responses to the question "How often did you send money to support parents or other family members while you were in college?"

Note: Difference in mean responses is statistically significant at $\alpha = .01$.

Source: The College Experience Study—Black Respondents.

them eligible for need-based financial aid programs like Pell Grants, and they may be more likely to bear significant economic burdens while they are in college.

HBCUs and a Distinctive Campus Environment

In addition to the role that socioeconomic status and access to financial support play in shaping students' ability to successfully complete college degrees, the type of campus environments that students encounter also shapes whether they successfully complete their degree programs. Do Black college students who attend HBCUs and PWIs encounter substantially different campus environments? Moreover, are their overall college experiences significantly different? Data from the College Experience Study corroborate scholarship showing that HBCUs may provide unique institutional cultures that promote student success. As education scholars Robert Palmer and Estelle Young note, "the cultural and social capital embedded in the fabric of [HBCUs] is a unique aspect of Black colleges that helps to foster an empowering educational climate."[8] What kind of campus environments have HBCU and PWI attendees encountered when they enroll at their respective colleges and universities?

Interviews with Black Americans who attended HBCUs and PWIs revealed that many members of both groups found their campus environments to be welcoming. Among Black respondents who attended PWIs during the 1970s and 1980s, a central theme that emerged from interviews was that many universities were working intentionally to promote diversity on their campuses. Lawrence, who attended the University of Minnesota in the 1970s, recalled that "at the time in the '70s, people felt . . . they looked for diversity, and the professors were all very open and, you know . . . Minnesota's a pretty liberal state. I never felt unwelcome on campus." Similarly, Krystal recalled feeling warmly welcomed as a student at Fordham University. She describes her time there during the mid-aughts saying:

I made friends quickly. It was a little weird for me being a minority [at Fordham University] at first, you know, because sometimes you just don't know, like, how other people may accept you. Especially when everybody's coming from different cultures. I was only 18 years old, and you grow up in the same area where you only see, you know, minorities. So going to a school that big, you just don't know. But, I made a lot of friends. It was a good experience. I joined lots of groups, you know. I'm still in contact with friends to this day.

Monique, who attended Iowa State University during the early 1970s, shared a similar experience: "I was apprehensive but excited at the same time, and I felt very welcome. The friends that I met, we're still friends today.... There was a White guy, and I wasn't expecting it, and he gravitated towards me and we became friends. . . . I always felt the difference, but never felt it was a difficult issue to deal with." Many Black students at PWIs describe approaching their racially diverse campuses with a level of apprehension, not knowing whether their presence would be met with enthusiasm or resentment. Moreover, even when their experiences were generally positive, Black students nevertheless reported that their difference was constantly felt on campus.

For Black HBCU attendees, there was an overwhelming sense that not only were they welcome on their college campuses, but that they were viewed as valued members of the campus community where they were seen as family and where the overall mission was to recognize and celebrate Black excellence. Lauren, a 2015 alumna of Bennett College, remembers college president Dr. Julianne Malveaux's description of Bennett College as an "oasis" where Black women would be celebrated. This seemed particularly extraordinary in a world that often failed to acknowledge or celebrate the accomplishments of Black women. Lauren described the Bennett College environment as particularly empowering: "To be able to be in a space where we are and we cherish that . . . we come into a room and, you know, our presence, you notice our presence. You know that we are here, and we're unapologetic about it."

April similarly describes the campus environment at her alma mater, Howard University, as one where there was "a very high expectation of Black excellence. Like, you are part of a larger legacy of Black excellence, and do not disappoint this legacy." She recalls that this theme was apparent throughout her campus experience as a Howard student during the 1990s and that the rich history of HBCUs figured prominently in campus culture:

Yeah [we were] getting it from the culture. So, the faculty members, orientation, and even . . . late-night conversations when there's a snow-storm. People talk about, "You know, we're sitting in the same place that Stokely Carmichael was sitting, like he sat in this classroom, blah, blah, blah!"

Campus traditions and mottos helped to define the campus experience for students at Black colleges, underscoring their status as part of a legacy of Black excellence. Recalling the impact of the campus environment at Tennessee State University, where she graduated in 1981, Jackie says, "Sometimes words don't even express the confidence instilled in me, the pride, the responsibility instilled in me for being at TSU and for being at an HBCU and understanding that my responsibility was to go out into the world and, as our motto says, 'think, work, and serve.' And, that was instilled in us and hammered in us the entire time. We not only dealt with [academics] but we dealt with, from a historical perspective, where Black people came from and our capability."

Ashley remembers unique campus traditions that offered valuable life lessons that she came to appreciate even more after graduating from Bennett College in 2009. There were traditions surrounding how students engaged with the campus landscape, and she recalls that respect for the campus extended "like even down to the grass." She continued:

> I don't know if you've heard, but Bennett Belles don't walk on the grass, and it has a lot to do with ancestry and how we took care of the grass and the yards and people's plantations. So, you don't walk through the work, the hard work that somebody else has taken care of. . . . If you look at Bennett's campus from afar, the courtyard is very drawn out, so there's like very little ways to walk or like get somewhere very quickly. And they said it's because there's no short cuts in life. I think when I was young, when I first got to Bennett, I was probably like, this is terrible. Like, if it's snowing or raining outside, like now you have to walk the long way to get to class or something like that. But, it's very much appreciated now because you realize the work ethic behind it.

These accounts support the notion that HBCUs have a rich legacy of fostering culturally tailored, socially inclusive educational environments that have embraced and empowered generations of students who hail from groups that are typically disempowered by the broader society.

The data also offer valuable insight into students' sense of "fit" in their college community, which is an important factor to consider when

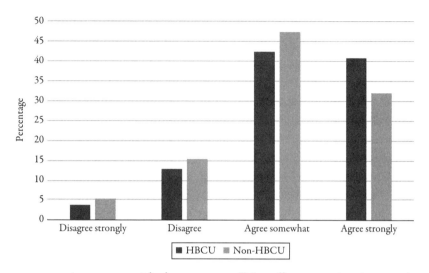

FIGURE 4.7 Agreement with the statement "My college or university was the best fit for me."

Note: Difference in mean responses is statistically significant at α = .01.

Source: The College Experience Study—Black Respondents.

thinking about whether students persist to earn a college degree. When asked about the extent to which they agree with the statement "My college or university was the best fit for me," respondents who attended HBCUs are significantly more likely to express strong agreement (40.9 percent) than their counterparts who attended PWIs (32 percent) (Figure 4.7). Respondents who attended PWIs, on the other hand, are slightly more likely to strongly disagree that their college or university was the best fit (5.2 percent), compared to those who attended an HBCU (3.8 percent). Although the majority of respondents express some level of agreement that their college or university provided the best fit for their needs, the rate of strong agreement among HBCU attendees is noteworthy.

Resources and Campus Infrastructure

For Black HBCU and PWI attendees, campus infrastructure and resources were a central aspect of their campus environments, setting the stage in which their institutions offered opportunities for intellectual development and personal growth. For HBCU attendees, recognition that their colleges and universities were chronically underfunded emerged as a noteworthy theme in interviews. Melvin, who attended Alabama's Miles College during the 1960s, pointed to unequal funding as a chronic challenge that HBCUs face: "Funding—getting the money for these kids to come. The predominantly Black colleges, as you know, do not get the kind of money that the predominantly White schools get. And, that's a fact." Gloria, who attended Cheyney University during the 1970s, concurs: "Even now when I look back at Cheyney—'cause I was looking at something a couple of months ago—they still have problems with financial aid. They're still having problems with funding, with state grants and government supports. And that was an issue then, and it's still an issue now when I look at them . . . they're underfunded."

The strain that limited financial resources places on HBCU campus environments emerged as a noteworthy theme, and HBCU attendees connected it to worn infrastructure and administrative challenges. Jermaine, who attended college during the early aughts, recalled the wear and tear on Lincoln University's campus: "the upkeep of the facilities was not great. Some of the dorms were really in disrepair, I would say. And so, it wasn't the greatest living environment." Jackie, who attended Tennessee State University during the late 1970s and early 1980s, recalled her father's hesitation about leaving her on campus with its signs of wear:

> We were standing outside. He was about to leave. He says, "I'll come back and get you. I'm going to stay a couple of days. I will come back and get you." And, I didn't understand. I said, "Come back and get me and go where?" And he said, "Jackie, look at these buildings." He said, "Some of the windows in the dormitory are broken." He says, "And, I'm really feeling like I don't want to leave you in this place like this." . . . We didn't have a whole lot of money, but we had a decent home to live in. And, I said, "Daddy." I said, "I see them . . . I just see myself being here." Now, he's got a tear coming down [his] face. I ain't never seen that. So I was like, "Oh my God, I'm going to cry. He's going to cry." . . . And, so I looked at him and I said, "Daddy, I'm going to be okay. . . . I think everything will work out."

Like many college students and alumni who recall the frustration of navigating campus bureaucracy, Crystal points to administrative challenges as an aspect of her college experience that she feels was particular to her attendance at an HBCU. Yet she remembers it with a sense of nostalgia:

Trying to register for school . . . that was a process. Trying to graduate. So, you'd go to registration, and they'd have—it's kind of like when you go to vote and, this is so horrible, but depending on what precinct you go to, they've got like the oldest people trying to check you in. And, you're in there for hours, trying to get registered for class.

And, I mean, the line used to wrap around the gym. That experience was nuts. . . . And then when we tried to graduate, the same thing. You're trying to get your cap and gown, and they're going through all your stuff. And, I remember I got up there and they were like, "Ma'am you have an outstanding bill." So, they wouldn't give me my cap and gown.

So, I was like, "What is it?" I had to go to the library, so I walked all the way across campus to go to the library. [They] tell me how much it was, 10 cents. I was overdue and I had a 10-cent bill, and they couldn't look it up in the system because there was no system. I was like, no. I had to walk across campus; I was like, "Let me be clear, I'm coming to the front of the line." So, that experience wasn't much fun, but it's just what makes it nostalgic because people talk about that still.

HBCU attendees generally did not view their institutions' strained resources as a detraction from the quality of their educational experience. Rather, many saw it as a mechanism for character building. For example, Bennett College alumna Ebony emphasizes:

The fact of the matter is, no institution is perfect. So, while there were times where there might have been . . . the plumbing was so old that the water was scalding hot or the water was too cold or we didn't have air conditioning or whatever—because there was always some kind of facilities challenge or not-enough-money kind of challenge that we had. At an HBCU . . . just with organization sometimes. Administration being so small, sometimes things fall through the cracks. But, those challenges further informed my experience as far as being stick-to-it-ive and knowing that I can overcome every challenge.

Highlighting a common conclusion among HBCU attendees who noted their campus' strained infrastructure, Ebony underscores the silver lining in this challenge: "The fact that everything wasn't perfect on campus really helped me to better prepare for the real world, because nothing ever goes [according] to plan." For many HBCU attendees, taking the challenges created by unequal campus funding in stride offered valuable lessons that they could draw on in their future lives.

For PWI attendees, their campuses' considerable resources and the broad range of opportunities that they offered emerged as central themes from their interviews. Julian, who attended the University of Michigan during the early aughts, noted, "On campus I just felt like it was a place where it was a lot of opportunity, a place where you could just try anything. At the time, I think we only needed like six or four people to start a student organization."

Yet Black students studying at PWIs frequently alluded to the work that they had to do on campus to advocate for Black students and to ensure that they were able to fully engage in the opportunities that their campuses offered and that they enjoyed full access to their considerable resources. When Valerie was at the University of Chicago during the 1970s, she developed valuable negotiating and organizing skills while advocating for programming that better catered to the interests of Black students. As she recalls,

> When we were there, the Black Student Union, we were able to have concerts on campus that they had never seen before. We had people like George Clinton [laughs]. They were not ready. . . . You know, think about it. The University of Chicago and George Clinton, the Funkadelic [laughs]. . . . They were not ready for something like George Clinton on the University of Chicago campus. They changed the rules after that, too. [laughs] Yeah, you had to get more approval before you could schedule to plan any concert.

For Black students at PWIs, working to fight for full citizenship on campus provided opportunities to develop skills like negotiating with administration, organizing campus protests, and building diverse coalitions of students to get things done. Cameron, who attended Otterbein College, described participating in protests in an effort to push back against microaggressions on campus. In participating in protests and other efforts to speak out against microaggressions and other aspects of second-class treatment on campus, Black students at PWIs gained experience pushing institutional boundaries and organizing efforts to alter the campus to better reflect their presence. For some, this work came with the additional lesson that success in fostering greater representation on campus in one instance might be met with subsequent adjustments to institutional rules intended to regulate the scope of student-initiated changes.

Campus Culture, Traditions, and the HBCU College Experience

Colleges and universities offer many young Americans their first experiences interacting directly with institutions as adults. The experiences that students have during college play a central role in shaping their sense of whether their school is a good fit and whether they will persist to degrees. Do HBCUs offer Black college students unique college experiences?

Data from the College Experience Study and the HBCU Alumni Study suggest that while HBCUs and PWIs generally offer welcoming campus environments, HBCUs offer especially inclusive spaces where students feel welcome, seen, and free to be their authentic selves. Wilberforce University alumnus Edward described being embraced by faculty and staff members during his first week on campus. He was particularly struck by the fact that they went to the trouble of learning his name and introducing themselves to him before he had an opportunity to begin to learn who they were. He summarized the surprising and emblematic aspect of his college experience in a pithy sentence: "[I'd] never been in an educational situation where people want to like me."

For Louis, who graduated from Lincoln University in the mid-1960s, there is a close connection between an inclusive campus environment and students' empowerment. Noting the significance of his college experience for shaping his ability to withstand discrimination and prejudice in the corporate world over a three-decade career, he says, "If you're going to a minority school, in addition to relationships you develop . . . it also helps to develop kind of like an inner strength, because it takes the inner strength for you to get through the things that you've gotta face in this world."

Isaiah, who graduated from Howard University in 2014, agreed, describing his academic and overall college experience as one "that affirmed my culture and affirmed who I am as a Black man in America." He emphasized his belief that his college experience "has set me up to be successful in spaces that are not predominantly Black and also has established a certain nostalgia when I am in spaces that are majority Black." These data suggest that HBCU attendees have found immense value in college experiences that were warmly inclusive and confidence-building. Respondents described these experiences as formative aspects of their development, helping them find their unique voices and, more generally, offering empowering preparation for life.

Candice recalls her HBCU experience as a refreshing change from the challenges of navigating through a high school environment characterized by tensions that made it difficult to live and learn as a student who did not fit neatly into categories forged by generational hardship and stereotypes about blackness. "When I went to Spelman it was like a breath of fresh air because there were girls who were like me. . . . These were girls who loved to learn." She continued, describing her college environment as affirming:

> I was in school with other girls whose parents had gone to college and were professional folks. There were girls who were super, super, super rich, so I wasn't the little rich girl in peoples' eyes. . . . I was just another girl that was at Spelman, so it was a really freeing experience for me, being in a place where girls were like me. . . . I just thrived in that environment because I could really just be my most authentic self, and I didn't have to dim myself so that other people didn't feel any kind of way. That was great.

For Black Americans, HBCUs offer unique environments for transitioning to adulthood, providing spaces where students may feel at ease bringing their authentic selves to bear in the pursuit of knowledge and personal growth. These data suggest that HBCUs seek to develop their students as holistic individuals in an empowering space, which may explain why many Black families, mentors, and communities guide their young people to them. By offering young people an experience of what first class treatment by institutions feels like and confirmation that it does exist, HBCUs may play a central role in the longer-term expectations that their students develop for their roles as democratic citizens.

Diversity on Campus

Interestingly, respondents who attended HBCUs and PWIs cite the diversity on their campuses as a valued part of their college experiences. Black PWI attendees noted that their institutions offered opportunities to connect with people with different racial and ethnic identities, as well as diverse intellectual perspectives. Mary, who attended Wayne State, a PWI in Detroit, during the 1960s, says, "What I remember most is the exposure to so many different ideas and people and things that I had just never been exposed to . . . growing up and going to high school. . . . So, going to the university exposed me to a lot of different ideas." Valerie recalls that, at the University of Chicago during the 1970s, "It was nice. They mixed it, in terms of your roommates and all. It was a mixed school, so you weren't paired with someone out of the same race, so that was good. You had exposure to other people." Craig, who attended Shippensburg University, was similarly impressed by the diversity on his PWI campus. "It was great seeing other people, other nationalities, races, how they lived, interacting with them, talking to them, finding out about their backgrounds, their history, things like that."

Some PWI attendees highlighted intentional efforts by members of their campus communities to include them. Terry remembers her first year at the University of Wisconsin–Stout during the late 1960s, where she was one of a few African Americans on campus:

> Okay, so . . . now, I'm the only African American student in my residence hall, and there's only like three African American females at the college. So, we're at an assembly and all of a sudden, I get nominated for vice president of the freshman class. I don't know anybody. I don't even know who nominated me, and the next thing I knew, I'm standing in front of the assembly hall, giving a speech on why I wanted to become vice president of the freshman class, and I was elected vice president of the freshman class. I don't know if it was because I was African American and they wanted diversity or what, but I ended up being in the international club. They wanted me to be a cheerleader. I said, I don't know how to cheer—I'm not a cheerleader.

For these respondents, having the opportunity to live and learn in PWI environments that made concerted efforts to include students from a variety of racial and ethnic backgrounds was a valued part of their college experience. Campus diversity and feeling welcome on campus represented one of the most memorable features of their PWI experience.

Black PWI graduates also note the diverse networks that they built during their college years and the role that diverse coalitions of students could play in achieving change on campus. Monique identified this as an important lesson that emerged from her experience at Iowa State University during the early 1970s: "One thing I learned—I guess, I learned it in college being a minority at the school—I learned that politics is not necessarily racially driven. I felt I was able to get a lot of things done with people who were not African American. I wish there was a way to see more of that nowadays, that kind of environment. Race was an issue, don't get me wrong. But it wasn't an issue used politically. That was the enjoyment of the college experience for me."

Another theme that emerged from interviews with Black PWI attendees is that there was considerable variety in terms of the type of campus experience that students sought. A number of PWI attendees shared that their status as nontraditional students who were primarily interested in making rapid progress toward graduation was central to their experience. Mary attended Detroit's Wayne State University during the 1960s, which offered a campus experience that catered particularly to students who were less interested in having a residential living and learning experience:

Wayne University was pretty much a commuter type university. At the time there was very little student housing. Most people traveled—were local and traveled to the university. And, so it wasn't like a college campus like Michigan State University or the University of Michigan. It was more people who either had jobs and were going to school part time and it wasn't a lot of community. . . . I was working. I was older.

Diversity similarly emerges as a valued part of the HBCU college experience. While the majority of students attending HBCUs were Black in 1976, 15 percent of HBCU students were non-Black. In 2020, 24 percent of HBCU students were non-Black.[9] West Virginia State University offers an example of an HBCU that is no longer predominantly Black. During the 2020–2021 academic year, 14 percent of its undergraduate population were minority students. Derrick, who attended West Virginia State University (then known as West Virginia State College) in the 1980s, recalls, "I learned to coexist with people from all parts of the country. People that didn't necessarily look or act like me because my HBCU, during the daytime, it was a lot more White students because it was local to West Virginia, which is only about 3 percent populated by African Americans." Gregory, who also attended West Virginia State during the 1980s concurred, recalling that

It was a bit different than other HBCUs—we used to say West Virginia State was White by day and Black by night because . . . the Black population [in West Virginia] had decreased so much since coal mining started to die down that there just wasn't as many Black students in the state, and the Black students in the state had the options of going to other places, whereas back in the '40s and '50s, there weren't that many options for Black kids. . . . It gave me a great ability to adjust and learn [in] two different environments. I had never been in an academic environment with White kids . . . and really be in a minority because up until I got to West Virginia State . . . during the day, I had never been in a setting where I was a minority.

Delaware State College (later Delaware State University) alumna Joyce had a similar experience during college, as a substantial proportion of Delaware State's nonresident student population were White. As Joyce describes,

Dover was a racist, White community. They did not come on campus. We had White students that came to campus, but they came and then they left. . . . I'm not saying this in a bad way, but . . . I think a lot of them are afraid of being around a bunch of Black people after dark. I'm just saying, perception. . . . I don't think I saw ten White people in my classes the whole time I was there. We knew that they were coming, the Dover people, the day people, and they would come and be a part, and do whatever, and then they went home, and then we did us.

A prominent theme in the data from Black HBCU attendees is that their colleges and universities offered an opportunity to gain close familiarity with the rich diversity of blackness, particularly the range of socioeconomic and geographical backgrounds that Black students brought to campus as they hailed from all across the United States and the African diaspora. Betty, who attended Hampton Institute (later Hampton University) during the 1940s, described the diversity at her HBCU as central to her personal and professional development: "Mixing with other Black students from various parts of the United States and the world—because we had Africans there, and we had kids from the West Indies there—I think I grew up a lot. I matured a lot. . . . Hampton made me a much better, a more gifted, a more intellectual [person]; and I became, I think, a very good English teacher."

Talladega College alumnus Kenneth, who came from a working-class background, said that at Talladega,

I was exposed to a Black middle class, or Black upper-middle class culture for the first time. A lot of my classmates had come from places like Charleston, South Carolina, or Atlanta, or Montgomery. Larger cities. Bigger high schools. More social class stratification. Many of them were, themselves, second- or third-generation college graduates, or came from families where there had been college graduates for a couple of generations, so it was a much more sophisticated environment than I had ever been exposed to.

Nathan says that his experience at North Carolina Central University during the 1980s and early 1990s helped him discover "that race wasn't the only dimension of difference and variability that mattered on college campuses. Socioeconomics was not just income and wealth but also a history of advanced or formal education within families. . . . There were kids at North Carolina Central who were fourth generation legacies at the institution whose great-grandparents had [attended]." He continued, "So, sort of class dynamics within the Black American community became more apparent to me when I was there than they had previously been." April gained a similar appreciation for the full scope of socioeconomic backgrounds represented at her HBCU, Howard University, during the 1990s: "There were a lot of very privileged kids at Howard, like I'd never met so many wealthy Black people before I got to Howard. . . . I never really thought about them existing in bulk. And, you know, you had folks who were really struggling [financially]."

Bennett College alumna Ashley describes the diversity at her all-women college as prompting her racial awakening, saying:

I don't think I ever noticed my blackness or cared about it when I was in high school because . . . all we pointed out were differences in high school. So, someone who was another color or another race, you know, they're just gonna identify you with Black. Whereas, in my [Bennett College] community, it's like, there's so many shades, or what we call flavors (laughs), of blackness and different things to be passionate about. Like our culture and African dance, African prints, like just all those little details that you don't think about. . . . So, going to Bennett, it just made me more proud, you know, to be Black.

Tiffany, who graduated from Clark Atlanta University in 2009, recalled the powerful impact that her HBCU's diversity had on her outlook on the world: "I would say it made it cool to be Black for me. Growing up, it wasn't that I was being told by people around me that were close to me that blackness isn't cool or 'don't be so Black.' But, I also wasn't getting the uplifting messages around being Black. . . . So, it was life-changing for me to see that Black people are not a monolith. That is in real color at HBCUs. I've seen so many beautiful, different types of Black people, being able to know that we will always be able to meet each other by being brothers and sisters in our culture first." As these data illustrate, Black HBCU attendees often described their campus experiences as steeped in appreciation for the full diversity of the Black experience and as valuable to their personal and intellectual development. This nuanced thinking about both diversity and blackness that HBCU attendees describe contrasts considerably with the prevailing thinking about diversity that respondents report to describe their experiences at PWIs.

Campus Culture and the Experiences of Black Students at HBCUs and PWIs

While Black Americans who attended HBCUs and PWIs point to the value of diversity for shaping their college experiences, those who attended PWIs frequently report having campus experiences characterized by social isolation and laced with microaggressions and, in some cases, outright racism. Indeed, the seemingly welcome presence of racially diverse students at many PWIs has not necessarily meant that Black students felt fully included as members of their college or university community or that they were subjected to equitable treatment on campus.

Black PWI attendees who were among few minorities on campus recalled feeling socially disconnected. Social isolation and experiencing race-based discrimination emerged as important themes in the interview data. Robyn, for example, who attended Trinity College during the 1990s, describes a feeling of separation from her PWI and a lack of knowledge about where to find support when she was navigating life on campus:

[T]here's a sense of not belonging, feeling sort of disconnected; sort of isolated. So, you know, my peer group were people who looked like me and had similar experiences and sort of gravitated toward each other and made it through together. . . . I didn't feel like there were advocates for me. Like, if I was looking for an advocate on campus . . . I would gravitate toward somebody that was like a minority teacher, right? I wouldn't know to ask them like, "Were you the first in your family to go to college?" You know, they weren't like, "Oh, you know, this program is for first-generation college students." There weren't those sorts of supports at that time.

Linda, who attended Normal Illinois State University (later Illinois State University) during the 1960s, recalled, "Well, I can't say I remember that [my college experience] was wonderful because it was about five thousand students, and only fifty of us were Black. And, so I guess I was feeling like I was rather isolated. I would say I remember that very well." Lawrence, who attended the University of Minnesota during the 1970s, agreed, saying:

I didn't have much of a campus life. My senior year, I did live on campus. It's a very big school. . . . It's one of the largest schools around. So . . . the good news is that you can always find some activity or something to do that was of interest. But it was a place where it was very easy to get lost if you let yourself get lost because there's no one overlooking what you're doing. You're there on your own.

As these examples illustrate, the social benefits of diversity at PWIs may have been lost on many Black students. Some put considerable effort into forming social enclaves with other Black classmates to combat the feeling of disconnection that the broader campus environment fostered, but others navigated their college experiences with little social support and without a sense of being part of a closely knit campus community.

During his first semester at a Shippensburg University, Craig experienced racial tensions as soon as he arrived on campus. Describing the start of his freshman year, he remembers that "The dorm that I was staying in had been vandalized by someone writing racial slurs and swastikas in the elevator. All the walls and stuff had to be cleaned out. So, we brought that to the attention of the dean of housing who had a meeting with our entire dorm, looking into it and getting to the bottom of it." Although Shippensburg worked to investigate the incident, Craig and his classmates would feel a sense of unease on campus that affected their living and learning experience:

> We were very upset about that because some of us had come from communities where we were used to being around a diverse group of people. And to have someone write the N-word and put swastikas up and things like that, it was very offensive to us. So we had a difficult time dealing with that, and we wanted them to take action to correct it because we didn't feel safe on our campus.

Mary describes an incident during her time at Wayne State University during the 1960s that further illustrates the kind of racism that the Black PWI attendees experienced:

> I mean, there were some . . . occasions, one occasion in particular that I remember where a White student who had befriended me and she apparently had some, I don't know, I thought later, some emotional problems. She came in one day and just called me all kinds of names for talking about Black people. And it was very distressing to me. And we, I had to take an exam that day . . . and she didn't, and she left. . . . Something had happened, and apparently [it] involved some Black people, and she was venting her anger at me.

As this example illustrates, experiences with racism can directly affect students' academic performance.

The social exclusion, racism, and exhaustion that many Black students have faced at PWIs have a substantial bearing on the nature of their college experience. For many of these students, in addition to the task of growing personally and intellectually during college, they must also fight to carry on in a complex and often troubling social environment. This exchange with Vanessa, who graduated from the University of California–Berkeley in the late 1980s, offers a powerful illustration of this theme:

Vanessa: So, I learned more out of the classroom than I did in the classroom. How about that?
Interviewer: Okay. In what way?

Vanessa: They were clear that they did not—administration, other students— did not want people of color there, and they fought every day to get us out.

Interviewer: So, in terms of politicking, as you were mentioning before. How exactly did that work? Was that with other students, or—

Vanessa: That was everything. Professors. Other students. I mean, you had to jockey to get enrolled in a classroom.

Interviewer: Okay. I see.

Vanessa: It wasn't just you sign up for a class and then you go to it. Oh, no ma'am. You had to politick to get an appointment with an academic advisor.

Interviewer: And, what did that look like?

Vanessa: You were doing whatever you had to do to get in there. Hook or crook. Um, trust me, there were a whole lot of favors going on.

When asked whether she felt welcome on campus, Vanessa said, "It was extremely hostile, and they were very clear that none of us belonged there.... Anybody of color." In addition to the isolation and feelings of not belonging that proved a powerful feature of the PWI experience for many Black students, exposure to racism on campus often made it difficult to live and learn as members of their campus communities.

HBCUs as Family-like Campuses with a Strong Sense of Community

While isolation, microaggressions, and racism emerge as challenging and exhausting parts of the campus experience for many Black students studying at PWIs, those who attend HBCUs overwhelmingly describe college experiences that take place in nurturing spaces where they are treated like family and where they feel as though an entire community is looking out for them. Jean, who graduated from Bennett College in the early 1960s, describes HBCUs as providing "a cocoon" for students that nurtures them during college and continues to support them over the long term. Describing life at Talladega College when she was a student during the 1960s, Gail describes a campus culture that felt familiar: "It was very formal, lots of dress codes about what you could and could not wear. No pants, except on Saturday. Lots of . . . very much *in loco parentis*. Chapel— required chapel attendance. Very much like a place where I'd grown up, with lots of rules about what's proper behavior, what a lady does, what a lady does not do, that kind of stuff."

While campus culture has become much less formal for more junior generations of HBCU students, those from younger age cohorts note the same sense of a campus culture that stressed Black community and excellence. Ashley recalled that taking pride in one's self and her Bennett sisters was part and parcel of life at Bennett College, where she graduated in 2009:

> That was our culture . . . keeping another sister in line. So, there were days where you would see one of your roommates or someone in your dorm wearing pajamas, and you're like, "Hey, like, maybe you should go and. . . ." It was very honest, and that's what I appreciated, like someone always having my back and being like, "Maybe you shouldn't wear that," or "Maybe you should do this. . . ." Because they were like your mom, or your aunt, or something, or your grandmother. So, there was always someone on campus that was keeping someone in line or having your back about something.

Chelsea, who graduated from Hampton University in 2009, recalled benefiting from a robust set of campus traditions that her university used to build a strong sense of community:

> As freshmen, when you come in you're given a class name—my class name was Onyx 10. And, your class name is passed down from the seniors that were graduating that year. . . . I think Hampton does a good job of making sure that [you] build relationships with your classmates. . . . Hampton did a great job of making sure they did things for our class, which was throwing different parties or different activities so we could bond with one another.

Savannah State University alumna Nicole recalled that professional development was woven into the campus culture at her HBCU: "We had this thing on our campus on Wednesdays, [it] was the dress for success Wednesday. We encouraged our students to wear—for men, wear suits, and women, professional wear as well. Our motto was, dress for success, dress for that future job, dress like you're already in that position that you want." Nicole described this campus tradition as contributing to the transformation that she underwent during college, fostering "growth" and "sharpening" that she views as crucial to her development. As these examples illustrate, HBCU attendees described campus experiences where they felt not only welcome and included but also valued and inspired as members of the college community.

A dominant theme that emerged from interviews is that HBCU attendees felt like family on their college campuses. This theme is illustrated powerfully in an exchange with Ebony, a 2008 Bennett College alumna:

Interviewer: How would you describe your relationship with your Bennett College classmates? Are you still in touch with them?

Ebony: Yeah. Those are my Bennett sisters. I would never call my Bennett . . . I would never use that, like "Bennett College classmate." Everybody is a Bennett sister. My Bennett Belle.

Black HBCU students overwhelmingly reported feeling safe on their campuses, protected from racism, and fully included in the joyful social life on their campuses. Participation in campus social clubs, pledging Greek organizations, and participating in their HBCUs' homecoming festivities were frequently cited examples of the rich and engaging culture that Black students benefited from as members of HBCU campus communities.

Ethan, for example, describes homecoming at Morehouse College as an unforgettable part of his college experience: "Our homecomings are tremendous—unlike any other homecoming at any other kind of school. But, our homecomings, you get thousands of people that come, a lot of them don't even go to the school. But, a lot of alumni and everyone, and it's just like, I don't even know how to put it into words. It was a life-changing experience for me." He described his first homecoming experience during freshman year:

So, I'm on the yard and they're playing . . . and there's thousands and thousands of people there. But, [the musical guest is] performing, and everyone starts going in unison to the Electric Slide, and then you see all these older people in their 80s, people in their 50s with their kids [who are] maybe in elementary school, everyone's dancing, everyone's having a good time. You see so much Black excellence all there at once. I literally broke down and starting crying. It was just such an emotional experience.

Moreover, many described the HBCU experience as an energizing one that does not stop at graduation. Jean, who is actively engaged in the Bennett College alumnae community, recalled the strength and refreshment that she and her college sisters continue to draw from the campus community: "Bennett was an empowerment tool for my life. I think of when we came back for one reunion. One alum who hadn't come in many years, she said, 'Oh, I'm ready to go back to New York and kick ass.' What she was saying was, 'I feel so empowered.'"

It comes as little surprise that the HBCU alumni community is a robust one that emphasizes paying forward the benefits that the broad HBCU community has provided by watching out for younger generations of HBCU alumni. Chanté, an alumna of Spelman College, describes her devotion to the community of Spelman alumnae, saying, "We're really close . . . professionally even, outside of friendships—if somebody's résumé comes across my desk that is any HBCU—but definitely if it's Spelman College—they are for sure getting their interview. . . . If I work somewhere, and there's a Spelman person there, I am bee-lining to them when I get there so we know we are together. We're a pretty close-knit group, period. But, I would definitely say we watch out for each other regardless."

Joyce, who graduated from HBCU Delaware State, underscores the "oneness" of the overall HBCU community, which she describes as a distinctive feature of the Black college experience:

> Now, when Howard is playing Delaware State, we are gonna kill Howard. It's just gonna happen like that—we're gonna rip your heads off. But, when I see a Howard grad, and we're in the same exchange, we're family. . . . You can be at work and you found out somebody went to A&T. You immediately have a connection. So, you wind up having a connection anywhere you go, 'cause that's how HBCUs train us to be. We are one. We in the struggle together. The same struggles that they have in Florida and they have at A&T are the same struggles that graduates of Delaware State are gonna have. We found out, through the HBCU connections that we have, that we all have to work together in order for us to get anywhere together. . . . There's just a connection. And, it's a good thing.

As these data illustrate, Black Americans who attended HBCUs describe their campuses as family-like environments that revolve around a strong sense of connectedness. This theme suggests that what political scientists Katherine Tate and Michael Dawson describe as "linked fate"—a group consciousness whereby the challenges or triumphs of one member of a group are felt as shared challenges or triumphs across the group—is a constitutive feature of HBCU campus culture.[10]

Protection from Racism off Campus

A central feature of the family-like experience that HBCUs provide is the campus work to provide students with a living and learning environment where they are as shielded as possible from racism. For more senior cohorts of HBCU alumni, many expressed appreciation for their schools' intentional efforts to protect them from the racism that existed off campus. "We were a pretty self-contained environment, and I think most of us were just fine with that," says Kenneth in describing his experience at Talladega College in the midst of Jim Crow in Alabama during the early 1960s:

> We had student stores. Or whatever clothing we needed, we bought in our hometowns, and we just didn't venture beyond the campus very much at all. We had opportunities to watch movies, so we didn't have to go and sit in the balcony of the segregated theaters downtown. We didn't need to go to church because we had . . . required chapel every Tuesday, and you were expected to go to chapel, so we were pretty self-sufficient. White Talladega was just sort of a foreign country, in a way.

Joyce, a 1979 alumna of Delaware State College, shared a similar description of the relationship that existed between her HBCU and the surrounding, predominantly White, Dover community when she was in college during the 1970s. In addition to limited mixing between Delaware State College and the surrounding community, she recalls local Ku Klux Klan activity as signaling that the community outside of campus was hostile to the Black students: "Remember, it was still a lot of discrimination [during the 1970s]—Ku Klux Klan would burn crosses on the school every summer." She continued, "Every summer they burned their crosses on the school at some point . . . for their hate-filled, racist situation, conglomeration they would have every summer. And they'd march over to the campus and burn the things and say whatever they say and then they leave. . . . That was every summer. Every summer that I was there."

Reflecting on the unique campus environments that HBCUs strive to foster, Gloria—who attended Pennsylvania's Cheyney University during the 1970s—said that HBCUs "pretty much understand how, as a minority person, if you don't feel included in things, you're always feeling separated. There I was included. I was never judged. I was never followed around the store. I was never called, um, a negative name. . . . You weren't exposed to racism." These data support existing scholarship suggesting that students at HBCUs report experiencing racism and microaggressions at lower rates than their counterparts at PWIs.[11]

HBCUs as an Extension of the Black Community

The close connection between HBCUs and the Black community is another powerful theme that emerged from interview data. Respondents recalled that HBCUs were important parts of their surrounding communities. As Kenneth, who attended Talladega College during the 1960s, observed:

> There was a very, very close relationship between the college and the Black community in Talladega. There were a number of students at the college who actually grew up in Talladega; and Talladega College, of course, was a major employer of Black folks there. And, because all of the cultural offerings that the college put on were available to the larger community. I don't recall seeing many youth, young people who were not college students attending cultural events in the time that I was there, but certainly adults who were not employed by the college would come and attend.

Candice echoes this sentiment as she recalls the close connection between Delaware State, where she spent time growing up, and the surrounding Black community: "In a lot of ways, Delaware State became an extension of what was going on in the Black community, like a resource for the Black community." She described this connection as similar to the connection between the Black community and the Black church "in that it was a place where Black people came together to be in community—[including] Black people that weren't even studying on the campus or weren't working on the campus—but it was ours, right? This place belonged to the Black community."

In addition to the Black communities that surrounded HBCUs, the more distant communities that sent their young people to far away campuses were also important members of the extended HBCU community. Gail noted the pride of her Macon, Georgia, community when she went away to college at Talladega in the 1960s:

> It was just not you going [to college], but you represented your whole community. So, there were all these people in my church, a lot of whom had not finished high school or even grade school, who were counting on me to make it. . . . I remember having this conversation with this older woman in my church, and she said, "What are you studying?" I said, "Psychology." She said, "Well, baby, I don't know what that is, but you do good at it, hear?" . . . So people would put money in your hand. . . . These were all domestics, who had nothing. They'd take money out of a knotted-up handkerchief and give you a dollar or two, and so I knew people were counting on me. It was a lot of pressure, but it was a lot of . . . it wasn't just about me succeeding or failing. It was about them.

The strong community of family, friends, and loved ones that supported HBCU students did not go unappreciated by their campuses. Black college alumni recall ways in which their campuses embraced their families and communities. For example, Derrick recalls how the West Virginia State yearbook helped to capture and honor his mother's pride when he became the first person in his family not only to graduate from high school but also to earn a college degree: "One of my greatest pictures in the world is in my college yearbook. It's a picture of me and my mother holding my diploma. This is a woman who grew up in rural Mississippi. She was born in 1936. She's no longer on this earth but now she's in my college yearbook. So, when I graduated so did she."

As these data illustrate, HBCUs have embraced Black college students, their families, and their communities, extending the reach of their commitment to Black excellence and providing oases from some of the challenges that Black Americans have faced as members of the broader society.

HBCUs, Identity, and Transformation

Another powerful theme that emerged uniquely from interviews with HBCU attendees was the notion that their college experience contributed to a change in their personal identity. Numerous HBCU alumni described having a clear sense of the standard that being a member of their HBCU community set. They frequently described their college experiences—and the culture and traditions that drove them—as transformative, both academically and personally. As Chelsea recalls of her experience in college, "I remember before coming to Hampton, I did have confidence in myself. But, Hampton really built, molded, and shaped me into just a different person in general." She continues:

> Hampton just changed me in the aspect of how I carry myself. We have this thing called "a Hampton Woman," and a Hampton Woman carries herself with class and with grace and with elegance. I feel like I do that more, and I'm more conscious of how I'm represented because I'm not only representing myself, but I represent my family, and I also represent the Black community.

Candice elaborated on this idea, noting widespread awareness of the qualities associated with alumnae of her alma mater:

> I have never been in any situation professionally where when I mention Spelman College people don't automatically feel that they know some things about me based on the reputation. . . . People know the kind of women that Spelman produced and were excited to have Spelman women in their department or at their institution or doing internships with them. So for me there have been a lot of benefits for having gone to Spelman.

Not surprisingly, among HBCU alumni who view their campus communities as extensions of their family, many expressed a commitment to defending their HBCU, and the larger of community of HBCUs, from detractors—much like people stand ready to defend their family members and other loved ones. Justin, for example, who holds HBCU and PWI degrees, describes his reaction to outsiders who dismiss his HBCU education as less consequential or impressive than his PWI education:

> I know [North Carolina] Central's not a ranked law school. I do know that, but I felt very offended [by disparaging comments]. But, that was just the beginning of just me coming to terms with the fact that I would always have to defend my HBCU, especially in predominantly White spaces. Especially because . . . Central's not like a Howard, it's not a Morehouse, it's not a Spelman. It's not a named, recognized HBCU

outside of North Carolina. . . . I feel like I'll always have to defend it, and that gives me another sense of pride for my school. Just like, okay, well now I have to prove to these people that Central is a good law school and that my training from Central alone could qualify me for this job and that it's not a blemish on my resume. And, I feel talking to my other law school classmates, they feel the same way.

These data illustrate the devotion that many HBCU graduates have to their schools and the strength of their sense of membership in the extended HBCU community. While appreciation for their college experience and connections with their alumni networks emerged from interviews with Black PWI attendees, those who attended HBCUs described a particular sense of loyalty to their HBCUs and steadfast connection to the broad HBCU alumni community.

Conclusion

In a society characterized by long-standing social, economic, and political inequality that particularly challenges Black and Brown communities, HBCUs have played a unique role in providing Black men and women with access to institutions that are boldly invested in their advancement. The research presented in this chapter reveals that Historically Black Colleges and Universities offer distinctive educational experiences that are driven by unique institutional cultures. The factors that shape these cultures include a keen appreciation for the history of Black colleges and their legacies for empowering Black people, campus traditions that have fostered community building over generations, and welcoming learning and living spaces that embrace blackness and that work in concert to recognize, develop, and celebrate Black excellence. The distinct educational culture that exists in HBCUs has been developed over the long history of Black higher education, and for the disproportionate number of college-educated Black Americans who have earned their degrees at Black colleges, this unique experience is part and parcel of higher education.

As generations of Americans who have been educated in Black colleges have concluded their studies and transitioned into the broader society— one that is characterized by chronic challenges like racism, discrimination, and structural inequality—many come to attach increasing value on the distinctive educational experience that they had in college and recognize the significance of HBCUs for nurturing and empowering young Black

Americans at a critical juncture in their personal and professional development. This could very well explain the powerful force of legacy ties that has shaped attendance at HBCUs across generations. Moreover, HBCUs have served a broad cross section of Black college students—from first-generation college students and those coming from low-income households, to fourth-generation college students and those hailing from the nation's wealthiest Black families. As such, they succeed in offering a unique educational experience that resonates with a diverse array of students who represent a broad cross section of the Black experience.

The data presented in this chapter suggest that students select HBCUs because they seek educational opportunity, an educational experience that unabashedly embraces blackness and that is centered on cultivating Black excellence, and a learning and living environment that is committed to not only their full inclusion but also to their holistic development. Academic environments that unabashedly embrace blackness and the issue of race, more generally, dwell in sharp contrast to many higher educational institutions that have struggled to deliver on the dual imperatives of diversity and inclusion, especially in the years since the 1964 Civil Rights Act prohibited race-based discrimination in college admissions.

While many historically White colleges and universities have sought to increase the number of Black students on campus, their efforts to promote diversity often stop short of providing programs and other resources to ensure that Black students are socially included and protected from the micro- and macroaggressions that have become all too common on PWI college campuses. HBCUs offer many Black students an opportunity to defer many of these types of interactions until after they have completed the initial transition into adulthood during their undergraduate years. In providing predominantly Black living and learning spaces, HBCUs offer Black students the opportunity to learn in environments where they are not a racial minority and where their identities are not reduced to stereotypes, as may be the case in other spaces where race is not considered with the same level of nuance or appreciation.

This analysis suggests that HBCUs offer Black students living and learning environments that were designed with them in mind. These spaces recognize blackness in its complexity—in a way that ventures beyond stereotypes to include appreciation for the diversity of the Black experience at home and abroad. Blackness is not viewed as a problem to be overcome but as an identity that is imbued with pride.

HBCUs also offer students an environment where both their racial identity and their shared commitment to learning and professional development are the norm. In doing so, they may help to promote future civic and political engagement by fostering a sense that their students are valued and empowered citizens. Do HBCUs offer students an academic experience that is similarly distinctive? To what extent do HBCUs offer access to politically empowering curricula? And what role do HBCU faculty members play in shaping these academic experiences? We turn to these questions in Chapter 5.

5

Investing in Black Excellence

HBCU Faculty and the Importance of Politically Empowering Academic Experiences

WHILE PWIS WERE GENERALLY DESIGNED with the purpose of cultivating the intellectual, social, and economic advancement of presumptively White, male student populations, HBCUs were designed to educate and empower students from historically marginalized populations. Considering the significance of higher education for democracy and the history of racial discrimination that long restricted Black people's access to college degrees in the United States, the work that HBCUs and their faculty members have done to ensure that Black Americans have access to college degrees has been central to the fight for democracy.[1]

Higher levels of educational attainment are associated with increased socioeconomic status, greater political interest, and a strong sense of civic responsibility.[2] By awarding degrees, colleges can open doors to professional opportunities and resources that facilitate civic and political engagement. Moreover, college faculty and administrators can develop curricula and degree requirements that promote an understanding of government, history, and the numerous pathways that students can take to democratic engagement. They can also offer students the opportunity to grapple with questions of identity, equity, and justice, while engaging with the various communities to which they belong.[3] Research suggests that such a politics-relevant curriculum has a positive influence on young citizens' political engagement in the years following college graduation.[4]

Using a combination of quantitative and qualitative data from the 2018 College Experience Study and the 2019 HBCU Alumni Study, this chapter examines the impact that HBCUs and their faculty have had on Black Americans' educational attainment and considers the possibility that Black colleges and universities provide distinctive academic experiences that help make their students especially well equipped to engage in civic and political life.

Persistence to Degree and Ultimate Educational Attainment

Perhaps the most obvious benefits that can be derived from college are the acquisition of knowledge and the completion of a credential that will provide access to personal and professional advancement. A valuable indicator of knowledge gained and credentials earned over the course of one's educational career is ultimate educational attainment. Do Black Americans who attend HBCUs tend to earn higher overall educational attainment than those who attend PWIs?

In line with previous research, the data in Figure 5.1 suggest that those who attend HBCUs earn graduate or professional degrees at higher rates than those who attend PWIs—27 percent compared to 22 percent. They are

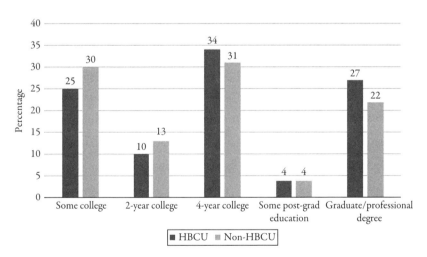

FIGURE 5.1 Educational attainment among HBCU and non-HBCU attendees.

Note: These differences between HBCU attendees and non-HBCU attendees are statistically significant at *p* = .05.

Source: The College Experience Study—Black Respondents.

also slightly more likely to complete a four-year degree, with 34 percent of HBCU attendees and 31 percent of non-HBCU attendees earning a four-year degree as their highest level of educational attainment. On the other hand, 10 percent of HBCU attendees complete their higher education after earning a two-year degree, while 13 percent of non-HBCU attendees do so.

When it comes to ending higher educational pursuits before earning a degree, 25 percent of HBCU attendees report "some college" as their highest level of educational attainment, compared to 30 percent of non-HBCU attendees. And, while Black Americans who do not attend an HBCU are more likely to conclude their higher education with the completion of an associate's degree, those who attend HBCUs earn bachelor's degrees, graduate degrees, and professional degrees at higher rates than those who attend PWIs.

While descriptive statistics suggest that HBCU attendees tend to persist to higher levels of educational attainment than non-HBCU attendees, it is possible that the difference could reflect factors like gender, age, or socioeconomic background, as opposed to institutional affiliation. Table 5.1 reports the results of multivariate analysis of the determinants of educational attainment among Black College Experience Study respondents.[5] The results of ordinary least squares regression analysis suggest that, in line with the literature on educational attainment, Black Americans who are women, whose parents have higher levels of education, and whose families place a greater emphasis on education are significantly more likely to attain higher levels of education. We also see that younger respondents are more likely to have attained high levels of education compared to those who are more senior, likely reflecting the fact that college degree completion has significantly expanded in the years since the mid-twentieth century. Last, the results also indicate that HBCU attendance is positively associated with educational attainment, as those who attend Black colleges tend to earn advanced degrees at a higher rate than those who do not.

Qualitative data provide greater insight into the academic experiences that Black students have at HBCUs and PWIs, which may shape their persistence to degrees and ultimate educational attainment. For both groups, challenging academics and some initial struggles with college coursework emerged as prominent themes in interview data.

Craig, who graduated from PWI Shippensburg University in the late 1980s, recalls a combination of faculty support and institutional structures that worked together to promote his successful progress toward degree

TABLE 5.1 Determinants of Educational Attainment

Gender	.265**
	(.091)
Year of Birth	−.020***
	(.003)
Youth Socioeconomic Status	−.098*
	(.047)
Parents' Education	.107***
	(.013)
Family Emphasis on Education	.191**
	(.063)
HBCU Attendance	.187†
	(.097)
R^2	.09
Adjusted R^2	.09
N	1,134

†$p \leq .1$; *$p \leq .05$, **$p \leq .01$, ***$p \leq .001$
Notes: Cells consist of ordinary least squares regression coefficients in the numerator and standard errors in parentheses. Analysis includes Black respondents who have completed at least "some college."
Source: The College Experience Study—Black Respondents.

completion. In fact, his university offered the opportunity to begin earning college course credit before he had enrolled as a freshman: "Some of my professors, they pushed me to strive for excellence. I ended up taking courses in the summer before I had even graduated from high school. I was enrolled as a freshman taking summer classes to get acclimated to college and build up credits." The encouragement that he received from faculty members and the opportunity to get a head start on the transition to college contributed to Craig's ability to successfully complete his degree.

HBCU attendees offer particularly rich accounts of how their college experiences contributed to their success in completing their degrees and to decisions to pursue graduate degrees. For Gloria, the watchful eye and constant encouragement of a counselor at Cheyney State College were crucial to her successful degree completion: "He just made it a point that I was gonna graduate from college. He would go downstairs and get the key from the housemother, come up to my room and say, 'Miss Williams, you're getting dressed. You're going to class.'" She recalled the counselor's surprising persistence in monitoring her progress and his extraordinary effort to ensure that she complete her degree. She recalled that "I would skip class. This is how spooky it gets. I would skip class. I would wait a few minutes and kind of say, he's gone, and go out the back door. . . . And, he'll be there at the door waiting for me. I don't know how he would know what door I was at. . . . He pretty much got me through college."

In addition to encouraging her to actively engage in classes, Gloria recalls the significance of her advisor's willingness to help troubleshoot in the area of academic challenges. When he noticed that she was having difficulty in math and other classes, he made sure that she had tutors for each area. This active support was central to her ability to complete her degree program.

Shawn, who completed his undergraduate work at North Carolina Central University in 1992, recalled having a faculty advisor who opened his eyes to the possibility of pursuing a PhD:

> I remember having a conversation with him, probably as a 17-year-old kid, where he announced to me one day, "Well, one day when you're getting a PhD." . . . I'm a 17-year-old kid from Mount Olive, North Carolina—I probably didn't even know what a PhD was. I said to him, "Oh, there's no way I'd ever do that." He just told me frankly that day, "Oh, there's no question about it. You're going to get a PhD. Why do you think we're investing all this time in you?" That's exactly what happened.

His advisor's bold prediction and assertion that his university's support for Shawn was geared toward an objective that extended beyond the completion of a bachelor's degree helped to reframe Shawn's perspective on the purpose and significance of the education that he was in the process of attaining at seventeen years old.

Other HBCU attendees described a close connection between their HBCU experiences and their success in graduate school. For Chanté, the confidence that she gained as an undergraduate at Spelman College created a strong foundation for pursuing a law degree at the University of Texas, particularly because it provided a sense of confidence and empowerment during the often challenging transition to graduate study. She explains:

So, I went from [a] homey, comfortable environment that I could grow in, [where] I could be myself, into like the whitest whiteness. I felt strong and sure of myself when I left [Spelman]. And so, I really liked the University of Texas. I wasn't sure how I was going to feel about it, but I loved it. It was a great time—I made a lot of great connections and learned a lot. It was awesome. But, a lot of that came from being sure of myself. I wasn't insecure about how I looked. I wasn't insecure about my academic ability. . . . [Spelman] really hammered home and drilled into us that we were capable, that we were enough, and honestly, that we were the best. So, I came there with that feeling, like you know what, I came here for a reason. Watch out University of Texas, because I'm here.

Like Chanté, Edward also describes his undergraduate experience at Wilberforce University as central to his success in graduate school. Describing his arrival as a graduate student at the University of Pittsburgh, he says:

I said to myself I'm going to this White school. Let me sit up here and be quiet and let these people do their thing and just sit here and absorb stuff. That lasted about two days because I found out I was as read as the professors and more than three fourths of the students. What I had done as an undergraduate had more than aptly prepared me for graduate school. . . . It was a very interesting experience and eye-opening because it reinforced how vital and important what I received at Wilberforce really was. Academically, socially, politically, all of the above. It helped build me into the person who is open and receptive and could compete.

These examples illustrate the value of HBCU experiences for not only preparing students for the rigors of graduate study but also for instilling in them the confidence necessary to succeed in it.

While experiencing undergraduate education with an eye toward graduate study emerged as a theme in interviews with Black HBCU attendees, those who attended PWIs generally reported that their educational experience was dominated by a square focus on undergraduate degree completion, rather than preparing for advanced study. Mary, who graduated from the nursing program at Detroit's Wayne State University in the early 1960s, describes her education as "good," saying that "I was fascinated. I learned a lot, and I learned things that fed my need to know about everything. I was an avid reader, and I did well in my English literature courses." Although Mary sounds like precisely the type of intellectually engaged, curious student who would be a prime candidate for graduate study, she did not find support for considering possibilities for extending her education and, instead, felt constrained by social limitations:

> At the time that I went into nursing school, in my mind there were only two avenues: either be a nurse or a teacher. And, my mother had been a teacher. But, I didn't see that there was any other road. After going to the university, I became interested in other things, but there was still limitations on what a Black woman could do in those years.

Robyn's experience at Trinity College, where she graduated in 1991, offers additional insight into the reasons why Black students at PWIs might find less support for transitioning to graduate study. Reflecting on the strengths and weaknesses of her undergraduate experience at Trinity, she says:

> [E]ven though it was a small institution, and we got a lot of interaction with our teachers, I don't think at the time I went to school it was an environment that really encouraged you to do internships or to do research. Or, perhaps because I was a first-generation student I didn't know to do those things. So, my focus was just to pass my classes and to graduate; but you know, [I] was sort of clueless as to what to do after that.

For Black students studying at PWIs, the early insight into possibilities for graduate study and a clear sense that their undergraduate experiences were a driving force toward success in graduate programs that emerged from interviews with HBCU attendees did not emerge as themes from interview data.

Rigorous Academics, Robust Support, and Democratically Relevant Curriculum

The creation and extension of knowledge and the cultivation of advanced cognitive abilities represent the core functions of higher education. In designing their curricula and devising the standards for advancing toward the completion of a degree, colleges and universities determine which ideas and perspectives gain attention and serious consideration by their students. Furthermore, they elevate chosen perspectives by curating what generations of college students devote their time to thinking seriously about, giving particular topics and questions weight and legitimacy in the academy and beyond. Do Black students studying at HBCUs have academic experiences that are distinct from those of Black students studying at PWIs?

Valuable Learning Opportunities and Challenging Academics

Black HBCU and PWI attendees emphasized the value of their higher educational experiences for providing opportunities to expand their intellectual horizons. The consensus among both groups is that their educational experiences offered valuable learning opportunities and challenging courses of study. Robyn, for example, described her undergraduate experience at PWI Trinity College as "very student-centered. They prioritize teaching over research and things like that for faculty, and so [there are] very small classes, high expectations, a lot of writing. I don't know if I want to say supportive, but . . . I guess . . . student-centered. I feel like I had a strong education in terms of it being challenging. . . . Really high-quality teachers, I felt, that were really passionate about what they study."

Similarly, April remarked on the value of her education at HBCU Howard University, describing it as a powerful supplement to the perspective on education that had been inculcated by her parents: "My parents told me, you want to do something, work hard, do it. You know, kind of pushed that you can do anything. But I felt like when I was at Howard, I got a road map on how to do it. So, it wasn't just . . . theoretically you could do it. . . . If I were to translate how I felt before I got there; and once I got to Howard it was like, this is how you do it."

Like April, other HBCU attendees offered a range of examples illustrating the extraordinary academic opportunities that they gained during college. As a student at Hampton Institute during the 1940s, Betty took courses in English and participated in speech choir where she had the once-in-a-lifetime opportunity to perform on stage with the legendary poet Langston Hughes. She also recalls that "My senior year at Hampton, Margaret Mead, the noted anthropologist, came to Hampton and she selected, I think, four or five of us to attend the University of Virginia in Charlottesville in 1949 to do social work." Betty's excitement about the possibility of working with the famous scholar was cut short when her parents flatly refused to allow her to pursue the opportunity.

Whether it was the notion of sending their daughter to a public university governed by state lawmakers who were firmly committed to racial segregation or discomfort with the idea of their daughter veering from her pathway to becoming a schoolteacher, Betty's parents steered their daughter in a different direction. Seventy years later, she concluded that all was well in the end, nevertheless musing, "But, my life would've been quite different, wouldn't it?" For students like Betty, HBCUs offered extraordinary learning opportunities that were especially noteworthy in light of the broader social dynamics that have limited opportunities for Black Americans.

A prominent theme that emerges from interviews with both Black HBCU and PWI attendees is that they found their academic work to be challenging. One indicator of academic rigor and the level of seriousness with which students treat their academic work is how frequently they attend class. Black HBCU and PWI attendees report relatively high levels of class attendance. However, there is a difference between institution type, with 81 percent of PWI attendees reporting that they attended class "very often," compared to 75 percent of HBCU attendees. This suggests that both groups of students maintain an active presence in the classroom setting but that HBCU attendees are less likely to report the highest levels of class attendance.

Joyce, who graduated from Delaware State University in 1979, helps illustrate this trend. She recalls that when she arrived at college "in 1974, I was not fully invested in education at the time. I did not realize I really, really, really . . . had to go to class, so I really, really, really didn't. I'm just gonna be honest." It was a faculty intervention that sparked an increase in her classroom attendance. She remembers that one of her professors "called me into his office one day and said he was gonna have a conversation with my momma. I said, 'That's unnecessary, because I'm gonna do this now.' And so I did." Her faculty member's willingness to monitor her progress— and to reach out to her parent if necessary—yielded a turning point in Joyce's classroom engagement.

Aside from the frequency of classroom attendance, data from interviews with Black HBCU and PWI attendees also provide insight into the aspects of their classroom experiences that made their academic work challenging. Like many students, Jasmine, who graduated from Hampton University in

2019, describes juggling a hefty academic load as the central challenge of her academic experience during college:

> It was very demanding. . . . [My last semester] I kid you not, I had a paper due on Monday, a paper due on Tuesday, either Tuesday or Thursday, something was always due on Wednesday, and I had some type of lab report due during the weekend. So, it was every other day I was writing four to five-page papers. . . . People always say, once you've finished Hampton, you can do anything.

For Black PWI students, the marked contrast between their academic experience during high school and college and difficulty navigating the resulting challenge emerged as a theme in interview data. University of Michigan alumnus Justin said, "I think there was some catching up for me to do and adjusting. I got I'd say like a B average in [high] school. But B in my school wasn't B college prep." Robyn similarly noted the challenge of her undergraduate education at Trinity college. Describing her initial struggle, she says, "I remember going from [being] a high school student that thought she was strong in all subjects to a freshman that felt she didn't belong in college, that it was very difficult, but never thinking of stopping because I knew my mother would be so upset with me." A first-generation college student, Robyn managed to persevere through the help of her social connections.

Developmental classes provide many college students with non-credit coursework in core areas like math and English to ensure their readiness for college courses. Existing literature suggests that Black and Brown students may be especially likely to enroll in developmental courses due to chronic inequality in the quality of US K–12 education that often leaves them needing supplemental academic support as they enter college. Approximately half of Black College Experience Study respondents report that they took remedial courses, with HBCU attendees reporting a slightly greater rate of enrolling in them "Very Often"—16 percent, compared to 13 percent of non-HBCU attendees. As institutions that strive to expand access to higher education, HBCUs may do a disproportionate share of the work needed to bridge gaps in college readiness.

Edward graduated from Wilberforce University, the nation's oldest private HBCU, in 1971. He noted the significance of developmental coursework to helping him successfully transition into college work. "I couldn't pass algebra to save my life," he recalled. Fortunately, the professor of his developmental math class matched him with an upperclassman who helped him get up to speed. "We sat down, and he talked to me like I actually had some sense. This was part of wondering why I couldn't do better. And then he just asked the right questions about how I studied and what I did. We kind of reorganized my time." This intervention helped set the stage for Edward to successfully complete his math courses, his undergraduate degree, and eventually a graduate degree. While HBCUs often operate with fewer resources than PWIs, they are nonetheless frequently called on to deliver courses and programs that help to bridge gaps left by public education systems that provide unequal access to quality elementary and secondary education to Black students.

In addition to developmental courses, HBCUs also offer targeted programs that deliver additional support to students viewed as being at higher risk of attrition. For example, the Office of the Vice Chancellor for Student Affairs at North Carolina Central University created the Centennial Scholars Program, which works to increase retention and graduation rates of Black male scholars. Brandon, who graduated from NCCU in 2016, explains:

> When I came to college my freshman year, I was automatically in a program called the Centennial [Scholars] Program, which is an African American male initiative that is designed to help Black men graduate on time, in four years, by providing academic and social resources for Black men because we all know Black men are the least likely to graduate and are also the least likely to be retained in school from year to year.

HBCUs have long worked to not only enhance the probability that students will graduate but have also worked to expand students' horizons by supplementing engaging classroom offerings with rare opportunities. During the 1940s, for example, when segregation precluded racial integration on college campuses, Hampton Institute and other HBCUs participated in exchange programs with PWIs. Betty, who graduated from Hampton in 1949, recalls that "we always had White students, about six of them every semester, that came from Antioch College. . . . And our students went to their college." These types of programmatic innovations, academic support mechanisms, and enriching classroom opportunities have played an important role in fostering academic success and intellectual growth at HBCUs.

Politically Relevant Coursework

In addition to the possibility that HBCUs have provided Black college students with challenging academic experiences and valuable support structures that fostered not only degree completion but also movement into advanced educational programs, it is possible that they have also offered their students access to curricular and co-curricular programming that can promote racial awareness and empowerment. Political scientists recognize that greater educational attainment tends to correspond to higher levels of political engagement. But it is worth also recognizing that the content of that education may have an important bearing on subsequent political and civic engagement.

Centering Black Perspectives and Experiences

Interview data suggest that a prominent focus on Black perspectives and experiences throughout their academic programming may help foster particularly empowering educational experiences for Black college students at HBCUs. April, a psychology major who graduated from Howard University in 1997, recalls that although the general structure of her Introduction to Psychology class was "kind of generic like everyone else's," the coursework that she encountered working toward her degree was distinctive: "In any of my other required classes," she noted, "I was still learning about Black people, so even if I took an Abnormal Psych class, or Cognitive Psych, or Brain and Behavior—those standard classes that you take in all psychology departments across the country—I still learned about Black people and Black theorists and researchers."

Candice, an English major at Spelman, also had a unique academic experience at her HBCU. Candice's work in the English department was shaped by a curriculum that prioritized non-canonical courses that might be marginalized elsewhere. She recalled her academic experience during college, noting that a diverse group of professors—consisting of mostly Black women, a few South Asian women, and a White man—approached teaching English in a way that emphasized Black perspectives:

What was interesting was that most of the classes that I took were outside of the canon. I didn't take a lot of canonical courses. I might have taken like one Shakespeare class and then maybe a broad survey course of twentieth-century American literature or something. But most of the courses that I took were . . . the South Asian professors specifically were looking at postcolonial theory and postcolonial writers. One of the most renowned scholars on Langston Hugues works at Spelman, Donna Akiba Sullivan-Harper, and I took one of her survey courses on Langston Hughes's works.

Candice enjoyed her academic experience at Spelman so much that she went on to pursue two graduate degrees. For students like April and Candice, the general education that they gained at their HBCUs was distinctive. While it offered standard information and skills associated with their majors, it also deviated from the norm observed at PWIs by centering Black perspectives and experiences.

In terms of Black studies, which expanded as a burgeoning discipline during the 1960s and 1970s, it took time for many academic programs to come around to dealing explicitly with topics like Black history and the politics of race. Describing her time at Talladega College during the mid-1960s, Gail underscores the virtual absence of curricular offerings that grappled with race and the Black experience, saying that, culturally, it was

a White school with Black students. . . . I don't think that anybody on that campus knew probably very much about Black history. . . . We got a very European education. Got a lot of stuff on Greece, and Rome, and in the humanities, we had a humanities festival every year, never a Black artist. Although the Amistad Murals were at Talladega. Nothing about Hale Woodruff, the Amistad, or what it was there. I think they replicated the European education that they had. I took a drama course from a Black woman my senior year. She was absolutely amazing, but we did Shakespeare. I learned a lot about Greek drama, but never anything about African American drama. Nothing.

Yet, for more junior cohorts of HBCU students who went to college during and after the 1970s, a concerted effort to center Black perspectives and the Black experience represented a central part of their academic experience.

In addition to the unique approach that HBCUs take in shaping the delivery of academic curriculum, HBCU students report participating in enriching co-curricular programming that further distinguishes their academic experiences. Many pointed to college-sponsored assemblies where students heard from political luminaries and other thought leaders. These programs offered students a unique opportunity to engage with some of the most important political figures of their time. Milton, a Howard University alumnus who graduated in 1968, recalled one such guest speaker in 1964:

> Freshman assembly brought in a speaker every Tuesday afternoon. And in February, it was a gentleman named Reverend Dr. Martin Luther King. Now, freshman assembly was mandatory. Yet thousands now claim they were in that auditorium when it only seated 2,000. [laughs] But, he was [in Washington, DC] to visit Lyndon Johnson on voting rights. And, he came and spoke to us before he went down to the White House that afternoon to meet with Lyndon Johnson. I think because of programs like freshman assembly, we became kind of aware of what was going on in the struggle.

Another example of such programming is the ACES seminar series that Vicky participated in when she was a student at Bennett College during the 1970s and that Ebony also participated in when she was there during the aughts. Both Vicky and Ebony recall that engagement with special guest speakers who included Nikki Giovanni, Ed Bradley, Oprah Winfrey, and Maya Angelou during the years that they were at Bennett was a staple of the series.

Kenneth similarly recalled that students had the opportunity to engage with a stream of prominent guests who enriched the learning environment at Talladega College during the 1960s. Among some of the luminaries who visited his campus were the Reverend Dr. Martin Luther King Jr., poet Arna Bontemps, and opera legends Leontyne Price and Martina Arroyo. Kenneth described the unique opportunity to connect with such inspiring Black figures as yielding the most "intellectually and culturally sophisticated environment" of which he had ever been a part.

Many HBCU students also point to special required courses that offer valuable insight into the history of their institutions, and they describe them as a central pathway by which they acquire a greater understanding of the significance of HBCUs to the broader social and political landscape. Hampton University graduate Chelsea described participating in a regular, two-part program that included a course called University 101, in which students learned about Hampton University history, the school's alma mater, and the Black national anthem. The series also included "Ogden," a professionalization seminar named for a prominent building on campus, which offered insight into a range of useful topics like internship and career opportunities and best practices for interviews.

Other HBCU students describe participating in similar programming as part of freshman orientation. At Delaware State during the 1970s, for example, programming for new freshmen included modules offering insight into Delaware's history and the racial dynamics of the local community. "During freshman orientation you learned all types of things," recalls Joyce:

> We had two separate things that I had to take as a freshman: I had to take Delaware history, and I had to take freshman orientation. Delaware history was just that, it told us about Delaware, what happened in Delaware, why it was the first state, yadda, yadda, yadda. But it also told us, basically, what not to do and where not to go and what not to say. The remaining of that came in our freshman orientation where we were all told about Delaware and Dover and what not to do and where not to go and whatnot. We were just told. A lot of us understood it anyway. I came from the South. Ain't nobody know more discrimination than I do.

Candice notes a similarly memorable emphasis on examining the dynamics of race and power in a required course during her time as Spelman. She remembers that

> People were really interested in political questions and thinking about Black feminism and what it meant to be a Black woman in America [and] in the world. We had an introductory course that all students take in the first year at Spelman called African Diaspora in the World, and it really was the first time for most of us we had thought about the African experience in terms of diaspora outside of our own lived experiences wherever we might have been from, and so that sense of

connecting Black women's experiences to those across the globe was just mind-blowing.

As these examples illustrate, HBCUs often weave consideration of Black history and the history of their institutions into the required curriculum that students take on their way to graduation.

Learning about Black History

A strong focus on Black history emerged from the interview data, as HBCU attendees—particularly those in younger age cohorts—describe engaging with curricula that prioritized ensuring that students left their studies with a strong understanding of history and that provided ample opportunities to examine connections between the Black experience and broader social dynamics. Ashley noted that the history curriculum that she encountered at Bennett College was unlike what she had been accustomed to in earlier educational settings:

> Learning Black history was important. That was the first time where you kinda hear a different scenario on the story that you might've read in eighth grade. You know, slavery was described very differently, and then other informal situations were just . . . experiencing it yourself. Like, going to a PWI for a community service project and realizing like how culturally we just handle things differently.

Crystal had a similar experience during her time at Tennessee State University. She remembers that history was closely intertwined with a focus on racial dynamics: "It is literally just like layers of history there. . . . There was a professor named Professor Jackson that taught a sociology class, and it was a Black nationalism class. And, he always had a King and Malcolm X debate, and the entire university would come to hear the debate." In this instance, engagement with two prominent Black historical figures was a prominent feature of a popular course, and it attracted campus-wide attention. Lorraine, who graduated from Virginia State College (now University) in 1973, especially remembers an assignment where she got the chance to engage with Black history in a way that she never had before:

One thing I can say that was unique when I went to Virginia State—I never had a Black history report in my life. It made me more aware of the history of the Black experience in America. I remember sitting in Black history classes being totally fascinated because all the things I was hearing, I never had heard before and that developed an interest in me to learn more about our history.

Many HBCUs also place a great emphasis on teaching history from a perspective that centers the experience of the African diaspora. This unique approach provides insight into Black history and American political development that differs from that which is typically attained in public elementary and secondary schools in the United States. Louis, a seventy-four-year-old alumnus of Lincoln University, recalls the emphasis that his college and other HBCUs place on history, saying, "You learn about Black history a lot. You're also made aware of the difference of how Black people are treated in this country." He continues:

> There's a saying, which I really believe is true that you've got to be several times better than your counterpart to be noticed and really excel in the corporate world because there's still a lot of prejudice that exists and discrimination and so forth. Basically it prepares you a lot for the society that you're gonna work in, you know?

Jermaine, who attended Lincoln University during the early aughts, had the same experience when he attended nearly four decades later. He recalls, "A lot of public schools don't really do a good job with teaching about—teaching accurate information on—African American history. Or even African history in general. At the HBCU, you will find professors that seem to be really dedicated to telling the whole story through the curriculum, rather than just glossing over it the way it's done in public high schools."

Elijah, who graduated from North Carolina Central University in 2014, recalls the impact that his HBCU's Ancient African History course had on him:

> It was eye-opening to me because it was just, it gave me a different perspective of just how the diaspora was an internal diaspora, like what does that mean for folks to move within that continent, that was like, who

was Mansa Musa? We had to learn about different dynasties. So that was interesting because I didn't know any of that. Then, I took a class on the diaspora and so what it means when people use the term "involuntary diaspora," "voluntary diaspora." What does that mean? What was the application? And so just Black people being dispersed everywhere. What does that look like in Europe? What does that look like in Latin America? What does that look like in Northern America? So, just understanding different forms or modes of being Black. And what does that look like in music? What does that look like for art? What does that look like for poetry? And, what does that look like politically through political struggle? . . . So, yeah, those are the kinds of things that I learned while I was there.

Nathan, a 1991 graduate of North Carolina Central University, gained a new appreciation for race, history, and inequality at his HBCU that significantly changed how he thought about politics in the United States. According to Nathan,

What it means to be Black race and perhaps more importantly what it means to be Black American ethnicity, I learned that it does not represent inherent inferiority, and in fact given the history of racial construction—institutionalized racial minority status in the United States of America—that there's something great and beautiful and wonderful and incredibly powerful about the fact that Black folks have not just "survived" but actually thrived in a system that, at best, was not designed for a particular population to succeed and, at worst, may have been specifically designed to assure failure. That's all stuff that I learned, in a rudimentary sense learned, and began to appreciate in value at North Carolina Central University, and that was not happening at [the PWI that he also attended].

For Lauren, who describes herself as having a long-standing passion for public service, learning Black history as a part of her work at Bennett College and North Carolina Central University had a powerful impact on her development. "Having to learn about Central, for example, and the activism around it. Learning about Black Wallstreet, I mean, I can go on and on and on. . . . I was just like, this started here in this community, and it makes you ask a bunch of questions. It really makes you . . . I guess for me, it really made me go hard in my books. Go hard in my work."

These data suggest that HBCU faculty and administrators work intentionally to give the study of history, race, and the Black experience a prominent place in their curriculum. They accomplish this by offering courses designed to focus on these topics and also by designing co-curricular and orientation programs that delve into them. HBCU attendees often remember these courses and programs as a central part of their educational experience and their outlook on the world.

Learning about Politics

What about engaging in formal coursework related to politics, government, or public policy? Figure 5.2 shows that Black Americans who attended HBCUs report engaging in coursework directly related to these topics at higher rates than their counterparts who attended PWIs. Sixteen percent of Black HBCU attendees say that they frequently took courses in government, politics, or public policy, compared to 13 percent of Black non-HBCU attendees. Additionally, 15 percent of HBCU attendees report

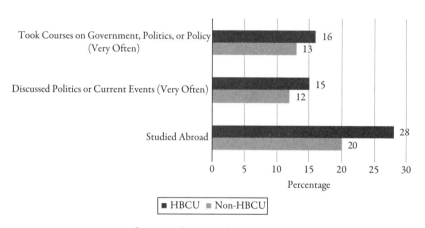

FIGURE 5.2 Percentage of respondents with high levels of participation in politically relevant academic experiences.

Note: The difference for "Discussed Politics or Current Events" is statistically significant at p = .05; and differences for "Took Courses on Government, Politics, and Policy" and "Studies Abroad" are statistically significant at p = .05.

Source: The College Experience Study—Black Respondents.

that they frequently discussed politics or current events in college, while 12 percent of their PWI-attending counterparts did so.

Multivariate analysis reinforces the finding that engaging in politically relevant coursework is correlated with HBCU attendance. Even when we control for factors like age, gender, parents' educational attainment, and youth socioeconomic status, which may shape the courses that a student selects, HBCU attendance remains positively correlated with having taken a course focusing on government, politics, or public policy during college (Table 5.2). What were these classes like for students at PWIs and HBCUs?

PWI attendees describe having valuable conversations in political science classes. For example, Krystal took a political science course when she was a student at PWI Fordham University during the mid-aughts. She described her political science professor as offering fresh perspectives on major political figures: "My political science instructor, he was very rebellious. He told the truth. [laughs] He was the first person I heard say that he didn't like Bill Clinton, and he didn't agree with how Bill Clinton

TABLE 5.2 Determinants of Taking a Course Focusing on Government, Politics, or Policy during College

Gender	−.055
	(.060)
Year of Birth	.009***
	(.002)
Youth Socioeconomic Status	.085**
	(.031)
Parents' Education	.043***
	(.008)
HBCU Attendance	.123†
	(.064)
R^2	.09
Adjusted R^2	.09
N	1,133

†$p \leq .1$; *$p \leq .05$, **$p \leq .01$, ***$p \leq .001$
Notes: Cells consist of ordinary least squares regression coefficients in the numerator and standard errors in parentheses. Analysis includes Black respondents who have completed at least "some college."
Source: The College Experience Study—Black Respondents.

ran the country. And, that was a shocker to me 'cause, you know, everyone loves Bill Clinton. Hearing that, it was like, wow this guy really has a voice, and he's not a follower." For Krystal, engaging with a professor whose perspectives went against popular sentiment was a memorable part of her PWI academic experience.

HBCU attendees offer numerous examples of the ways in which their coursework provided ample opportunity to learn about and grapple with politics, government, and policy; and they often described these opportunities as helping to reshape their perspectives on the racial dynamics of the United States and the world. Milton, a 1968 graduate of Howard University, recalled his experience as a Government major studying under trailblazing Black social scientists during the turbulent 1960s:

> Now it's called the Department of Political Science, but it was the Department of Government under Emmett Dorsey, who was a leading Black political scientist in America. And I took every course I could from him. And he encouraged us to take other courses in sociology and history particularly. And so, I had a semester with Nathan Hare, which was like nothing else I could describe . . . he was one of the activist professors who was helping to bring about social change, and boy was he into it.

Alexis, a 2014 graduate of Spelman College who majored in political science, identifies her political science training at Spelman as central to her long-standing engagement in politics: "I think that my experience at Spelman has definitely helped galvanize the desire for me to want to give back to my community because it exposed me to things about my community that I didn't know were affected by politics." During college, Alexis earned a prestigious White House internship that she describes as a political dream. Reflecting on that experience, she said: "Spelman kind of put me in a space to see those political dreams—then see myself in those political dreams."

Engagement with politically relevant coursework was not limited to enrollment in political science classes. Courtney, an alumna of Spelman College, majored in sociology. She recalled that politics "was always a topic of conversation in our classes regardless of the topic of the class or the specific course. Those kinds of things made their way into the discussion." Courtney also highlighted politically relevant course work that helped to shape her view of the world. For example, she describes a course called African Diaspora and the World: "It was a beautiful course that I would love for every college student to take." Reflecting on what she gained from the classes that she took at Spelman, she says, "It was really my time at Spelman that I learned about feminism . . . from the lens of Blackness. That is still something that is very important to me, issues of intersectionality. I don't think there is a week where I don't reflect on intersectionality or Black feminism in some way."

Reflecting on her academic experience at Spelman College, Candice describes the striking awakening that her HBCU experience inspired: "You always see these narratives played out in movies and TV about the freshman who comes home from college and they're super militant. They like learn all this stuff. That's really how I felt. I felt like the world had just opened up in a lot of ways, and I just had some incredible professors who were really invested in the teaching of Black women, like what it meant to be producing Black women leaders in the world." She recalled that attention to politics and policy was virtually ubiquitous in her college experience, saying:

> There was a lot of interest in thinking about how policy impacted Black women, and I just think even if not a particular focus of a class there were always meta conversations about policy and government at all times, right? We could have been reading *The Bluest Eye*, and somehow we would be talking about policy and practice. You know, just how things affect Black women from outside institutional structures—all those things are at play all at once.

Ethan also noted the bespoke approach that HBCUs took to teaching politics and history in a way that prioritizes the Black perspective. He says:

> Learning about politics and everything, and everything I'm learning is kind of from a Black perspective—from my perspective—which I liked. . . . Things are catered for my eyes. They talk about all these standardized tests and all that being catered for a White audience. It's proven that they're written on that basis, but everything at Howard was written for me and how I thought of things. So, in that instance, I think it was a little bit easier, more understandable. I can connect more with the work.

It seems logical that this style of integrating consideration of power dynamics and policy decisions throughout the curriculum could render HBCU alumni particularly well versed in and comfortable grappling with them.

Courses offering insight into international issues and opportunities to engage with other cultures also represent important parts of a politically relevant curriculum. Many students gain valuable experience engaging with other cultures and gaining a global perspective on politics through study-abroad programs. Survey data reveal an interesting gap between HBCU attendees and non-HBCU attendees when it comes to participation in study-abroad opportunities: while 28 percent of HBCU attendees report that they studied abroad during college, only 20 percent of non-HBCU attendees report that they have done so. Lauren, a 2015 graduate of Bennett College, described participating in the college's study-abroad program as the highlight of her college years:

> Through that experience I was able to travel to Europe, and it just really opened my eyes to what else is out there. And just being a representative of myself, and my family, and my institution, and connecting with other young people across the country who had accompanied me on that particular trip. It was a great experience—something I will cherish for the rest of my life. Being able to take that back and to be an advocate for global education, being heavily involved with our global center, whose main mission was promoting and increasing awareness about global education . . . that was a real highlight for me.

As was the case with learning about Black history, many HBCU alumni interviewees shared how completing various graduation requirements—from attending mandatory assemblies, to working in internships, to doing community service—helped to awaken their political consciousness. When working to satisfy her HBCU's senior internship requirement during the late 1980s, Tennessee State University alumna Crystal found a new passion. As she recalled, "prior to me just trying to fulfill my senior practicum, I never paid attention to politics. My second day on the job I was like, 'Ooh, I like this!'" She subsequently pursued a law degree and a career in state and national politics. For students interested in government, politics, and public policy, HBCUs have provided their students with powerful opportunities to delve into these topics.

Justin, who completed an undergraduate degree at the University of North Carolina–Chapel Hill, a PWI, and graduate degrees from HBCU North Carolina Central University and PWI Duke University, asserts that his experience at both institutions has changed him in ways that he describes as "conflicting." He elaborates on this reflection, observing that his HBCU and PWI campuses both promoted community engagement among students, but he notes that they did so in different ways:

> Central made me more of a people's person, like it trained me to be a lawyer, it trained me to talk to people, it trained me to get out into the community and do the good work. And, Central is very much a public interest law school. So everything that they focused on was about helping others and making sure that you're giving 110 percent of yourself because you never know, somebody else might need that motivation later on. Versus like . . . Duke is more so like, well let's take a look from the back room and see how these policies might affect people, but not really actually getting your hands dirty with the work. And, Central taught me how to get my hands dirty.

In addition to academic requirements that fostered engagement with Black history and politically relevant topics, community service requirements, which I will examine at length in Chapter 6, emerged as a core feature of HBCU curriculum that promotes a unique educational experience.

Teacher, Mentor, Coach, Parent: HBCU Faculty Members and the Many Roles They Play

For Black HBCU and PWI attendees, faculty members are central players in their academic experience during college. Data from interviews with Black PWI attendees highlight faculty members as key figures who shape the curriculum and offer challenging classes, and they report valuing the opportunity to learn from their college instructors. While data from interviews with Black HBCU attendees echo these sentiments, they further reveal a sense that faculty members are the heart and soul of the HBCU experience.

The racial composition of faculty at HBCUs has changed over time. During the 1960s, small schools like Talladega College were home to a small number of Black faculty. Gail opines that Talladega's isolated location in rural Alabama may have made it difficult to recruit and retain the precious number of Black PhD holders in the United States, particularly when competing for talent against other HBCUs located in more metropolitan locations. Kenneth, who also attended Talladega College during that decade, pointed out that the small size of Talladega's faculty at the time placed considerable limits on intellectual diversity. Talladega embraced a traditional curriculum that was light on subject matter devoted to examining the Black experience. Describing racial dynamics of her faculty at Talladega during the early 1960s, Gail recalls:

> It was the first time I ever had White teachers. But, I was not even conscious of that, I thought about that later. Why did I not think that was extraordinary? I didn't. . . . A good many of them, I found out later, were . . . Jewish refugees. Which I found out later was not just unique to Talladega, but was across the board at HBCUs, that these were people who were refugees from Germany, and we had some faculty who had been in concentration campus. But, I didn't know that either.

While Talladega was slow to pivot toward a curriculum that grappled unabashedly with issues related to race, larger HBCUs like Howard University were giving students access to some of the nation's foremost Black social scientists who were shaping how a generation of young people—and the nation—thought about race, institutions, and Black power. As Milton recalls from his time at Howard during the 1960s, his HBCU's Political Science department not only provided access to prominent scholars, it also offered additional opportunities for students to delve into political issues, such as participating in congressional internships during the summers.

While most PWIs strictly prohibited or limited the existence of interracial teaching forces and student bodies before 1964, HBCUs have been traditionally open to students, faculty, and staff coming from a range of racial and ethnic backgrounds. Candice recalls working with a racially diverse faculty as an important part of her experience at Spelman College during the late 1990s and early aughts:

> I have a lot of instances of Black women faculty who were [like family and invested in their pursuit of excellence]. I had a very, very, very

progressive White male philosophy professor who was that way and was a mentor to so many Black women on that campus, and I think he just kind of really understood what it meant to be in that space. And, he understood his privilege and his position.

Interviews with Black Americans who attended HBCUs highlighted the prominence of HBCU faculty and the significance of having the opportunity to learn from scholars who were well known and well regarded in their fields. Linda, who graduated from North Carolina Central University in 1975, recalled having a professor who was a pioneer in the field of African American studies: "Dr. Earlie Thorpe was one of my professors, and he was very outstanding. As a matter of fact, Harvard University had a plane for him, a private plane, where he would go to Harvard and teach Black studies there, which was a new program here in the United States. Not many colleges were teaching Black studies in the US. And, Harvard would have him come there, fly him up to Harvard to teach."[6] As this example illustrates, Black faculty have been recognized as making distinct and powerful contributions to the academy, and HBCU students have been particularly aware of the unique opportunity that they have in working with their faculty.

HBCU Faculty in the Classroom

Interviews with both HBCU and PWI attendees suggest that members of both groups viewed their faculty as extremely serious about academic excellence. They report that faculty members made clear their expectation of strong academic performance and pushed students to meet lofty goals. According to Brianna, a 2018 graduate of HBCU Savannah State University, "Teachers definitely didn't play that when it came to like, you know, academic honors and stuff like that. I can vividly remember teachers taking all the electronics up. Computers, watches, anything that beeps or rings, you know, in an envelope in the front of the room."

Veronica offers a similar example of the lofty demands that she and her classmates encountered from their HBCU faculty. She describes a love-hate relationship with the chair of the honors program whose standard for excellence translated into a lofty hurdle that she had to clear before graduation. She recalls:

He made me rewrite my senior thesis the night before gradua-tion. . . . I hated him for about ten years after graduation. I loved him in the last twenty years. And, I loved him then. You know, that's why I stayed up all night rewriting that thesis and crying because Dr. Williams said that I got to do this. [The faculty] inspired you, they encouraged you, they stayed on you to . . . make sure that you were excelling. They let you know when they knew that you were not doing your best and you were not working as hard as you could or should be. They'd let you know.

According to April, faculty members' willingness to invest heavily in students was widespread, but it came with one simple condition: students needed to demonstrate that they were taking their work seriously. As April recalls, "No matter where you go to college, there's a shaping that's involved. But there was . . . I guess that this is specifically at Howard, mediocrity was really looked down upon. It was like, mediocrity was horrible when I was there. That was something that was very clear. If you wanted a professor to stop investing in you . . . seem as if you accepted mediocrity."

Raven, an alumna of Bennett College, had little experience taking courses from Black faculty members prior to entering her HBCU. She recalled that "to go to an environment where I had Black teachers, and I had people push me, and I had individuals tell me that I could do anything or be somebody" was transformative. Raven recalled one sociology professor in particular who started the semester by asking students to share their career aspirations. "I said, I'm from Seattle, Washington, and I want to be a lawyer, and I want to be secretary of state." Later that term, she missed class, and her professor showed up at her dorm room:

Yes. She showed up at my door, and I was like, first off, how did you find out where I live? But, why are you here? And she just looked like, "Aren't you from Seattle?" I was like, "Yeah." She was like, "And I know that you were raised by your grandmother." Yes. So she was like, "Do you think that your grandmother who raised you pretty much as a single parent, and you flew 3,000 miles away to school, and you're not going to show up to my class?" She was like, "You told me you wanted to be a lawyer. . . . You think a lawyer can just not show up in court or not show up to a case or anything? Not show up to a mediation?" She was like, "You better be in my class the next hour."

Many HBCU alumni recall such encounters as reassuring and valuable hard lessons that helped them to grow academically. In many cases, the faculty inspired the students and helped them forge ahead through demanding semesters. As Ethan, a 2013 graduate of Howard University, remembered, "There's a lot of teachers like that at Howard. If I'm having a rough week and say I'm not in a professor's class, I'm going to pop in their class just to get a shot of that energy that I need to get me through."

Interviews with Black PWI attendees often revealed a different classroom experience. Cameron, a thirty-year-old alumnus of Otterbein College (now University), a private liberal arts college in Westerville, Ohio, noted the challenges that came with being the only Black person in his classes:

> In most of the classes you'd be the only Black person or Latino in a lot of the classes because it was predominantly White. Sometimes the professors would make insensitive comments. So that basically was the bulk of it. Just in class and people from different towns who may not be exposed to different cultures may make certain comments to people of color. One experience was someone came to me and said, "Oh your hair. Can I touch your hair? I've never touched a Black person's hair."

While faculty members figure prominently in HBCU attendees' accounts of their educational experiences, Black PWI attendees frequently point to their interactions with guidance counselors and college administrators as central to their experience. Julian recalls that the University of Michigan's School of Kinesiology took great pride in their low teacher-to-student ratio. He noted that "I just felt that in terms of the counselors and the administrators they knew me. And, so that made it pretty welcoming to me." Krystal offered a similar reflection on her experience at PWI Fordham University, saying, "I remember the attention that I received from instructors when it came to choosing my major and advisors. If I ever wanted to change a major or if I wasn't sure what I wanted to do, they would help me pick a minor. There was a lot of support from the staff in general."

Not all students, however, felt that the support they received was adequate. Students like Jason, who went to Long Island University, felt that the counselors at his school misled him: "Don't believe in the guidance counselor. Speak for yourself, ask more questions." Jason, whose dream was to become a lawyer, felt that his counselor's advice to major in political science because that was the major that he needed to choose to become a lawyer was a lie. "I believed it. And, when I found out the truth, it was too late—I wasted a whole five years on a major I didn't really want. . . . You don't need political science as a major. You could technically be any major." Looking back on his experience he says ruefully, "I wish I would've talked to my mom about it more and asked her for her opinion. We could've found out the truth about it so I could've continued my dream of being a lawyer." As this example illustrates, some Black respondents who attended PWIs felt that they lacked trusted sources of guidance and support that HBCU attendees often report that they found in their faculty.

Faculty as Valuable Mentors

In addition to the curricular work that takes place in the classroom, students benefit from having the opportunity to talk with faculty members about ways to connect what they are learning in the classroom to long-term career possibilities and their broader lives. Extraordinary levels of faculty mentorship and support proved a common theme in interviews with HBCU alumni. When it comes to discussing career plans with professors, HBCU attendees are slightly more likely to report that they do so with the greatest frequency—with 28 percent saying that they discussed career plans with faculty members "very often," compared to 27 percent of non-HBCU attendees.

"They were invested in you, I guess, so to speak," said Nathan, an alumnus of North Carolina Central University. When he changed his major to Health Education, he met with the chair of the department who took the time to welcome him:

> He asked me questions about where I came from, what my experiences were like growing up, absolutely positively completely and totally understood some of the mechanisms that might serve as constraints to my success at a place like [a PWI] in ways that I, at the time, didn't and said to me in no uncertain terms—and I remember this even until today— "Well, we are a family here in Health Education. You're one of ours now, and we're going to take care of you."

This exchange illustrates the importance of HBCU faculty members' capacity to identify with the lived experiences of students from groups that are traditionally marginalized in higher education and to offer careful, intentional mentoring to help marshal them to their degrees.

April had a similar experience during her freshman year at Howard when she was on track to earn a "B" in her psychology class. The professor pulled the first-generation college student and aspiring psychologist aside. April recalls:

> And [she] said, "I think you're going to get a B in this class." And I was like, "Okay, good." And she said, "No, aren't you a psychology major . . . you need to get an A." I was like, "Why do I need to get an A, I'm already in college?" And she was like, "You've got to go to grad school . . . you can't get to grad school if you don't have A's in your majors." Mind blown. Didn't understand it, didn't cross my mind.

April describes how the conversation opened her eyes to the process that she would need to navigate to pursue her career goals and completely changed how she approached her academic work. "That was very much a first. . . . Because yeah, she really looked at me like I was crazy. And, this was not a Black professor, this was a Japanese-American professor. She was like, 'You clearly know this work, you just haven't turned in all of your assignments. . . . You could get an A if you turned in all your assignments.'"

This was a prominent theme in discussions with HBCU alumni. They emphasized how faculty members invested in them and frequently went beyond the call of duty to foster their intellectual growth. Whether it was teaching extra class sessions on weekends to help students prepare for exams, providing opportunities for students to present at scholarly conferences, or demanding honors thesis rewrites the night before graduation, faculty members went to extraordinary lengths to marshal their students to excellence. Elijah, a 2014 graduate of HBCU North Carolina Central University, who later pursued a graduate degree at a PWI, recalled that numerous NCCU faculty members "really took time out, going out to eat with us, having conversations, encouraging us to go to conferences and present our research, staying up late to teach us how to research and go through documents." He described it as a remarkable experience that was distinctly related to his enrollment in an HBCU.

Black HBCU attendees also describe the work that their faculty members did to help prepare them for life. One of the central factors that drew Lauren to Bennett College was the inspiring leadership of Dr. Julianne

Malveaux, an economist and the college's president, who impressed her and her mother with her vision for the Bennett Belles:

> Just her dynamic nature and her overall, just competence and wanting to excel and wanting Bennett to be this oasis for Black women in this cultural atmosphere really, really . . . turned my head. It really did. . . . I remember when I first got to Bennett and we were part of orientation class before school started. Dr. Malveaux talked about how it was her mission and goal to have every freshwoman have a passport for that year. And, my mom really took that and ran with it, so before I even started school, I had a passport. . . . That was the first time I had been exposed to that.

Gregory recalls the impact that one faculty member, his ROTC colonel at West Virginia State, had on his life after establishing a reputation on campus as a student leader who did not hesitate to push back against campus rules and regulations that he considered to be unfair—such as the women's dorm director's decision to ban him from visiting the dormitory. At one point, as Gregory was lobbying the university's leadership to fire the woman from her job, the colonel summoned Gregory to his office where he took the opportunity to offer him a life lesson. Gregory recalls:

> And what he told me was something that was a lifelong lesson that nobody had ever told me. . . . He said, "Let me tell you something. . . . What you bear is the burden of visibility." And, I said what the hell is that? And, he said, "You are a known figure amongst the student body on this campus, and whatever you do, everyone knows you . . . and so you have a burden to carry because you are visible, and because people think more of you." Soon thereafter, university leadership encouraged him to direct his leadership and advocacy talents in a different direction by getting involved in student government.

According to Tennessee State University alumna Maxine, "the instructors that we had not only taught education, but they prepared us for life, being a decent human being." Considering the challenges that Black students were likely to face after leaving their college campuses, this was an especially important investment. Maxine notes that her HBCU education made it easier to grapple with "a life where, basically, you were considered a second-class citizen. It prepared us and showed us how to deal with that without the anger and going through the feeling that the world owes you a living. It prepared me for how to deal with life and the injustices that life had to offer."

Justin, who attended two HBCUs and two PWIs in the course of completing his undergraduate degree in 2010 and graduate degrees in 2018, offered a particularly valuable perspective as someone who had attended both types of institution. He recalled:

Most of my professors at [North Carolina] Central and Fayetteville State were Black, and most of the students are Black. And so, there was a more intimate relationship. Professors looked out for you. Like there'd be sometimes in class where we didn't even get to the material because there's a significant event happening in the world and professors wanted to make sure they addressed it. . . . Or if you go up to a professor after class, it's not like a "Oh, come to my office hours" kind of thing. It's more so just like a "Hey, let's talk right now. What's up?" So, our professors, they seemed a lot more available. They can relate a thousand times more, and it really helped me enjoy my time being there because I was like, okay, well the professors are here for me. These other students are here for me, and I can make it through it.

HBCU faculty members challenged students with rigorous course curricula and high expectations. But alumni also described their faculty in familial terms, as extraordinarily supportive, and not hesitating to intervene when students were not delivering excellence. This level of extraordinary, and parent-like, investment from faculty was a common theme in interviews with Black Americans who attended HBCUs.

Joyce, who graduated from HBCU Delaware State in 1979, emphasized that "the faculty and students had a relationship that was like parents and children. It was family. They took care of us. . . . They would take us by the collar, they would reprimand us when need be—like [my professor] did for me when I wasn't going to school. They would keep up with us." Andrea, who graduated from HBCU Dillard University in 2003, echoed this sentiment: "Your professor is basically your mom or your dad, and if you don't show up to class, they're calling you on your phone in your room, and trying to figure out why you didn't come to class."

Tennessee State University alumna Jackie recalls when she got the flu shortly after arriving on her HBCU campus in 1977. Being away from home for the first time, she did not tell her parents that she was ill because she did not want to worry them, but she becomes emotional when she remembers that

> My math teacher calls my dorm room, and he said, "I'm calling because it's so unusual for you not to be in class." And, I explained that I was ill, that I sent my roommate to get my homework. He said, "Yep, she picked it up." He says, "But, I went home and I talked to my wife about you and how you never miss class, you're always on time and da da da da da." He says, "So, if you're able or if you can send someone down to the lobby"—because we didn't have co-ed dorms. Girls were in one dorm, guys were in the other on the other side of the campus—he says, "if you can send someone down, my wife has made soup for you and I have some other goodies for you because I know that you don't have family here." He says, "And, I just wanted you to know that it's important to me that you're okay."

Clark Atlanta University alumna Tiffany recalls a similar instance when her professor went above and beyond to ensure that everyone took advantage of a special learning opportunity:

> One of my favorite professors, Professor Gwendolyn Morgan, she actually—true story—during our freshman year, we were supposed to go on a civil rights tour trip to Birmingham on a Saturday morning. The buses were supposed to leave at six in the morning. She realized, I guess around 6:30 that the bus was not filling up at the rate she wanted it to. She literally walked into our dorms and started banging on people's doors to get them up. . . . It was out of love and just the genuine concern for us and our development. She wouldn't stop at anything to make sure that we got what we needed out of our institute and out of our experience, which was great.

Edward, an alumnus of Wilberforce University, credits his HBCU's faculty with not only offering individualized attention that promoted his academic success, but also demonstrating that they "really cared" about him. Early during his time at Wilberforce when Edward's active social life conflicted with his academic progress, his developmental English professor interrupted plans with his friends:

This lady rolls up on me in a car, says, "Mr. Scott, did you find that English book?" I said, "No, Ma'am." She says, "Mr. Scott, we need to have a conversation." I say, "What's up?" She says, "I had a conversation with your mother." I said, "You didn't call my mother." She said, "Is your mother Florence Scott?" And, I said, "Yes, her name is Florence Scott." "Should I tell you what she told you at the Greyhound bus when she put you on the bus?" And I said, "Please do." "She said that if things don't work out here, you're to go straight to Colorado Springs with your grandmother." I said, "I guess you did talk to my mother."

She took me to her house. She fed me and then she took that English book out and we read from cover to cover. And then she took me back to campus. When she let me out of the car, she said, "The next time you go to sleep in my class"—this is 8:00 in the morning in English class in a room that was about 10 × 10 in the basement of a building that's as old as . . . and had a steam pipe going straight through it, and it's hot and steamy in that room—she said, "the next time you go to sleep in my class, you're going to be going to Colorado Springs."

At first blush, such reports of the extensive lengths that HBCU faculty members go to as they invest in their students and work to foster Black excellence seem too extraordinary to be commonplace. But, as Bennett College alumna Ashley asserts, "You didn't feel like they were picking favorites because everyone got treated the same way." By all accounts, the faculty are the heart and soul of HBCUs, and they wear a multitude of hats in their roles as educators. Melvin, who graduated from Miles College, an HBCU in Alabama, during the 1960s, pointed to the central role that faculty members play as driving a key challenge facing HBCUs: "The biggest strain [on HBCUs] is keeping the good professors there because the predominantly Black schools cannot afford to pay them like . . . the predominantly White schools."

Conclusion

As the heart and soul of higher educational institutions, faculty members shape not only the curriculum with which students engage but also their classroom experiences. Data from the College Experience Study and the HBCU Alumni Study suggest that faculty members play a central role in the academic experiences that students have at HBCUs and PWIs. Moreover, these data suggest that faculty members and their unique approach to education are especially prominent features of the distinctive HBCU educational experience. While Black Americans who studied at PWIs and HBCUs report that they valued the considerable academic opportunities that they encountered during college and felt challenged by their courses, HBCU attendees underscored the value of expanding their understanding of the Black experience through history, political science, and even general coursework that was driven by faculty members who were invested in their intellectual growth and their achievement of excellence. Many HBCU faculty members are pioneers in their fields who introduce their students to new perspectives on race and who design courses that grapple seriously with issues facing the Black community. Moreover, the data reveal that HBCU faculty have routinely gone above and beyond the call of duty to provide support and mentorship that have been integral to students' success at completing their degrees and, in some cases, attaining advanced degrees.

In many respects, the content of HBCU academic coursework—from formal courses to orientation programming to required co-curricular opportunities—is political, as faculty and students often approach the full range of subjects from a perspective that centers on the Black experience. Aside from this type of valuable, politically relevant academic experience, do HBCUs offer their students distinct opportunities to engage in politics during college? Chapter 6 grapples with this question.

6

Building Citizens, Shaping Democracy

The Political and Civic Value of the HBCU
Educational Experience

SINCE THE MID-TWENTIETH CENTURY, BLACK Americans have made strides in the political arena. In addition to the increasing representation of African Americans serving in elected and appointed governmental positions, which I will examine at length in Chapter 7, Black Americans have been active participants in determining who will exercise political power.

Despite declines in the overall rates at which Americans participate in mass political activities like voting, volunteering on campaigns, contacting elected officials, and participating in protests, this pattern does not hold for African Americans.[1] Since 1960, the rates at which African Americans volunteer for political parties or candidates, donate money to campaigns, attempt to influence how others vote, and express high levels of interest in public affairs have increased.[2] As important legal victories like the Civil Rights Act of 1964 and the Voting Rights Act of 1965 helped to remove de jure barriers that had long obstructed African Americans' participation in politics, increasing educational attainment has enhanced African Americans' ability to make their voices heard in the political arena.

Political scientists recognize that, among the central determinants of mass-level political engagement—which include individual-level characteristics like age, gender, race, income, and occupation—educational attainment represents one of the most reliable predictors of whether someone will engage in political activities.[3] Education provides valuable human capital, which facilitates high levels of political involvement. In addition to providing access to politically relevant knowledge, higher education can also provide access to a variety of skills and experiences that facilitate political participation, such as public speaking, organizational skills, and leadership opportunities.[4] Moreover, people with higher levels of education are more likely to have access to social networks that promote political participation, and political parties, candidates, and interest groups are significantly more likely to recruit them for participation in political activities.[5] Thus, higher education is connected to democratic engagement in important ways.

Is it possible that HBCUs do a particularly good job of providing the types of knowledge, skills, and experiences that scholars recognize as the building blocks of long-term political engagement? Given their distinctly political history and their commitment to the inherently political mission of African American empowerment, it seems plausible that HBCUs may represent unique agents of political socialization that go above and beyond the call of duty, providing their students with distinctive experiences that provide a strong foundation for subsequent political engagement.

For example, as we saw in Chapter 5, many HBCUs use their curriculum to promote community service by making it a requirement for graduation.[6] Others promote direct engagement in political and civic work by sponsoring voter registration drives and extending social services like adult learning programs, day care, and food pantries to their communities.[7] Some HBCUs have even provided formal incentives to encourage faculty members to promote political and civic engagement. At Albany State University, for example, university leaders have made efforts to consider faculty members' use of service-learning opportunities in teaching when making promotion and tenure decisions.[8]

Compared to their counterparts who attended PWIs, do Black Americans who attended HBCUs gain a unique college experience that provides greater access to political knowledge, skills, and experiences that can help foster active engagement in politics? Using data from the 2018 College Experience Study and the 2019 HBCU Alumni Study, this chapter draws on a combination of quantitative and qualitative data to examine the possibility that HBCUs have provided educational experiences that have helped to foster long-term political engagement among their students. I suspect that by providing their students with access to particularly empowering political experiences, HBCUs play an important role in helping to cultivate democratically engaged citizens.

Political Efficacy

Are HBCU attendees more likely to report high levels of political efficacy—feeling that they have what it takes to influence government when compared to their counterparts who attended PWIs? Figure 6.1 offers insight into this question, displaying survey data indicating respondents' perceptions of whether they have the knowledge and skills necessary to engage in meaningful political participation (internal efficacy) and whether they feel that elected officials and government will be responsive to people like them (external efficacy).

Twenty-eight percent of Black Americans surveyed who attended an HBCU strongly agree with the statement "I consider myself well qualified to participate in politics," compared to 22 percent of those who did not attend an HBCU. Similarly, 11 percent of respondents who attended an HBCU strongly agree that "Public officials care about what people like me think," while only 5 percent of respondents who attended a PWI strongly agree with the statement.

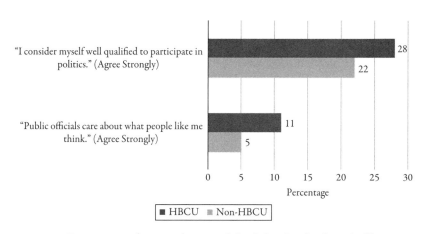

FIGURE 6.1 Percentage of respondents with high levels of political efficacy.

Note: The difference for "I consider myself well qualified to participate in politics" is statistically significant at p = .01; and the difference for "Public officials care about what people like me think" is statistically significant at p = .001.

Source: The College Experience Study—Black Respondents.

Multivariate analysis corroborates this finding that HBCU attendees report feeling more efficacious when it comes to the prospect of engaging in activities aimed at shaping government outcomes. Table 6.1 displays ordinal logistic regression results for the determinants of political efficacy. The dependent variable is an index of political efficacy, and the model controls for gender, year of birth, household income, and educational attainment. The results suggest that men, older respondents, those with higher household incomes, and those who have higher levels of educational attainment are significantly more likely to express high levels of political efficacy. The model also suggests that HBCU attendance is positively associated with high levels of political efficacy.

As these data illustrate, Black Americans who attend HBCUs are significantly more likely than those who attend PWIs to report high levels of confidence that they have what it takes to influence government and politics and that government actors care what people like them think. This

TABLE 6.1 Determinants of Political Efficacy and Participation

	Efficacy	Participation
Gender	−.449***	−.102
	(.110)	(.113)
Year of Birth	−.007*	−.019***
	(.003)	(.004)
Household Income	.041*	.044*
	(.017)	(.018)
Educational Attainment	.103**	.165***
	(.036)	(.038)
HBCU Attendance	.275*	.492***
	(.116)	(.121)
Log Likelihood	−2,246	−1,588
N	1,133	1,134

$\dagger p \leq .1$; $^*p \leq .05$, $^{**}p \leq .01$, $^{***}p \leq .001$
Notes: Cells consist of ordinal logistic regression coefficients in the numerator and standard errors in parentheses. Analysis includes Black respondents who have completed at least "some college."
Source: The College Experience Study—Black Respondents.

is an especially important finding because political efficacy is positively associated with higher levels of political engagement.

Mass-Level Political Engagement

Are there significant differences between Black Americans who attended HBCUs and those who attended PWIs when it comes to engaging in mass-level political activities? Figure 6.2 displays the percentage of survey respondents who report ever having participated in five political activities: voting in presidential elections, volunteering for a political candidate, contributing money to a political cause, contacting a government official, and participating in a protest. Robust majorities of respondents who attended HBCUs and non-HBCUs report that they voted in virtually "all" presidential elections since they have been eligible to do so—63 percent of HBCU attendees and 59 percent of non-HBCU attendees. On

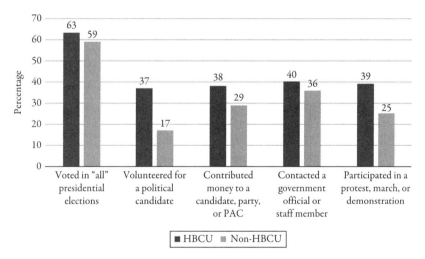

FIGURE 6.2 Percentage of respondents who have participated in various political activities.

Note: The differences for "Volunteered for a political candidate" and "Participated in a protest" are statistically significant at $p = .001$; the difference for "Contributed money" is statistically significant at $p = .01$; and the difference for "Voted" is statistically significant at $p = .05$. The difference for "Contacted a government official" is not statistically significant.

Source: The College Experience Study—Black Respondents.

his engagement as a voter, Tyrone—an alumnus of HBCU Florida A&M University—said:

> I vote. I definitely vote. I let my opinion be known by voting, okay? If there's a petition that's being filled out that's for a just and right cause, I do add my name to the petition. Especially, for example, here in the state of Florida. They're having to deal with those people who were incarcerated but who are now out, have done their time, and they're trying to get their voting rights back. I did sign a petition for that.

Fellow HBCU graduate Maxine, an alumna of Tennessee State University, considers voting to be a responsibility. "First of all, growing up the way I grew up, there were a whole bunch of Black folks that are dead, and they were killed because they tried to register to vote. And so, I feel an obligation to vote. And I feel that that's one way that I can make my little voice heard, is by my vote. So, I think that as a citizen, I have not only a right to vote, but I think that I have a responsibility to vote."

Black PWI attendees also express a commitment to making their voices heard through voting. Valerie, who attended the University of Chicago, describes her commitment as rooted in a family tradition: "I guess it's because of my family. One of my aunts participated in the March on Washington, and she was written up in the paper and everything.... Most of [my aunts] are teachers, and they believe in education. They believe in the power of politics, and so it's just been something that's been instilled in me all my life."

Beyond voting, Black Americans who attended HBCUs and PWIs report engaging in other forms of democratic engagement, but those who attended HBCUs do so at higher rates. While 17 percent of non-HBCU attendees say that they have volunteered for a political candidate, more than twice that proportion—37 percent—of HBCU attendees report having done so.

Money has come to represent a particularly powerful force in American politics, as the cost of campaigning has increased precipitously, and financial contributions have become an increasingly powerful mechanism for gaining access to elected officials. Twenty-nine percent of respondents who attended PWIs report that they have contributed money to a political candidate, party, or political action committee; 38 percent of HBCU attendees have made such contributions. When it comes to directly engaging with elected officials, HBCU attendees are only slightly more likely to report that they have contacted a government official or staff member compared to non-HBCU attendees: 40 percent and 36 percent, respectively. Last, 39 percent of HBCU attendees report having participated in a protest, march, or demonstration, compared to 25 percent of non-HBCU attendees.

The multivariate analysis presented in Table 6.1 models the determinants of political engagement. In line with the dominant literature on political participation, these data suggest that older respondents, those with greater household income, and those with higher levels of educational attainment are significantly more likely to participate in political activities. Moreover, the analysis also suggests that, controlling for each of the aforementioned variables, Black Americans who attended an HBCU are significantly more likely to take part in political activities than those who attended a PWI. I also consider the possibility that there may be political or democratic implications of attending public or private HBCUs using an interaction term to explore whether attending public versus private HBCUs reveals significant differences in terms of political efficacy and political participation. As the analysis shows, no significant differences emerge for political efficacy or political participation (see Table A.6.1).

Qualitative data provide additional insight into these findings. Joyce, an alumna of HBCU Delaware State, is an active poll worker. "I work election polls every election," says Joyce. "I'm up at four o'clock in the morning to be here about five so that we can open by six o'clock a.m. I've done that for the last ten years. I do voter registration for my church." Joyce also works with one of her local senators as part of a citizen's coalition that helps him identify challenges in the community and helps him find solutions to address them. Raymond, a 1980 graduate of HBCU North Carolina Central University, has also actively participated in the democratic process and reported a high level of political and civic engagement:

> I recently served on the board of elections as one of their regional directors. When we had elections, I was the one that visited the precincts to make sure everything was done properly or if they had some type of dispute, I would be one of the ones that would go out to see if we can resolve the allegation. I did that probably for fifteen years.

Jerry, who attended Chicago State University, a PWI, expressed having less energy to devote to politics. When asked about the extent of his engagement in politics he replied: "I just vote and go on about my business, 'cause I know there's nothing I can do about [challenges he sees]. . . . I contribute a little money, but I don't participate in events."

Interest in Elite-Level Political Engagement

Does the high level of political engagement among Black HBCU attendees hold when we move beyond participation in mass-level political activities to consider engagement in elite-level activities, namely running for political office? While we know that people are significantly less likely to run for political office than they are to engage in mass-level activities like voting and contacting elected officials, the survey data presented in Figure 6.3 indicate that Black Americans who attended HBCU participate in elite-level political activities at higher rates than their counterparts who attended PWIs.

Twenty percent of HBCU attendees say that they have considered running for political office, compared to only 12 percent of non-HBCU attendees. When it comes to actually serving in a government position, 14 percent of non-HBCU attendees report having served on a local government board, council, or committee, compared to a full 27 percent of HBCU attendees. Extremely small proportions of both groups report

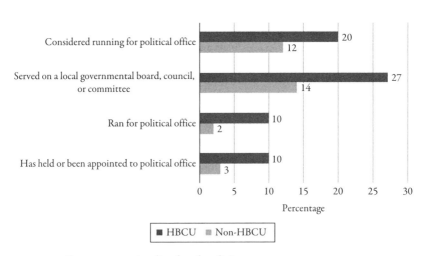

FIGURE 6.3 Engagement in elite-level politics.

Note: These differences are statistically significant at $p = .001$.

Source: The College Experience Study—Black Respondents.

having actually run for or been appointed to political office, but HBCU attendees, again, report engaging in these activities at higher rates than their counterparts who did not attend HBCUs: 2 percent of PWI attendees say that they have run for political office, while 10 percent of HBCU attendees report that they have. Similarly, 3 percent of non-HBCU attendees say that they have held or been appointed to political office, compared to 10 percent of HBCU attendees.

For an additional indicator of inclination to engage in elite-level political activity, I incorporated a behavioral item into the College Experience Study to try to gauge survey participants' willingness to engage in a low-stakes activity geared toward exploring the possibility of running for office. This item asked respondents, "Would you like to receive a list of resources for learning more about running for political office?" Thirteen percent of Black survey respondents who attended HBCUs opted to access resources for running for office, while a full 21 percent of attendees who attended HBCUs opted to access the resources (Figure 6.4). Once again, the data suggest that Black Americans who attended HBCUs are significantly more likely to engage in political activities than those who did not.

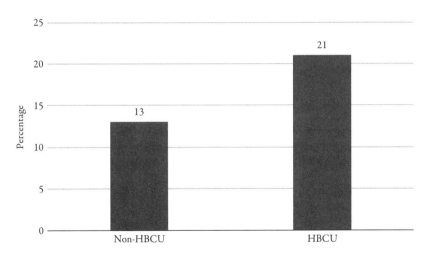

FIGURE 6.4 Percentage of respondents who opted into seeing a list of resources for learning more about running for political office.

Note: This difference is statistically significant at $p = .01$.

Source: The College Experience Study—Black Respondents.

Attitudes about Citizenship, Government, and Other Political Issues

Do HBCU attendees and their PWI attending counterparts hold different attitudes about citizenship, government, and issues like equal opportunity, race, and the pathway toward racial progress? This section compares HBCU attendees' and non-HBCU attendees' responses to a number of questions related to such issues (Table 6.2).

Feeling Like a "First-Class" Citizen

The College Experience Study asked respondents to indicate the extent to which they agree with the statement, "Generally, I feel like a full and equal citizen of this country with all the rights and protections that other people have." Respondents who attended an HBCU express agreement with the statement at slightly higher rates than those who attended a PWI: 21 percent of HBCU attendees indicate strong agreement, compared to 19 percent of non-HBCU attendees. We see a similar trend in agreement with the statement "I'm proud to be an American." Forty-eight percent of HBCU attendees strongly agree with this statement, while 44 percent of non-HBCU attendees do (Table 6.2).

We see similar trends when it comes to attitudes about government. HBCU attendees express faith in lawmakers at a higher rate than non-HBCU attendees: 39 percent agree (either "strongly" or "somewhat") with the statement, "We can trust lawmakers to make our society more equitable," compared to only 28 percent of PWI attendees. Similarly, 56 percent of HBCU attendees agreed that "Government has given me opportunities to improve my standard of living," while 49 percent of non-HBCU attendees agree with that statement.

Table 6.2 also compares Black PWI attendees' and HBCU attendees' attitudes about democracy in the United States. When asked how satisfied they are "with the way democracy works" in the United States, 43 percent of non-HBCU attendees say that they are either "somewhat satisfied" or "very satisfied," compared to a majority of HBCU attendees (51 percent). These data suggest that respondents who attended HBCUs are slightly more likely to report confidence in their status as citizens, pride in being an American, trust in lawmakers, and satisfaction with democracy than those who did not.

TABLE 6.2 Perspectives on Citizenship and Attitudes toward Government

	Disagree Strongly	Disagree Somewhat	Agree Somewhat	Agree Strongly		Total
ON CITIZENSHIP						
"Generally, I feel like a full and equal citizen of this country with all the rights and protections that other people have."						
HBCU Attendees	19%	25	35	21	=	100%
Non-HBCU Attendees	18%	30	33	19	=	100%
"I'm proud to be an American."						
HBCU Attendees	4%	9	39	48	=	100%
Non-HBCU Attendees	5%	15	36	44	=	100%
ATTITUDES ABOUT GOVERNMENT						
"We can trust lawmakers to make our society more equitable"						
HBCU Attendees	25%	36	29	10	=	100%
Non-HBCU Attendees	31%	40	24	4	=	99%
"Government has given me opportunities to improve my standard of living."						
HBCU Attendees	15%	29	42	14	=	100%
Non-HBCU Attendees	19%	32	39	10	=	100%

	Not at All Satisfied	Not That Satisfied	Somewhat Satisfied	Very Satisfied		Total
ON DEMOCRACY						
"On the whole, how satisfied are you with the way democracy works in the United States?"						
HBCU Attendees	14%	35	39	12	=	100%
Non-HBCU Attendees	21%	36	35	8	=	100%

Notes: The total percentages may not equal 100 percent due to rounding. The difference for "We can trust lawmakers" is statistically significant at $p = .001$. The differences for "I am proud to be an American," "Government has given me opportunities," and satisfaction with "the way democracy works" are statistically significant at $p = .05$. The difference for feeling like a "full and equal citizen" is not statistically significant.
Source: The College Experience Study—Black Respondents.

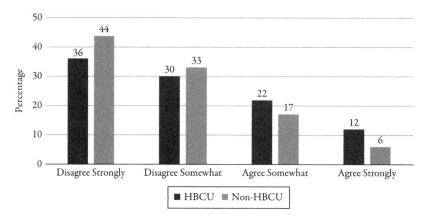

FIGURE 6.5 Percentage of respondents who agree with the statement "Blacks have a great deal of power in American politics."

Note: These differences are statistically significant at $p = .001$.

Source: The College Experience Study—Black Respondents.

When it comes to respondents' views on race, do these differences persist? When asked whether they agree that "Blacks have a great deal of power in American politics," Black survey respondents who attended PWIs are more likely to disagree (Figure 6.5). While 36 percent of HBCU attendees strongly disagree with this statement, 44 percent of non-HBCU attendees strongly disagree with it. Conversely, 6 percent of PWI attendees strongly agree that Blacks have a great deal of power in American politics, while 12 percent of HBCU attendees strongly agree with this statement. These data suggest that HBCU attendees may be more likely to view Black Americans as having greater agency than their counterparts who attended PWIs.

The College Experience Study also asked respondents to share their perspective on the best approach for Blacks to use to achieve racial progress (Figure 6.6). The majority of Black respondents felt that Blacks should organize both among themselves and with other racial groups. However, non-HBCU attendees were slightly more likely to hold this position— 63 percent, compared to 59 percent of HBCU attendees. Eighteen percent of HBCU attendees and 22 percent of non-HBCU attendees felt that Blacks should work with other racial groups to achieve progress. Last, 15 percent of non-HBCU attendees believed that Blacks should organize among themselves to achieve progress, while 23 percent of HBCU attendees expressed this view.

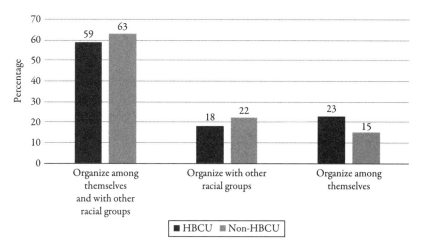

FIGURE 6.6 Respondents' beliefs about the best way for Black people to organize to achieve progress.

Note: These differences are statistically significant at *p* = .05.

Source: The College Experience Study—Black Respondents.

Another indicator of Black Americans' views on race is their feeling of closeness to various racial groups. Figure 6.7 shows the percentage of survey respondents who report feeling "very close" to six racial groups—Black Americans, White Americans, Hispanic Americans, Asian Americans, Blacks in Africa, and Whites in Europe. Black survey respondents who attended HBCUs and PWIs report feeling very close to Black Americans

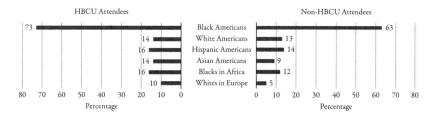

FIGURE 6.7 Percentage of respondents who feel "Very Close" to various racial and ethnic groups by HBCU attendance.

Note: The differences for "Blacks in Africa" and "Whites in Europe" are statistically significant at *p* = .001. The difference for "Black Americans" is statistically significant at *p* = .01. The difference for "Asian Americans" is statistically significant at *p* = .05. The differences for "White Americans" and "Hispanic Americans" are not statistically significant.

Source: The College Experience Study—Black Respondents.

at much higher rates than they report feeling "very close" to any other group—63 percent of non-HBCU attendees and 73 percent of HBCU attendees. Both groups report feeling "very close" to the remaining five racial groups at much more modest levels. Respondents who attended HBCUs express feeling "very close" to all of the groups at higher rates than those who did not attend HBCUs. One possible explanation for this trend is that HBCU attendees may feel greater comfort and familiarity when it comes to thinking about race issues and relating to other racial groups, at least in part, because they have participated in institutions where the topic of race is not only acknowledged but embraced and actively engaged.

While these results cannot be taken as evidence to suggest that HBCU attendance causes high levels of political efficacy, engagement in mass-level political activities, or an inclination to run for political office, they do suggest an interesting pattern: for this pool of Black Americans, HBCU attendance is correlated with these three important democratic outcomes. Moreover, these data indicate that HBCU attendees and non-HBCU attendees alike report frustration with the ongoing struggle against racism and race-based discrimination in the United States.

Building Efficacy, Confidence, and Lasting Social Networks during College

In addition to their role in providing academic opportunities that support the development of knowledge and skills that can empower developing citizens, colleges and universities also offer opportunities for social engagement that can foster personal growth and development. Such opportunities can yield lasting connections with a valuable network of faculty and classmates that can facilitate civic and political engagement. For many young people, college years mark their initiation to independent living, and these years often involve formative experiences that provide a foundation for long-term perspectives. College campuses provide an important context in which many young people gain a sense of their position in society.

Given the potential of colleges to shape the early development of citizens, it is important to ask whether certain higher educational institutions offer unique campus cultures and social experiences that provide a particularly empowering context for political socialization. College experiences that yield substantial personal growth can foster the development of confidence that sets the stage for high levels of political efficacy—an important factor driving whether people engage in political activities. Nina, who graduated from Spelman College in 2001, credits HBCUs with equipping students to feel as though they can affect real change in the world:

> I think that [HBCUs] groom leaders, and we give people the confidence and the tools and the ability to feel like we can compete and that we're worthy of being in positions of leadership. Whether that's being the COO of Starbucks or Stacey Abrams running for governor of Georgia. We have lots of women in our ranks who we're very proud of and who are examples of what's possible.

Tennessee State University graduate Tiffany agreed, pointing out the effect that her HBCU experience had in shaping her confidence:

> It gave me truck loads more confidence than I entered with—and, I wasn't lacking for confidence when I got there. But, I think that I had misplaced confidence. And so, I do not do so well a couple of times to realize that, you know, confidence comes from hard work. Confidence comes from being competent in what you're doing. I just thought confidence was a popularity contest when I first got there.

A prominent theme that emerged from qualitative data was that HBCU attendees viewed their college experiences as helping to strengthen their confidence through engaging academics and a nurturing campus environment driven by a faculty that was invested in their success (see Chapter 5). It seems plausible that such confidence contributes to the foundation for the high levels of political efficacy that we saw earlier in the chapter—a characteristic that is associated with high levels of political engagement.

In addition to the value of confidence for promoting political engagement, the social and professional networks that students gain from their time in college can also contribute to higher levels of political engagement. People may be tapped by those in their social network to engage in political activities; and they can also seek help from members of their social networks to support political endeavors like running for office or advocating for a political cause.

Participating in team-based activities is one form of campus engagement that could yield the types of networks that promote civic and political participation. Intramural, club, and intercollegiate team sports provide college students such opportunities, and the data presented in Figure 6.8 show that while 33 percent of non-HBCU attendees report that they played a team sport during college, a full 50 percent of HBCU attendees do.

At many American colleges and universities, Greek letter organizations serve as a pillar of campus social life, offering valuable opportunities for social engagement and the development of lifelong friendships and networks. Each year, thousands of Black college students pledge and become new members of sororities and fraternities, including the "Divine Nine"—historically African American Greek letter organizations that are associated with the National Pan-Hellenic Council. Have there been significant differences in the rates at which Black HBCU and PWI students join fraternities and sororities? Among College Experience Study respondents, 10 percent of Black PWI attendees report that they participated in a sorority or fraternity during college, while a full 25 percent of HBCU attendees report that they have participated in a Greek letter organization.

Interview data underscore the significance of Greek letter organizations on HBCU campuses. Ethan, who pledged Kappa Alpha Psi at Howard University, recalled how fierce the competition was to gain membership in the "Divine Nine" fraternity at his HBCU. He recalled, "It's very, very competitive, I'll tell you that. Three-hundred people applied for 13 spots." Gail, a 1966 alumna of HBCU Talladega College, noted, "I'm an AKA [a

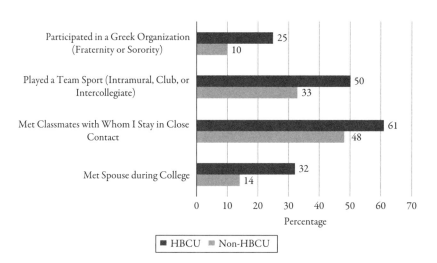

FIGURE 6.8 Social inclusion and lasting connections.
Note: These differences are statistically significant at $p = .001$.
Source: The College Experience Study—Black Respondents.

member of Alpha Kappa Alpha Sorority, Inc.]. . . . That was a big part of the social life on the campus. There were movies on campus. There were dances on the campus, so that they kind of created an environment where we didn't have to leave the campus if we didn't want to." This type of social programming was particularly valuable for Black students living on the rural southern campus during the racially segregated 1960s.

For many college students, Greek letter organizations provide an entrée into civic and political activity. As Jackie, who graduated from HBCU Tennessee State University in 1981 and who pledged Delta Sigma Theta there, shared: "So, you can't be on a Black campus and not be engaged politically in some activity or organization because our campus is as political as they get. So organizations, like we call it, run things on the yard."

Most of the HBCU alumni interviewed who were members of sororities and fraternities during college mentioned that a substantial portion of their experience centered on community service activities. For example, Ethan participated in outreach with his fraternity brothers at Howard: "Me and a couple of my friends started a nonprofit in DC helping high school football players try to have a path to go to college." From starting nonprofit organizations, to serving as tutors, to raising funds for struggling communities after Hurricane Katrina, HBCU students and their Greek organizations have made valuable contributions to the civic landscape through their service activities.

Beyond community service, Greek organizations also served to help mobilize their members for political engagement. Ralph, who graduated from HBCU Shaw University in 1958, recalled the emphasis that his fraternity brothers placed on political activism in the midst of the civil rights movement:

> Because my fraternity had leaders all out in the community, anytime we had a frat meeting we had some of our fraternity leaders come by, and they would talk to us about the different politics—not only in the city of Raleigh but in the state and also in the nation. And, they would always tell us that we have to get involved. Okay, maybe not now, but when you graduate, you go back home to where there might be some kind of political strike, you have to get involved.

Ralph noted that the late 1950s marked an important juncture in the history of HBCU political activism. His fraternity brothers were discreet about their work to mobilize their Shaw University brothers because, at the time, students enrolled in the private, religious institution were discouraged from engaging in political activities. This soon changed as students got involved in marches and sit-ins with the Student Nonviolent Coordinating Committee (SNCC). By that point, the Shaw University faculty and administrators supported the students' activism.

For many college students, Greek letter organizations provide the opportunity to hone leadership skills that could come in handy in future political endeavors. Marcus, who graduated from HBCU West Virginia State College in 1988 and pledged Kappa Alpha Psi fraternity, remembered that his fraternity "taught me Robert's Rules of Order, how to manage finances within an organization, how to care—meaning how to grow your membership. In that respect, I learned a lot about being political and being strategic at Western State."

Greek affiliations also serve as a powerful source of support for political candidates. As Joyce, who graduated from HBCU Delaware State College in 1979, noted about then-US Senator, now Vice President Kamala Harris:

> Even though I'm not a Howard grad [like Sen. Harris], she's my sorority sister. She automatically has the 800,000 of us in her corner. That's the impact of the oneness of an HBCU. I don't have to know you, but once I know you're an AKA, you are my sister. Once somebody knows you're a member of Omega Psi Phi, that's your brother, and you can get a meal anywhere you go, you can have a place to lay your head anywhere in the world you go. That's the kind of oneness.

Reflecting on the nature of this sense of unity, Joyce points to the role that Black Greek organizations have played in countering the nation's history of institutional racism: "I think because of Jim Crow and because of slavery and because of the things that we as a people went through, the sorority and fraternity lives were a different focus and meant more to us because it finally made us understand we were important, and we had things to promote as well."

How about forming lasting friendships and connections while in college? Figure 6.8 shows that Black survey respondents who attended HBCUs report that they formed lasting relationships at higher rates than their counterparts who attended PWIs. While 48 percent of Black PWI attendees met classmates during college with whom they stay in close contact, a full 61 percent of HBCU attendees indicate that they did so. Milton, who graduated from Howard University in 1968, describes his classmates and the network that he gained as one of the greatest benefits of attending his HBCU. "I mean, one of our classmates was the premier of Bermuda. How many other folks can say, 'Oh, I had a classmate who was president of a country'?" His college friend group included people who achieved great success as future business leaders, political leaders, and military generals, and he actively works to keep these connections alive.

One of the most consequential connections that many people form during college is meeting marriage partners. Respondents who attended an HBCU are significantly more likely to have met their spouse during college than those who attended a PWI: 32 percent of respondents who attended an HBCU marry someone they met during college, compared to a much more modest 14 percent of respondents who attended PWIs. Marcus, who graduated from West Virginia State College in 1988, credited his HBCU with providing him with the "greatest gift of all." He declared, "I went to get a degree, and I came back with a wife."

Gregory, who graduated from West Virginia State College in 1986, recalled meeting his wife during college as one of the most valuable aspects of his college experience: "Me and a bunch of my friends all met our spouses in school. Overall, the majority of us are still married to this day, which is also another great thing for African American marriages or relationships." Ethan had a similar experience at Howard University where he met his fiancée: "I'm a champion for that with all of my line brothers. They all met their fiancées or wives at Howard as well. . . . Dating and relationships are a big part of HBCU as well. A lot of people go there to find a future husband or a future wife. So, for me, it worked out so far." These data suggest that HBCUs may foster campus climates that promote feelings of full inclusion and full citizenship while also providing students with access to social opportunities and networks that can translate into valuable personal, social, and political capital.

Building Political Skills through College Programming and Activities

The college classrooms and related curricular programs discussed in Chapter 5 are not the only places where college students gain politically relevant knowledge and skills. They can develop such tools by participating in programs and activities on campus. College years provide many young

TABLE 6.3 Participation in Political Activities during College

	Disagree Strongly	Disagree Somewhat	Agree Somewhat	Agree Strongly		Total
"I had significant political experiences that have shaped my views of government."						
HBCU Attendees	19%	24	34	22	=	99%
Non-HBCU Attendees	29%	30	29	12	=	100%
"Politics was a central part of life at my college."						
HBCU Attendees	30%	36	22	13	=	101%
Non-HBCU Attendees	46%	28	17	8	=	99%
	Never	**Occasionally**	**Often**	**Very Often**		
How frequently did you participate in a campus club, organization, or student government group?						
HBCU Attendees	29%	33	17	21	=	100%
Non-HBCU Attendees	48%	22	16	13	=	99%

Notes: The total percentages may not equal 100 percent due to rounding. The differences are statistically significant at $p = .001$.
Source: The College Experience Study—Black Respondents.

people with the opportunity to have significant political experiences that shape their views of government. Data from the College Experience Study and HBCU alumni interviews offer insight into the nature of Black Americans' politically relevant experiences during college, paying particular attention to the experiences of HBCU attendees compared to PWI attendees.

To what extent do HBCUs and PWIs provide campus environments that foster democratic engagement? Table 6.3 provides insight into College Experience Study survey respondents' engagement with politics during college. Among those who attended HBCUs, a full 56 percent agree (either "somewhat" or "strongly") that they had significant political experiences during college, compared to 41 percent of non-HBCU attendees. When

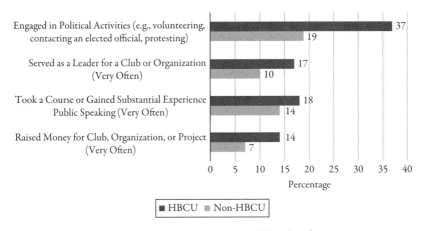

FIGURE 6.9 Percentage of respondents with high levels of participation in politically relevant academic experiences.

Note: Difference for "Took a Course or Gained Substantial Experience Public Speaking" is statistically significant at $p = .01$; and the remaining differences are statistically significant at $p = .001$.

Source: The College Experience Study—Black Respondents.

asked directly whether politics was a central part of life at their college, 35 percent of HBCU attendees agree with the statement, compared to 25 percent of PWI attendees. Thus, data indicate that HBCUs may provide distinctive campus environments that are particularly conducive to fostering student civic and political engagement.

Central to the value of colleges and universities for fostering democratic participation among students is the fact they often offer numerous pathways for engaging in politically relevant activities. Organizational and group activities can help students build valuable networks while also transmitting transferrable skills like organizing events, working on teams, and serving in leadership positions (Figure 6.9).

The College Experience Study asked respondents how frequently they participated in a campus club, organization, or student government group during college. Thirty-eight percent of Black respondents who attended HBCUs report that they participated in such organizations "often" or "very often," compared to 29 percent of PWI attendees. HBCU alumni reported participating in a broad range of campus organizations such as marching band, traveling choirs, collegiate and intramural athletics, royal court, and Greek letter organizations. Each of these activities offered numerous opportunities to build the kinds of networks and skills that could have a positive effect on long-term political engagement.

Chanté, who graduated from Spelman College in 2003, had an opportunity to gain a global perspective during her college years as a participant in her HBCU's Model United Nations program, which was a collaboration between Spelman and Morris Brown College. "We had a team, and then we traveled to Rio de Janeiro in Brazil. That was the first time I'd ever left the country . . . that kind of gave me more of a global experience and realizing that nations conduct their governments in different ways and have different needs and different priorities and trying to navigate that, come up with policy with all of that in mind." Chanté's dual-HBCU Model UN experience offers just one example of the kind of programming that HBCUs have offered to give their students opportunities to expand their perspectives on the world.

Given their significance for the Black community and their commitment to empowering young Black citizens, HBCUs are a frequent destination for many of the nation's most prominent political figures. Faculty and administrators organize campus visits that offer students ample opportunity to learn from role models who have made significant contributions as leaders in politics, civic life, business, the arts, and beyond.

Such opportunities offer particularly valuable opportunities for students to gain insight from political figures, and interviews with HBCU alumni revealed an impressive roster of political luminaries who visited their campuses. HBCU campus visitors mentioned in interviews include civil rights icons like Reverend Dr. Martin Luther King Jr., Rep. John Lewis, and Nelson Mandela; former presidential candidate Jesse Jackson; political activist Angela Davis; former presidents Gerald Ford, Bill Clinton, and Barack Obama; former first lady Michelle Obama; and numerous state and local political figures and candidates. Joyce, an alumna of Delaware State University, recalls that many of Delaware's politicians made their way to her HBCU's campus, including Senator and later US Vice President and President Joe Biden.

> We would see the governor, he'd come, and Joe Biden. He was there all the time. But it wasn't politics, it was just, "Oh, there's Joe! Hey Joe!" We knew that if there was something that Delaware needed, that Joe would make sure we had it. . . . Him and [his son] Beau, they were there all the time, if there was something—every graduation, Joe was there, whether

he was speaking or not. . . . We knew who he was, and we realized that he was a senator. But, being the only HBCU in Delaware, I expected that. As opposed to Norfolk State and Hampton—Virginia has a lot of HBCU schools. We were the only ones [in Delaware]. Therefore, I expected the government to be there. I expected the state senators to be there, because where else you got to go? We the only ones he got.

As Joyce's comment suggests, HBCUs may be prioritized as a destination for political figures who wish to engage with the Black community and who wish to demonstrate their commitment to Black young people.

Gaining Politically Relevant Skills during College

Among campus clubs and organizations, student government offers a particularly valuable opportunity for political socialization during college. Not only does it offer participants the opportunity to learn how to develop and execute a campaign strategy and how to participate in institutional governance, it also manages to capture the attention of some students who may not be interested in politics but who vote as a result of their interest in campus politics.

April, who graduated from Howard University in 1997, recalled deciding to forgo high-level engagement with student government at her HBCU because it seemed especially intense:

I thought those folks were crazy because I just thought they were that invested because it was Howard Student Association. But I didn't understand until I had been there a few years how much power there was both as a student, but how it gave you access to other avenues of politics. Because the president of the Student Association automatically became a board member [and] was also able to attend the Board of Trustees meetings. So, it gave you access to all of those trustee members, and that's how folks got connected into a whole bunch of other things.

Isaiah, a Howard University alumnus who graduated in 2014, emphasized the immense value of experience gained from running for a student government office, asserting that his experience campaigning for student government at Howard prepared him for a later campaign for public office. As Isaiah asserted, "If you can run a Howard campaign or if you can run for office at Howard, you can run for office anywhere." Recalling his own experience running for a leadership position in student government, he recalled that because of his experience at Howard, subsequent campaigns were relatively simple:

> There were no surprises for me as far as what to expect from people that were running against me, what to expect as far as putting together a strategy or campaign. When I talked to other friends of mine that did not go to Howard and, on a larger scale, that did not go to an HBCU, when they talk to me about what their student elections were like, it paled in comparison to the campaign life and lifestyle of a Howard University campaign. And that definitely showed in my level of preliminary preparation before I actually started going to training for new candidates. And, I think it really helped me during the campaign.

April, who also graduated from Howard University in 1997, echoed Isaiah's sense that running for a leadership position in campus government at Howard was particularly valuable training for future campaign work. April recalls that "By the time I was like a junior or senior, it was known that you tried to become a student body president at Howard if you plan on becoming the mayor of a major city."

One of the most valuable experiences that students can have—particularly when it comes to fostering high levels of political engagement and perhaps even setting the stage for elite-level engagement—is serving in a leadership role for a campus group. When asked how frequently they served as a leader for a club or organization on campus, 10 percent of non-HBCU attendees report that they did "very often," compared to 17 percent of HBCU attendees (Figure 6.9). Developing skill and comfort with speaking in public is another valuable tool that students can develop during college. Fourteen percent of non-HBCU attendees say that they took courses or otherwise gained public speaking experience "very often" as college students, while 18 percent of HBCU attendees report that they did so. Jackie, who graduated from HBCU Tennessee State University in 1981, reflected on the relationship between HBCU attendance and leadership development, saying:

> We're a family, where you get focused, where you know what you have to do, where you find yourself, where you find your voice. You may have

some political aspiration. You may just want to be a strong leader (because I think any kid who wants to go to college is a leader already). But you may develop some stronger leadership skills during that experience. And, I'm not saying you don't get that at a larger [PWI]. I'm saying it's so much easier to attach to it at an HBCU.

From this perspective, HBCUs are especially adept at helping Black college students acquire valuable leadership skills.

In addition to fostering the acquisition of leadership skills, college is also a time when many young people build valuable advocacy skills by engaging in campus activism. Yet, this tradition seems to be especially ensconced in HBCU campus culture. Diane, who graduated from Hampton University in 1980, described her mother's experience at that same HBCU during the 1940s when she took part in protests calling for more student empowerment and greater representation of African Americans among Hampton's faculty and administration:

> They had always had White college presidents, and they were protesting to have a Black college president, and they did end up getting a Black college president during her time at Hampton. . . . And then she talked about a protest to have sororities and fraternities at Hampton because they didn't have them at one time. . . . They thought that that would tear the community spirit of Hampton apart, and the administration didn't want it. But the students protested during that time, and that's how they ended up getting sororities and fraternities at Hampton. I think that started in '47.

Candice also described student activism on campus as a memorable part of her college experience at Spelman College. She recalled tensions between students and Spelman's administration when it came to empowering political conversations and activism around issues like policing and police brutality:

> I think Spelman was definitely an institution that was encouraging of a lot of these political conversations, but I also know that Spelman has its limitations, right? I think as progressive as the institution is in comparison to maybe many other HBCUs, there is still that politics of

respectability. There's still that, so I think that the campus promoted a healthy amount of political action and engagement, but I would also say that there's also a conservatism as well that I think a lot of students push against.

Another example of political activism on campus is the Black Lives Matters social movement, which captured the attention and engagement of many HBCU students across the country. Jasmine, who graduated from Hampton University in 2019, recalls that her cohort of students continued the university's long-standing tradition of campus activism. The year after George Zimmerman was acquitted for the murder of unarmed Black teenager Trayvon Martin, the freshman class took a photograph with all of the students on the football field holding their hands up in a "don't shoot" gesture. These examples of the advocacy work that HBCU students engage in on campus illustrate the range of activities that have provided an opportunity to acquire knowledge, skills, and inclinations that may contribute to a strong foundation for future political and civic engagement.

Last, given the increasing significance of money in American politics and the increasing imperative that successful candidates and high-level participants in the political arena be comfortable raising money, gaining fundraising experience during college provides another valuable tool for future political participants. While 7 percent of non-HBCU attendees reported that they raised money for a club, organization, or project during college, 14 percent of HBCU attendees did so. Brian, who graduated from University of Maryland–Eastern Shore, participated in fundraising efforts to support his HBCU's hotel restaurant management (HRM) program: "We were building and raising money for the new HRM building where they have the kitchens and extra rooms and such. We did a lot of fundraisers at night, where we would cook for donors and have elaborate meals, and it was really something special."

While the financial challenges that many HBCUs face due to factors like the history of inequitable government funding, possessing smaller endowments, and the racial wealth and income gaps that often limit Black alumni members' capacity to donate funds to their schools, they may also offer HBCU students unique opportunities to gain experience with fundraising and other advocacy work geared toward supporting their HBCUs.

Direct Engagement in Political Activities during College

The College Experience Study and HBCU alumni interviews provide insight into Black Americans' experience in political activities during college. The study revealed a striking difference in the rate at which HBCU attendees and non-HBCU attendees report having engaged in political activities like voting, volunteering for a political candidate, contacting an elected official, or participating in a protest or demonstration during college. While 19 percent of non-HBCU attendees report that they participated in such activities when they were college students, a full 37 percent of HBCU attendees report having done so.

Table 6.4 uses multivariate analysis to further examine the relationship between HBCU attendance and engagement in political activity during college. The first model suggests that, among survey respondents, those

TABLE 6.4 Determinants of Engaging in Political Activity During College

	Model I	Model II	Model III
Gender	−.074	−.040	−.029
	(.148)	(.149)	(.150)
Year of Birth	.012*	.013**	.012*
	(.005)	(.005)	(.005)
Youth Socioeconomic Status	.158*	.117	.106
	(.076)	(.077)	(.078)
Parents' Education	.069***	.043*	.039†
	(.020)	(.021)	(.022)
Parent Attended HBCU		.612***	.496**
		(.179)	(.189)
Grandparent Attended HBCU			.400*
			(.201)
HBCU Attendance	.881***	.742***	.729***
	(.149)	(.156)	(.156)
Log Likelihood	−594	−588	−586
N	1,134	1,134	1,134

†$p \leq$ .1; *$p \leq$ .05, **$p \leq$ .01, ***$p \leq$ .001
Notes: Cells consist of binary logistic regression coefficients in the numerator and standard errors in parentheses. Analysis includes Black respondents who have completed at least "some college."
Source: The College Experience Study—Black Respondents.

who are younger, those who hail from a more privileged socioeconomic background, and those whose parents have higher levels of education are significantly more likely to engage in political activities during college. We also see that HBCU attendance is positively associated with higher levels of participation in political activities.

To what extent might one's HBCU lineage relate to participation in political activity during college? The second model in Table 6.4 includes an additional independent variable—whether either of the respondents' parents attended an HBCU. Results suggest that having a parent who attended an HBCU is also positively associated with engagement in political activity during college. The third model incorporates grandparents' HBCU attendance as an additional independent variable, and we find that—like having a parent who attended an HBCU—having a grandparent who attended an HBCU is also a significant predictor of engaging in political activity during college for Black survey respondents.

These data suggest that higher educational institutions offer valuable opportunities to gain skills that can prove useful in the development of politically engaged citizens. And, this appears to be particularly true for Black Americans who attend HBUCs or whose parents or grandparents attended them.[9]

To be sure, the prevalence of HBCU student political engagement has varied over time. Betty, a 1949 graduate of Hampton College (later University), described the relative quiet on campus during the immediate postwar period: "World War II had just ended when I went to college—it ended in August of 1945, and I went to college in September. And, I think everybody had been so upset about World War II that we, sort of, stayed in a little shell and just tried to be happy at college and not get involved in any political activities."

This changed for subsequent generations of HBCU (and PWI) college students. In recent years, not only have college campuses helped to encourage student voter participation, they have devoted considerable campus resources to helping students participate in democracy. For many students, college represents the first opportunity to vote in presidential and down-ballot elections, and many HBCUs work to mobilize voter participation.[10] Some campuses provide polling locations right on campus, offering students convenient voting access. And, others offer shuttles to help students reach off-campus polling sites.

A number of alumnae from Bennett College discussed a prominent motto on their college campus: "Bennett Belles are voting Belles." As this popular saying illustrates, voting was viewed and treated as a constitutive part of the identity of a Bennett College student, and it left a profound impact on the college's alumnae. Marcus offers a similar account of the emphasis that his HBCU, West Virginia State College, placed on voting: "There was always, always, always an encouragement for us to register to vote, and how our ancestors died for us to have that right to vote and be counted as a whole person for our ability to make change within the country. And, if we allowed our voices to remain silent, then that's what they would be, silent."

Tiffany, who graduated from HBCU North Carolina A&T in 2019, noted the heavy emphasis that her peers placed on voter registration: "If you're not registered to vote and you go to A&T, you just didn't . . . you'll ruin the entire day because at least three or four people will ask you, 'Hey are you registered to vote?'"

Crystal, who graduated from Tennessee State University in 1990, distinctly remembers the extraordinary mobilization that took place on her HBCU campus. "In 1988," she recalls, "Jesse Jackson was running for president. He came to Tennessee State and talked to all the student body. Then they took a caravan of us . . . of all the students down to the voter registration election place, and we all registered to vote. So, I registered to vote in 1988 because Jesse Jackson came to Tennessee state because he was running for president. Totally awesome."

HBCU faculty have been known to act as particularly powerful mobilizers for voter engagement. Ashley, a 2009 graduate of Bennett College, remembers faculty member and then–North Carolina state representative (later US Congresswoman) Alma Adams encouraging students to participate in politics:

> She was known to have a megaphone or like the, I forget what you call it, the electronic one. And she would go into the lunchrooms while we were eating and be like, "Bennett Belles are voting belles." And that was her thing. Like, she was very passionate about it. So, seeing that, I think naturally you just wanna engage with her. . . . So, everyone in some way had a way to get into politics or get into voting or help out a campaign, even if it wasn't her, maybe somebody else.

Indeed, the robust presence of political role models on campus made a strong impression on a number of HBCU graduates. Raven, who graduated from Bennett College in 2013, describes the active political engagement that existed on her campus among both faculty and students: "There were professors on our campus that were state representatives and board members who were senators. I was a Political Science major, so being involved on political campaigns and interning with the mayor's office and kind of seeing the civic change that we had registering students to vote. I think 93–95 percent of our campus was registered to vote." Olivia, who also attended Bennett College and graduated in 2014, recalls the long-standing tradition whereby Bennett Belles marched together to the polls. Others recalled that Bennett College alumni in the surrounding Greensboro, North Carolina, area would come to the campus to also join in the march to the polls, demonstrating a level of solidarity and support for their younger sisters that left an impression.

Tiffany, a 2009 graduate of HBCU Clark Atlanta University, remembers the excitement on campus during the 2008 election that ushered Barack Obama, the nation's first Black president, into office. "This is when Vote or Die [was popular]. Barack Obama got elected during my senior year, so it was very, very prominent on our campus to vote. People wore shirts. There were voter registration drives. When Barack Obama got elected, on his election night, oh my gosh, the campus. . . . I'm sure like many other campuses around the nation, shut down."

Other HBCU attendees described working on political campaigns during college. They supported presidential, congressional, state, and local candidates by helping with mailings, phone banking, event planning, and staffing fundraisers. Andrea, who graduated from HBCU Dillard University in 2003, recalled, "We were out there holding campaign signs, and you get a little bit of money to help do that, especially when you're a broke college student. That was always fun to do, and that's how you learn about the city." She continued:

> I think they were just using us as cheap labor, but a lot of those politicians would come to our campus and, of course they would give their little speeches. Because, they were trying to lure us to help them with their campaigns, to go out there and rock the vote—get people in the community to vote. . . . So, they used young, educated, Black young men and women to go out there and rock the vote. So, getting us out there and

encouraging the elderly, or encouraging people that wouldn't normally go and vote, to go and vote.

As these examples illustrate, HBCUs have helped to provide their students with a wide variety of opportunities to engage in politics. They also have provided access to political role models who help to demonstrate the ways that citizens might engage in political activities at a higher level. For many, this emphasis on political engagement was seen as part and parcel of the identity of a member of that school's community.

Social Movement Activity

For young people across generations, college years have marked a period of political awakening, and college students have stood at the forefront of numerous social movements in the United States. From the US civil rights movement of the 1950s and 1960s, to the Black power movement of the 1960s and 1970s, to the quest for South African liberation and the campaign that led to Nelson Mandela's freedom in 1990, to the Million Man March in 1995, to the Black Lives Matter movement that began in 2013, HBCU students have been at the center of related youth activism efforts in the United States.

For the generation of Americans who attended college during the 1960s, the turbulent political context brought many opportunities to get involved in political activities. Evelyn, a sixty-nine-year-old alumna of PWI Central Michigan University, attended college during the late 1960s. She says:

> It was during the '60s when I first started college, so it was a lot of protests that we were involved with. Martin Luther King was alive back then, and so it just was a lot of protests. President Johnson was the president. I know I'm dating myself, but yeah, we were involved in the politics as far as the marching and things like that. And I sat at a lunch counter when I went to Mississippi.

Ray, a seventy-year-old graduate of PWI Stony Brook University who also attended PWI UC-Berkeley, described politics as central to college life during the 1960s: "At Berkeley, that's all it was, you know. I was there in '67 through '68 . . . that's when everything was going on there. . . . I was involved in a lot of things. I had friends who were Black Panthers, friends who were with different White activist groups. Most of my friends were involved politically 'cause I was kind of bent that way."

Generations of HBCU students have become mobilized to engage in political experiences during their time in college. Milton, who attended Howard University in the late 1960s, described the era as "the most pivotal change period in the history of HBCUs." He recalled a great amount of tension between administrators and activist—predominantly junior—faculty and students who were advocating change on campus and in the broader society, using tactics like campus takeovers and protests. Milton notes the difference between this era of activism and that which characterized previous generations: "My parents could just not fathom how a bunch of students are going to dictate to the president and the board and take over the university. . . . My aunt and uncle in Detroit, they were both activists in their day, in the '40s, on campus. But it was a different kind of activism."

Of her time at Howard University in Washington, DC, during the 1980s, Tanya recalls, "There was a lot of activism on campus because when I was in school, apartheid was in South Africa, so there was a lot of protests in front of the South African Embassy. I remember friends going down there and getting arrested and put in plastic handcuffs and ended up paying like $30 to get out of jail. It was symbolic, but I do remember that." She also described Howard as a politically charged educational hub:

> Barbara Bush was the honoree at one of our graduations, and I remember the graduates standing up and turning their backs on her. Lee Atwater was appointed to our board of trustees, and I think he worked for George [H. W.] Bush . . . and the students protested that. They were in the administration building, and they shut it down because they didn't want him on the board of trustees.

More recently, HBCU students studying at North Carolina A&T mobilized to protest the use of political gerrymandering in North Carolina that resulted in unequal representation in government institutions. Kiara, who graduated from A&T in 2019, said, "Well, first of all, our school has a gerrymandering problem. There is a, what do you call it? The district or whatever. The line goes straight through campus. So, half of campus votes on one polling area, the other half of campus votes on another polling area." The student government association, Kiara recalls, took up the issue with state lawmakers.

HBCU students have also mobilized in response to government actions targeted at HBCUs. For example, some respondents describe mobilizing in response to proposed cuts to HBCU funding, sharing that they signed letters and contacted state legislators in relation to the issue. And, in some cases, highly engaged and mobilized students decide to run for public office. One Winston Salem State University alumnus recalled having a classmate who ran for city council as a college student and who went on to serve as a state legislator.

Town/Gown Relations and a Culture of Community Service

> There's so much history that runs through Clark Atlanta's campus . . . people can't deny that we all have a part there. It's not just for collegiate people who are going onto higher education. Every Black person owns Clark Atlanta or owns the AUC [Atlanta University Center] in a way.
> —Tiffany, Clark Atlanta University Alumna ('09)

HBCUs have traditionally worked to empower local African American communities, and their students—who study, work, and worship in their cities—often become integrated into surrounding communities. During the 1950s, for example, some HBCUs developed radio and television programming that would expose their communities to political issues and promote greater engagement in the fight for civil rights. Talladega College aired a radio show that "delved into controversial topics such as voting rights and segregation in the workplace . . . [at a time when] African Americans were not encouraged to vote by mainstream radio stations or newspapers so the role of HBCUs was critical to civic engagement and political activity of Black citizens."[11] Bethune-Cookman College offered members of their community information on the importance of voting and aided their efforts to combat voter disenfranchisement and to fight for their civil rights.[12]

HBCUs have a long legacy of serving as a resource for their local communities. As Nathan, a 1991 graduate of North Carolina Central University, recalled about his HBCU's Health Education Department:

> They were active in doing good, important work. For instance, they started a blood drive, I want to say, in 1987, that has continued even until today on campus; and in the broader community they were actively

involved in voter registration . . . and used students to go out and help register people and assist in providing transportation in collaboration with the local churches. . . . They were involved in a prenatal education program with the county health department.

The idea that service was embedded in their school's culture was a central theme that emerged from interviews with HBCU alumni. As Courtney, a 2009 alumna of Spelman College, put it, "It was very clear to all of us that service was our duty." Veronica, who graduated from Tennessee State University in 1988, further illustrated this notion by pointing to the alma mater that guided her HBCU's work: "The motto of the university is 'Enter to learn before serve.' And so, service is a part of what the University teaches. You know, you're getting this degree for a reason. It is of course to better yourself, to better your life, to better your family. It's also to give back and serve your community."[13]

Nicole, a 2019 graduate of Savannah State University, recalled the impact that her HBCU had in the local community: "When they see our college's name, they know that we're coming to help, and they can use us, so they use us to make things run smoothly . . . whether it's a back-to-school bash in the park, just different things. When Savannah State is there, they know that we're there to help, and we'll help get the job done." Like Nicole, many HBCU attendees note that their colleges provided valuable opportunities to become familiar with their surrounding communities and to contribute to them. Of her time at Spelman College, Candice noted:

> There was a sense of everybody here should be doing something to give back. When I first got to Spelman, we were surrounded by housing projects, and there were a few elementary schools that were very close by, that were like mostly Title I schools, if not all, and mostly Black kids. There were a lot of organizations that did work within the schools, like tutoring. There were a lot of local churches that had after-school or weekend programs. I worked as a staff person, counselor, for one of the local churches in the area. . . .
>
> Most of my friends, if not all of my friends, were doing something in the community, some kind of outreach work. We had a Bonner Scholars office . . . where there was a group of students on campus who were doing that for scholarship money. Not just for the scholarship, but because they considered themselves to be community servants. I just don't

remember there being a culture of people not being in the community. It was just what was expected.

As these examples illustrate, engagement with and service to the surrounding community is a prominent feature of the HBCU college experience that makes civic engagement a central part of their students' educational experience. Such opportunities help students connect their academic exploration of topics like Black history, politics, and inequality to on-the-ground efforts to strengthen the community.

In interviews, HBCU alumni placed strong emphasis on the extent to which community service was a central part of their college experience. For virtually all, such service is viewed as a tacit requirement that is expected of them and all members of the campus community; and for many, it is a formal requirement for graduation. Amber, who graduated from North Carolina Central University in 2017, recalled that—in line with the university's motto, "Truth and Service"—students were required to complete 100 hours of community service to graduate. The university took great care to ensure that all students completed this part of the curriculum, even setting up a formal online portal where students could log their volunteer hours and learn about service opportunities. Amber noted the seriousness with which NCCU takes its service requirement, remembering that her status as a transfer student did not exempt her from the requirement to fulfill the full 100 hours of community service required for graduation.

Some HBCU alumni view their unique college experiences as directly tied to their engagement in political and civic activities. Angela, an alumna of HBCU Prairie View A&M University, says:

> Going to the college that I went to allowed me to open up my mouth and hear that I have a voice; understanding my voice can be heard. Sometimes you have to speak a little louder, sometimes you have to speak a little softer. However, you still are given that voice, and it's up to you. Having that college experience, on figuring out what's the best way to communicate that voice, and when it's a good time, and when it's not a good time. And then determine, you know, what avenues do we use?

Lorraine, who graduated from Virginia State College in 1973, concurs, pointing to her HBCU experience as a significant influence on her perspective on politics:

When I was in high school, I used to listen to the news, and I was interested. But when I went to Virginia State, it opened up a whole new
world after I got some knowledge of Black history. Today, I'm very much
interested in politics. I see a lot of things going on today that I cannot
believe are happening, so I'm very much interested and sometimes I get
frustrated and just tired of seeing the same thing over and over and over
and over and over and over and over on the news and nothing being
done about it. I find it kind of frustrating, and I have a big question mark
in my mind, "Why is all this stuff being allowed to happen?"

In particular, the widespread expectation of service may create a strong
foundation for HBCU graduates' long-term civic and political endeavors.
As Gail, who attended Talladega College in the 1960s, noted, "I don't
know whether it came from Talladega, or our changing consciousness over
the last fifty years, but I think there was an expectation of leadership ... you
were expected to do more than just get a good job, but to contribute something to your community." She continued, "I certainly try to instill that in
my grandchildren—that it's not enough for you to do well. If you're not
making a difference in the lives of Black people, then you're not successful.
You're not doing what you need to do." As these examples illustrate, political and civic engagement are a matter of tradition for HBCUs, and it
seems plausible that their legacy of leadership, activism, and service could
contribute to a uniquely empowering educational experience for HBCU
students.

Conclusion

Many have recognized that HBCUs have provided valuable higher educational access to millions of Black Americans, helping to increase educational attainment and enhance the life chances of a group that historically
has been marginalized by American higher educational institutions. It is
important to note, however, that the significance of HBCUs does not
stop there. As this chapter has illustrated, HBCUs have also empowered
African Americans and the Black community by providing an educational
experience that fosters civic and political engagement.

The evidence presented here suggests that HBCUs provide their
students with unique college experiences that foster active engagement
as political citizens and a commitment to giving back to the various
communities of which they are a part. Of course, Black students can gain

valuable opportunities for community engagement at both HBCUs and PWIs. But, empirical evidence suggests that among African Americans who have attended college, those who attended HBCUs are more likely to report having had college experiences that supported active democratic engagement.

Furthermore, qualitative data provide greater insight into how HBCUs work to foster community outreach and engagement and political participation. As such, this analysis suggests that HBCUs act as important agents of political socialization and transmitters of human capital by helping students build politically relevant skills, promoting confidence in one's ability to make valuable contributions to the world, and including students in their strong commitment to service.

7

Foundations for Leadership

HBCUs and the Cultivation of Black Political Elites

HBCUS HAVE PRODUCED GENERATIONS OF American leaders who have made valuable contributions to numerous fields. According to the Thurgood Marshall Fund, nearly 13 percent of Black CEOs, 40 percent of Black engineers, and half of Black professors teaching at PWIs were educated at Black colleges. These figures are even more pronounced for Black Americans working in law and government, as approximately 40 percent of Black members of Congress, 50 percent of Black lawyers, and 80 percent of Black judges attended HBCUs.[1] What role have HBCUs played in the development of Black political leaders? Do Black elected officials who attended HBCUs report having experiences markedly different from their counterparts who attended PWIs? This chapter uses qualitative data from in-depth interviews with Black political elites in the United States to gain insight into this question, revealing key features of the HBCU educational experience that Black leaders identify as helping to shape their pathway to public service.

Political scientists have provided valuable insights into the forces that shape political elites' capacity and motivation to embark on a career in public service.[2] In terms of shaping one's ability to run for office and serve as an elected official, education offers a pathway to valuable resources such as time, higher levels of income, and greater professional autonomy.[3] For Black Americans, a group that has historically been marginalized in elite politics, higher education is a particularly valuable democratic resource that can provide knowledge and skills that facilitate high levels of political engagement. As we saw in Chapter 6, HBCUs can provide access to political role models who can inspire students to participate in political activities.[4] They can also help foster strong feelings of ethnic community, which are associated with higher levels of political engagement.[5]

Political scientists have also shown that substantive policy interests play a role in Black citizens' reasons for seeking elected office. In their study of Black political elites, political scientists James Conyers and Walter Wallace found that, when asked to share their primary motivations for running, Black elected officials report a strong desire to remedy social injustices.[6] Conyers and Wallace also examined whether the racial dynamics of the college that elected officials attended shaped their political attitudes. Interestingly, they found that Black elected officials who were younger were significantly more likely to support racial independence (as opposed to integrationism) than were their older counterparts. The one exception to this trend was the group of older Black elected officials who had attended predominantly White colleges: they were also more likely to favor racial independence over integrationism.[7]

In the United States, the racial and ethnic diversity of political institutions is also a matter of democratic significance. Scholars of political representation have highlighted the importance of descriptive representation—which results when elected officials and their constituents share relevant identities, such as race, gender, or socioeconomic status—for addressing the policy needs and preferences of various communities.[8] For Black Americans—as is the case with other identity groups—the presence of elected officials in government institutions who share their identity can shape how their interests are represented in the halls of power. Scholars have shown that Black political empowerment, as evidenced by the presence of a Black mayor leading one's city, corresponds to higher levels of political engagement and efficacy, which is associated with higher levels of engagement with politics.[9] Moreover, the perspectives, experiences, and priorities that Black elected officials bring to their work in public service also play a role in how they represent their constituents.

Of course, sharing demographic characteristics is no guarantee that the dominant interests or preferences of a group will be reflected in an elected official's decisions. Indeed, there are instances in which elected officials' actions may deviate from the preferences of constituents who share their demographic background. Scholars describe such instances as illustrating "symbolic representation," which offers an important reminder that the election of officials with particular demographic characteristics does not preordain any particular policy outcome.[10]

Nevertheless, as political scientists Paula McClain and Jessica Johnson Carew assert, "the importance of descriptive representation comes in terms of the increased substantive representation that can flow from it, as well as the increased political efficacy and engagement that it can produce among those who are descriptively represented."[11] They go on to note that a combination of heightened engagement in politics plus the work of representatives actively seeking to bring a group's preferences to the legislative agenda can promote democracy and more effective representation of those with marginalized identities.[12] Other scholars have emphasized that political representation of a constituency by an elected official is largely driven by representatives' work to achieve strong connections with their constituents.[13] Given the value of one's formative years as a period for establishing a social network that could result in lasting social bonds, an elected official's college experience could be particularly important to their effectiveness as a candidate and later as a public servant.

This chapter draws on data from the Political Elites segment of my 2018 College Experience Study, which involved in-depth interviews with thirteen current and former Black elected officials to gain insight into how their college experiences may have shaped their pathway to politics and their approach to public service. Given that this study includes thirteen current and former Black political elites, my aim is not to make causal claims but to draw upon these case studies to better understand the features of HBCU and non-HBCU college experiences that can shape advanced political engagement in the United States.

Of the thirteen interview subjects featured in this chapter, seven attended HBCUs and six attended PWIs. Ten of the thirteen interview subjects were members of the 115th US Congress, two were state legislators, and one was the former mayor of a small southern city.[14] All interviewees are members of the Democratic Party. In terms of demographics, all thirteen interview subjects are Black Americans. The group includes nine men and four women, and while the men interviewed had both HBCU and non-HBCU college experiences (seven and two interviewees in each respective group), none of the women interviewed attended an HBCU.

The age distribution is similar for HBCU attendees and non-HBCU attendees, with each group including at least one respondent born in each decade from the 1930s through the 1960s. The most senior HBCU attendee was born in 1934 and the most senior non-HBCU attendee was born in 1937. The youngest HBCU attendee was born in 1965, while the youngest non-HBCU attendee was born in 1966. While the elected officials interviewed do not offer a representative sample of Black elected officials in the United States, the data nonetheless provide valuable insights into the higher educational experiences that contributed to the development of prominent Black political leaders.

Choosing a College and Paying for Higher Education

For the Black elected officials included in this study, a number of factors shaped their decisions to attend an HBCU or a non-HBCU for their postsecondary education. Not surprisingly, factors like a school's reputation, family connections and familiarity with an institution, and a school's location and distance from family loomed large among the factors that HBCU and non-HBCU attendees considered. For both groups, the influence of parents and family connections were the most commonly reported factors shaping the decision about where to attend college.

However, family influence and extended family connections were particularly prominent forces for Black elected officials who attended HBCUs, with four of these seven interviewees in this category describing this as highly significant. North Carolina Representative Raymond Smith describes "a family tradition of attending historically Black colleges" as part of the appeal of attending North Carolina A&T. His mother and cousins had attended A&T, while various aunts, uncles, and cousins had attended other HBCUs. Smith also notes that schools in his neighborhood were not integrated until 1969 when he was in the fourth grade and that "all of my teachers, my principals, individuals who lived in the neighborhood who were doctors and lawyers—they all had attended HBCUs." When preparing to matriculate into college, Smith, an accomplished student athlete, received numerous offers from PWIs, but he saw going to North Carolina A&T as "a no brainer." Describing his decision, he said:

> I had my heart set on attending an HBCU, and I guess it was years of exposure to them, knowing what I was getting myself into, having friends and more classmates than others who I attended high school with who attended A&T. . . . I knew I was going to a historically Black college; I had no interest in attending a predominantly White institution.

For Congressman Jim Clyburn (D-SC), growing up in his father's church in Orangeburg, South Carolina, where two prominent professors from nearby South Carolina State University were members, made an impression. He spent considerable time with them on the historically Black campus: "That's how I became accustomed to South Carolina State— going over there, after church on Sundays, spending the whole afternoon, playing football or whatever we played on the lawn where they lived." Former Chapel Hill, North Carolina, mayor Howard Lee's first awareness of HBCUs came when a cousin gained admission to Tuskegee Institute at the age of sixteen. His interest in college sports first brought his attention to another HBCU—Florida A&M—when he was a teenager, and Lee's mother, who was a teacher, introduced him to HBCUs like Bethune Cookman, Howard University, Shaw University, and Saint Augustine's College, which his community held in great esteem.

As a first-generation college student, North Carolina State Representative James Gailliard was planning to attend Boston University, but a chance encounter with an influential Black college leader led to a change in course. After graduating from high school, Gailliard met civil rights icon and long-serving Morehouse College president Dr. Benjamin E. Mays at an event in Philadelphia. Gailliard recalled the life-altering conversation:

> He just said, "You remind me of a Morehouse man. You should go visit." And, so I did. And, I was just blown away by what I encountered when I got there. I think the real changing point of my life was attending Morehouse. I don't think my life would remotely look anything like it does now had I not gone specifically to Morehouse.

Elected officials who attended non-HBCUs described having much less familiarity with HBCUs and did not report the same level of encouragement by parents, relatives, and social connections to attend a particular college or type of college. One elected official's parents actively discouraged attending an HBCU because they believed that HBCUs were less prestigious than PWIs. The majority of the elected officials interviewed who did not attend an HBCU were first-generation college students, and HBCUs did not figure prominently in their formative years. Congressman Gregory Meeks (D-NY) attended Howard University Law School after doing his undergraduate work at Adelphi University, a PWI. Meeks recalls that "I did not consider a historically Black college because, to be quite frank, I was the first in my family to go to college and I did not know of anyone who had attended."

In addition to the role that parents, relatives, and other social connections played in shaping Black elected officials' decisions about where to attend college, college reputation was another important factor. For those who attended HBCUs, a legacy of civil rights activism attracted many to Black college campuses. Congressman Meeks, who attended Howard University Law School in the 1970s, recalled the pull of attending the law school where icons like Thurgood Marshall had learned how to fight for social justice through the law. Awareness of Howard Law School's reputation for cultivating lawyers who were experts in areas like criminal law and litigation were central to his decision of where to pursue legal study.

Black elected officials who did not attend HBCUs also reported that institutional reputation was central to their decision of where to pursue postsecondary education. For Congressman Bobby Rush (D-IL), who had been active as a cofounder of the Illinois chapter of the Black Panther Party, Roosevelt University was a solid match. Named in honor of President Franklin D. Roosevelt and First Lady Eleanor Roosevelt, the college was founded on the principle of racial, religious, and gender inclusion. Rush's decision to attend Roosevelt University was shaped by the fact that it was a liberal college that reflected his progressive values. Congresswoman Eleanor Holmes Norton (D-DC) reported a similar fit with Antioch College, which had a reputation for providing a rigorous intellectual experience that prepared students for pursuing advanced study in a graduate or professional degree program, which was her goal.

Another common factor shaping the elected officials' decisions about where to attend college was school location and distance from their family. This theme was especially prominent in the interviews with HBCU attendees, as four of the seven interviewees in this group mentioned this was a central factor shaping their decision. The question of whether to attend college in the North or the South was central to many respondents' thinking. For Congressman Clyburn, South Carolina State had been his childhood dream school, but as he neared the point of embarking on his college studies, the fact that many young Black Americans living in the South during the late 1950s and early 1960s ventured north for college led him to strongly consider leaving his home state and pursuing a college degree in the North.

While his mother also supported this plan, a conversation with one of his high school teachers helped to change his mind. Clyburn recalls the occasion that "Miss Lucas . . . [who] was my Bible Teacher" asked her students to write a page about their dreams and goals for the future. After reviewing Clyburn's paper in which he mentioned his plans of going north for college, she said, "I read your paper and I'm very, very disturbed by your paper. If all Black children should get educated, leave the South, things will never change. The only way for things to change is for those Blacks who get educated to stay in the South because that's where battles have to be fought. You can't fight from up North." Clyburn recalls the conversation: "Here's this White woman telling me how this Black man ought to conduct himself. I'll never forget that conversation. But, it had everything to do with me changing my mind." The prospect of being better able to help improve the situation in the South led Clyburn to enroll in HBCU South Carolina State.

Mayor Lee echoes Clyburn's recollection of the pull of the North for Black prospective college students in the South during the mid-twentieth century. "During my time as a youngster, the greatest dream of most Black folk was to grow up and get the heck out of the South as soon as they possibly could." Lee explored northern and southern possibilities for higher education and applied to Ohio State, a PWI, and Clark Atlanta University, an HBCU in Atlanta.

Racial segregation was another factor that emerged from interviews with members of each group; however, the nature of the impact that segregation had on their decisions about where to attend college varied, as it acted as a factor that pulled students toward Black colleges in some instances, while pushing students away from Black colleges in others.

A final theme that emerged from conversations with Black elected officials who attended both HBCUs and PWIs was the central role that meeting the cost of college played in shaping their decisions about where to go. North Carolina State Representative Raymond Smith, for example, who earned a bachelor's degree from HBCU North Carolina A&T in 1992, used the G.I. Bill to pay for his education.

Mayor Lee, on the other hand, supplemented a $100 scholarship at HBCU Clark College with a variety of jobs to pay for his education: "I had to work and could not stay in the dormitory the first two years, which made it difficult, and that contributed handsomely to my inability to perform academically." A cousin helped him get a position parking cars during special events at a golf club in Atlanta. He also worked as a bartender and waiter at the Biltmore Hotel in Atlanta, and during summers he worked as an assistant chef at a hotel in Atlantic City. He recalls: "I paid my way through, barely. When I got to [HBCU] Fort Valley [State College], there was not a similar opportunity, so I had to work in the dining hall . . . and my parents were starting to make a little more money by that time and they were able to help. So, that's how I muddled my way through."

For elected officials who did not attend HBCUs, paying for college loomed similarly large in their decisions about where to go to college. When Congresswoman Stacey Plaskett (D–Virgin Islands) applied early decision to Georgetown's foreign service school—an institution noted for being one of the best places for studying diplomacy and international affairs—the availability of financial aid was a central question. She recalls that "I knew that where I went was going to be determined by money. So, I applied to a bunch of Ivy League schools where I knew I would need need-blind admissions as well. I got into most of them, and because Georgetown's early decision was nonbinding I was able to use the packages that I got from the other schools to negotiate with Georgetown."

While elected officials who attended HBCUs and non-HBCUs highlighted a number of shared factors that shaped their decisions about where to go to school, there were some notable differences between the groups. One theme that emerged from interviews with HBCU attendees was the fact that HBCUs offered a second chance for students who struggled academically. For example, Mayor Lee described a shaky academic start at his first HBCU, Clarke College, which led to his being asked to leave due to poor grades. At his mother's encouragement, he decided to try to talk his way into Fort Valley State College.

"So I got on a bus and went to Fort Valley and walked into the registrar's office and told my story and he laughed. But after we talked, he became interested and he wanted the president to see me." His meeting with the college president was an important turning point in his life:

Amazingly enough, [the registrar] took me across the hall and we met the president. And, they sat there and looked at me and said, "You really have to be out of your mind. You just flunked out of a college, you've proven you can't do the work, and you're just not college material." So I kept talking, and finally they made a decision. "You come here. We're on the quarter system. You make anything less than a C in any course the first quarter, and you're out." That was the pressure. So, I came in, first quarter, all Cs [laughs]. And from that point on of course, the next quarter, I hit the honor roll and I was off and running.

This example illustrates the commitment that many HBCU's have demonstrated to recognizing students' potential and extending valuable educational opportunity—and even second chances—at critical junctures in students' transitions into adulthood.

For elected officials who did not attend HBCUs, the needs of nontraditional college students and an interest in completing a degree quickly emerged as central themes when it came to their decisions about where to attend college. Congresswoman Bonnie Watson Coleman (D-NJ) and Congresswoman Karen Bass (D-CA), for example, first enrolled in college programs after high school and then left their programs to join the workforce. As Congresswoman Coleman recalls:

> I didn't really have a good experience the first year or so at Rutgers . . . so I came out and got a job. I spent years taking a course here, taking a course there. . . . But it was at a time where you didn't necessarily have to have a degree to get into certain first-level professional positions. And I started doing really well, working hard and moving up really quickly in the system. And, at some point, a good friend of mine just told me to finish this degree. That's how I happened upon Thomas Edison. She was actually a member of the Board of Trustees. So, finally, I sat down with Thomas Edison because it's an adult learning institution, and we plotted my way to finish my degree. They did it around my schedule.

Thomas Edison College offered Congresswoman Coleman the opportunity to complete a rigorous program of coursework while continuing to move up on her professional trajectory and also balancing family responsibilities.

Congresswoman Bass shares a similar account of integrating college into her life as a nontraditional student. After high school, Bass attended PWI San Diego State for two years where she was engaged in activism related to the war in Vietnam, global independence struggles, and fighting racism in San Diego. She recalls:

> I didn't pay a lot of attention to my academic studies. I left after two years and after that, I kind of went back and forth to college. . . . I worked

for a while, traveled to Cuba, went to nursing school because nursing school was quick—it was twelve months—and I could go back into being a political activist.

Congressman Rush was another nontraditional college student for whom speed in completing his degree was essential. As he recalls, "I decided to go to Roosevelt University because they had an accelerated degree program. I went to Roosevelt because I knew that some of my life skills that I had learned or acquired in the movement, in the military, I'd apply those and get credits for those. I was a young man in a hurry, so that accelerated degree program really appealed to me."

For a number of the Black elected officials who attended PWIs, they placed less emphasis on having a deep campus experience and more emphasis on completing their degree as quickly as possible so as to focus on other priorities with which they were engaged outside of college. Those who attended HBCUs, on the other hand, were often more amenable to heavy engagement in campus life and receptive to experiencing their college experience as a central part of their development and identity as they transitioned into adulthood.

College Experience, College Coursework, and Politics on Campus

What kinds of college experiences did Black elected officials have at their respective HBCUs and PWIs, and to what extent was politics part of their coursework and campus life? Common themes emerged from interviews with those who attended HBCUs and PWIs—particularly the central role that faculty members played in shaping their college experiences and a robust interest in politics during their college years.

For those who attended PWIs, the influence of key faculty members was the most frequently cited factor that shaped their college experience. Congressman Rush recalls the significance of the friendship that he developed with Professor Frank Untermyer who taught political philosophy at Roosevelt University as central to his college experience. Congresswoman Bass similarly notes the role that her mentor, Professor Peter Bohmer, played in helping her to develop a keen understanding of political economy during her time at San Diego State University.

For Congresswoman Plaskett, having the opportunity to learn from a Black woman professor at Georgetown was a particularly important part of her college experience. As she notes, "I'd never had a Black female teach me—someone who looked like me—before I got to Georgetown.

And I remember it was my junior year, and her name is Gwen Mikell—
she still teaches at Georgetown ... and she is an anthropologist. I can remember sitting in the class and it was maybe a month into it, slamming
me that, oh my God, this Black woman is teaching me! And, she was
such a ... I mean, I couldn't get into her class until junior year because
the best in the foreign service program, the anthropology [program],
everyone wanted her."

While having the opportunity to learn from Black faculty was an unusual experience for many PWI students, those who attended HBCUs
had regular opportunities to learn from Black professors, and these
faculty-student relationships were central to elected officials' experiences
at HBCUs. The central theme that emerged from interviews with elected
officials is that those who attended HBCUs recall having engagements
with faculty that seemed parental or otherwise family like. Describing the
relationships between students and faculty at his HBCU, North Carolina
A&T, State Representative Smith notes that "the relationships that you develop between your professors and your students are absolutely personal.
It is not just business, it is personal." Smith describes this as the "secret
sauce" that makes HBCUs special, noting that for his own daughters who
are HBCU students, "the relationship that they have developed with their
classmates, their professors, is absolutely personal. My daughters can get on
the phone right now and call any one of their professors and have a conversation." State Representative Gailliard expanded on this theme, noting that
during his time at Morehouse College:

> [T]he faculty were very paternal and maternalistic regarding students. It
> was not uncommon for professors to have students over at their home
> on a weekend and sit down with them over a meal and review the lesson.
> It was a very hands-on feel. You could touch the faculty. They were very
> involved in your overall life, and they were parenting us. They weren't
> just educating us. They were parenting us.

The sense that HBCU faculty were invested in the holistic development
and well-being of their students is a frequently recurring theme among
elected officials who attended HBCUs.

Elected officials who attended HBCUs and PWIs report similar levels
of engagement in political science courses and other politics relevant classes
including courses in history, speech, and international relations. The study
of history was particularly prominent among elected officials who attended
HBCUs. Moreover, data from interviews with elected officials who

attended HBCUs reveal the theme of HBCUs acting as a type of "cocoon" for their students, offering the opportunity to gain valuable life lessons, regardless of one's major. For example, State Representative Smith, who attended three HBCUs over the course of his education, recalls learning valuable lessons about being Black in America from professors whose expertise might make such conversations unexpected, such as accounting professors. He recalls that "we had professors that would . . . talk to us about how to prepare ourselves for a life outside of the cocoon called the college campus and especially the Black college campus. . . . We had those conversations in those classrooms in every HBU that I've ever attended."

In addition to engaging in politics-related coursework during college, Black elected officials who attended HBCUs and PWIs also report that engagement in politics-related experiences outside the classroom was an important part of their college experiences. Data from interviewees who attended HBCUs pointed to the presence of political leaders on campus as one important avenue for early politically relevant experiences, but this differed by generation. Mayor Lee, who attended HBCU Clarke College and then HBCU Fort Valley State College in the 1950s, noted that political role models were few and far between when he was a college student: "I can't recall a single elected official because we didn't have that many Blacks, and not many Whites would show up. There were basically no Blacks in the political arena of the South." Lee pointed to Black voter disenfranchisement as a likely explanation for the trend, noting that low levels of Black voting and the influence of voter suppression meant that many elected officials in the South saw little reason to invest time in Black young people. Further, he asserted:

> Even if you voted for someone—those who had the privilege of voting—there was no return on that investment because the congressmen never responded. They never did anything, like the congressman I wrote. My parents voted for him but he never even considered me to be important enough for him to respond, and that registered heavily with me as well to recognize that politicians are very discriminatory in their whole behavior.

Elected officials who attended HBCUs after the passage of the Voting Rights Act, on the other hand, recalled having access to major political leaders who visited their campuses as guest speakers. State Representative Gailliard recalls that a steady stream of "industry leaders, political leaders, religious leaders, heads of states . . . would speak to us. They would challenge us. . . . They would really help give us a broader understanding of society as a whole." He offered an account of a particularly memorable occasion when President Ronald Reagan visited Morehouse College: "One year, the then-president Ronald Reagan came to speak to us. And, the president came and he made a comment that it was his understanding that Morehouse was the Harvard of the South. And our [college] president corrected him and said, 'No, Harvard is the Morehouse of the North.'"

Data suggest that engagement in campus activism as well as advocacy efforts off campus were important parts of the college experience for both the elected officials who attended HBCUs and PWIs. Advocating for civil rights and protesting racial violence and discrimination was the primary focus of student activism for elected officials who attended HBCUs. For example, Congressman Clyburn participated in the student movement when he was an HBCU student at South Carolina State, being arrested after a sit-in in February 1960. Nearly twenty years later, State Representative Smith engaged in protest marches in 1979 during his freshman year at North Carolina A&T, shortly after conflict between the Ku Klux Klan and the American Nazi Party on one hand, and the Communist Workers Party on the other, resulted in a shootout about a mile away from his HBCU's campus in Greensboro.

For elected officials who attended PWIs, assuming formal student leadership positions to help demand better support for Black and Brown students on campus was a central theme that emerged from the data. During the 1970s, as head of the Black Student Union at PWI Adelphi University, Congressman Meeks engaged in efforts intended to "level the playing field" for African American and Hispanic students, including advocating for greater affirmative action on campus and the creation of ethnic studies departments at the university. Elected officials who attended PWIs also reported engaging in activism around broader social equity issues. During her time at San Diego State during the early 1970s, Congresswoman Bass advocated for criminal justice reform. That same decade, Congressman Dwight Evans (D-PA) was chair of the Black Student Union at La Salle University and led student activism related to the Vietnam War and civil rights. He also led student engagement with local Philadelphia politics. During the 1980s, Congresswoman Plaskett was a student organizer for South African apartheid protests at Georgetown.

While connections with faculty, the opportunity to engage in politics-related coursework, and access to politically relevant experiences were components of elected officials' college experiences at both HBCUs and non-HBCUs, HBCU attendees described greater involvement in the broader campus experience during their time on campus. This was particularly true about social activities, as those who attended HBCUs described participating in student government, athletics, and Greek organizations as central to the culture on their campuses. Describing the engaging social experience that he had in college, State Representative Smith laughs, "If anyone ever tells you that they had more fun in college than I did, they're lying. I had an absolute ball. Being a young undergraduate on an HBCU campus is an experience that I don't think most people can appreciate.... It was probably the most comfortable space that I had been in outside of being in spaces with my own family."

For a number of the leaders interviewed, the extraordinary comfort that HBCUs provided their students was central to their living and learning experience and played an important role in their inclination to engage on campus. Expanding on the impact that his sense of comfort at North Carolina A&T had on his experience during college, Smith continues:

> I didn't have to watch my language. I didn't have to be concerned about how someone would perceive my behavior. I wasn't concerned about being judged by others because everyone there had a very similar background to mine, so it was comfortable. I'm glad to say it was reminiscent of being with my family, and I consider my A&T family as my family because of that. And, for me, going to class and seeing the professor who looked just like me, the chancellor looked just like me, the custodian just like me, my classmates looked just like me. That experience gave me a sense of comfort that I did not experience in other aspects of my life— the camaraderie, the brother hood, the sisterhood.

In addition to elected officials who attended HBCUs' feeling that enjoying extreme comfort on campus was integral to the value of their college experience, the data also reveal their sense that those who do not have the benefit of HBCU education are at a loss socially. State Representative Smith recalled feeling sympathy for his Black friends who attended nearby PWI University of North Carolina–Greensboro who had to make special efforts to create a sense of social comfort on their campus:

> In the midst of this primarily White campus, they had an organization called the Neo-Black Society where they would go in the basement of this dormitory and they would have parties so they could listen to music

they liked. And I thought it was honestly—I thought it was pretty sad. But, you know, it was what they had to do. Frankly, a lot of them spent a lot of time over at A&T, I guess because of the cultural comfort of being in an environment that you didn't have to challenge all the time.

Indeed, Smith recalled that Black PWI students from UNC-Greensboro, Elon University, and University of North Carolina–Chapel Hill would come to North Carolina A&T to hang out because the social environment on their campuses "just was not the same."

Three of the elected officials interviewed attended both HBCUs and PWIs, and their experience attending both types of institutions yielded valuable insight into some of the contrasts between the social experiences that they offered Black students. State Representative Smith, who attended PWI Eastern Carolina University for graduate school after his HBCU experience at North Carolina A&T, noted the contrast between his PWI and HBCU experiences: "I took a couple of courses at ECU in grad school, but it just wasn't the same. . . . It was strictly business. It was, you go to class, you just get your grade, keep 'em moving. You just don't develop those relationships like you do at HBCUs."

Data from interviews with Black elected officials who attended PWIs suggest that a lack of inclusivity for Black and Brown students on their college campuses prompted them to engage in activism that yielded organizing skills that they would continue to draw upon. For Congressman Meeks, experience advocating for greater social inclusion for Black students at predominantly White Adelphi College provided a valuable opportunity to build negotiating skills, which were valuable assets that he could draw upon in future political and justice oriented endeavors. Recalling his activism at Adelphi, he says:

> We were very upset that a number of the student activities—whether it was movies or concerts or anything about the people they were putting on—had nothing to do with anything that we or the African Americans on campus could relate to. . . . We ultimately negotiated a deal with the school that if we could make sure that at least at Adelphi you would have two concerts that catered to our African American and Hispanics, one each semester, as well as bringing in an African Studies Unit . . . we had something that we could deliver that was going to change the lives of the students. That I learned from Adelphi University.

While elected officials who attended both HBCUs and PWIs offered a clear sense that HBCUs provided Black students with a more equitable and inclusive academic and social culture on campus, they also acknowledged that HBCUs and PWIs differed in terms of the living and learning environments that they offered. Mayor Lee, who attended Fort Valley State College in the 1950s, recalled that access to internship opportunities and active recruitment from corporations and other professional fields that extended beyond the more familiar areas like teaching were more difficult to come by when he was in college, although, he suspected, students at some HBCUs like Howard and Florida A&M might have had greater access to such opportunities.

A number of elected officials described some of the challenges that they encountered at HBCUs as formative to their development. For example, State Representative Gailliard recalled that "I never once lived in a dorm that had air conditioning. That's unheard of in this day and age; but we weren't sent to Morehouse so that we could be comfortable in air-conditioned dorms. We were sent there to become changed people. And the trappings around us didn't really matter."

Black elected officials who attended HBCUs describe the unique campus environments that HBCUs provided as helping to shape their understanding of Black people and instilling a sense of confidence, which would prove crucial to their future work as leaders and advocates. State Representative Gailliard noted how impressed he was by the diversity of Black experiences that he encountered for the first time as a student at Morehouse College: "My very first roommate was third generation Morehouse, and I was blown away that there was a Black guy, seventeen years old like me, whose dad and granddad had gone to college. . . . It was just giving me a sense of value that I came from a good stock of people that had really done well in the past. It also gave me a sense of legacy that I didn't have." He also noted that Morehouse offered a holistic approach to education that extended beyond the classroom, which he describes as life changing:

> I was taught the value of looking professional—I learned that at Morehouse. . . . The value of being able to properly communicate and enunciate and be able to present my argument, the value of debate. . . . You develop the art of conversation. . . . The value of experiences and exposures. . . . The value of networking, how to navigate the

corporate board room, and at the same time, the hood. . . . We had dress codes back then . . . you didn't come to class in tank tops and shorts. That didn't happen.

Mayor Lee echoes this sentiment about the broad scope of his education as an HBCU student:

The one thing that I will always appreciate about my HBCU experience is that it was a standard that every week we had to go to what we call Vespers services. And, every week we had to dress up to go to Vespers services. We were expected to conduct ourselves in a respectful manner toward other people, both other students as well as our faculty. The one thing I appreciate about Clark is that everybody was referred to in a formal manner—Mister, Miss, Mistress, Doctor.

Lee views his HBCU experience as integral to his development as a leader: "What I experienced on that campus in many ways prepared me for what I've been able to experience as I've paved my journey through the political arena." State Representative Smith concurs, making a direct connection from his HBCU experience to his work as a public servant: "The way I lead is through a level of confidence that was built through my experience at an HBCU. I'm not intimidated by anyone's education. I don't care what your degree says—I know I can compete with the best because the first person I conquered was me."

Running for Office and Approach to Public Service

For the Black elected officials included in this study—both those who attended HBCUs and PWIs—a combination of parental and family influence and a deep interest in social issues were central to the development of their interest in politics and public service. Among those who attended HBCUs, Mayor Lee recalled that his grandmother told him the story of his birth in 1943 when an aunt who would die less than a year later looked at him and told the family, "This is going to be a senator one day." Growing up, he wanted to become a prominent speaker like his grandfather, who was an inspirational speaker known to mesmerize the church on Sundays. State Representative Smith describes his parents as "community servants" who were among the Black leaders that he engaged with his entire life, and Congressman Meeks had the opportunity to observe his mother engaging in leadership as the head of one of the tenants' associations in a Philadelphia public housing community.

Similarly, elected officials who attended predominantly White colleges were heavily influenced by their politically engaged family members. Congresswoman Norton's parents were Roosevelt Democrats who inspired her interest in economic inequality and political systems. Congresswoman Coleman's father, John S. Watson, was a prominent New Jersey state legislator, and she gained early political experience helping with his campaigns. When her father passed away in 1996, she decided to help continue his legacy of service. She recalls, "When he died . . . the seat he once held suddenly became available. I needed to keep him alive, and that was my way of doing that and to honor him. So, I ran for the seat he once held in the state legislature. I did it out of a respect for the work that he did."

Family ties also helped to shape Congresswoman Plaskett's pathway to public office: "I come from a political family," she notes of a family that includes two uncles who were prominent grassroots labor organizers. A keen interest in political issues is another theme that emerged from interviews with Black elected officials who attended both HBCUs and PWIs. Civil rights and racial segregation were particularly influential in shaping their pathways to public service, along with economic inequality, voting rights for eighteen-year-olds, Vietnam War protests, and struggles for independence around the world. Some of the elected officials even trace the beginning of their political engagement as far back as middle school and high school.

While the data suggest no major differences in the factors shaping the Black elected officials' interest in politics and public service, clearer distinctions emerge when we consider their experiences running for office. For those who attended HBCUs, receiving support from friends, classmates, and the HBCU community was a central theme that emerged from interviews. State Representative Smith, who attended North Carolina A&T, described receiving "a tremendous outpouring support" from his college classmates and remarked that "that Aggie network is very, very powerful. Very powerful." Indeed, Smith was encouraged to consider running for office in the first place by a fellow North Carolina A&T alumnus who was transitioning out of office. State Representative Gailliard also received support from his HBCU college network when he first ran for office, estimating that approximately 5 to 10 percent of his campaign's financial support came from his HBCU network.

For Congressman Clyburn, enthusiastic support from his HBCU classmates was the signal that made him confident that he had made the right decision in deciding to run for Congress in 1992. When considering whether to throw his hat into the ring, he gathered a group of his closest friends and fellow HBCU classmates at a Washington, DC, restaurant called Joe and Mo's, "and they all pulled out their checkbooks and wrote checks." After dinner much of the group left and then a prominent pollster arrived, whom Clyburn's friends had contacted. Using the financial support that his friends had provided, the pollster ran her first poll for Clyburn, launching a collaboration that would last for more than twenty-five years.

This contrasted significantly with the experiences of Black elected officials who had attended PWIs. Robust support from their college networks did not emerge from data regarding their first political campaigns. This seems, at least in part, related to the fact that a number of the elected officials in this group had been nontraditional students who were focused more on completing their degrees than engaging in campus life and building enduring social relationships during their college years.

In addition to the role that college networks and relationships played in shaping first political runs among Black elected officials, the data also reveal differences in terms of the experiences that interviewees had navigating through their early years in politics. Those who had attended PWIs generally describe deciding to run for office after engaging in a progression of work and volunteering activities that seemed to lead to running for political office. For those who attended HBCUs, data reveal a theme of deciding to run after experiencing race based discrimination.

In one particularly powerful case, Mayor Lee describes deciding to run for mayor of Chapel Hill after trying to purchase a house in a predominantly White section of the city. He had tried unsuccessfully to convince the city board to pass an open housing ordinance, and afterward a friend encouraged him to run for mayor. He and his wife were eventually able to purchase the house, and his family received death threats for nearly a year and had to have police officers stationed at the front door of their house at night for protection: "We had to put the school on alert because of all the threats that our kids were going to be killed walking to or from school. My wife got a call one night, I was somewhere making a speech, and they said, 'We just want to warn you, you need to make funeral arrangements for your husband, 'cause he ain't coming home.' That kind of thing." Lee began to seriously consider running for mayor and one night assembled a group of about fifteen friends and neighbors in his basement to consider the possibility. At one point, a neighbor—a professor at UNC–Chapel Hill—stood up and said, "You know, I just don't think the time is right for a Black mayor." Lee recalls that:

> That set a chill down my spine because I said to him, "All my life I have been told the time is not right, and so let's make it right." And, that's when I decided to run, just that night. . . . And from that point on our goal was to put together the most hard-hitting, broadly prospected campaign and to run a campaign that had never been run in Chapel Hill.

Lee won the election, becoming the first Black mayor of Chapel Hill, North Carolina.

Public Service and Support for Black Colleges

When asked to describe how they approach their jobs as elected officials and which issues they have prioritized, Black elected officials who were educated at HBCUs and PWIs are more similar than not in the themes that emerge from their responses. Among leaders in both groups, a commitment to making a difference is the central factor driving their work in politics, and they are particularly interested in providing effective representation for African Americans. PWI graduate Congresswoman Norton, for example, describes wealth generation as a particular area of focus, especially when it comes to ensuring that African Americans have the opportunity to generate wealth. Fellow PWI graduate Congresswoman Coleman describes her commitment to ensuring that "government being what it is supposed to be for everybody" as central to her work in public service:

> Creating a level playing field and eliminating those barriers that are placed in your way for reasons that are beyond your control—like, being Black and being female. Or looking at what government should be doing for those who have the least among us. You know, that was always my passion. . . . It's good work. It's work that you do on behalf of others. . . . If you care about your brother and your sister, then public service is probably a good choice for you.

Coleman's work as the founder of the Caucus on Black Women and Girls illustrates her commitment to being an advocate for those whose perspectives are most often left out of the halls of power, particularly African American girls and women.

HBCU graduate Congressman Donald McEachin (D-VA) identifies environment and energy policy as central priorities, while fellow HBCU alumnus Congressman Al Lawson (D-FL) considers reparations and achieving restorative justice for African Americans whose communities were destroyed by racism to be an important policy priority. A strong common theme that emerged from both groups was the idea that public service is more than just holding public office. It is also noteworthy that Black elected officials who had graduated from HBCUs and non-HBCUs described supporting Black colleges as another policy priority. A full nine out of the ten Black members of Congress interviewed are members of the Congressional Bipartisan HBCU Caucus.[15]

When asked to share their thoughts about what role one's higher educational experience might play in shaping how they work as elected officials, a number of the interviewees suggested that they viewed college experiences as having a bearing on how public officials engaged with their work. Among those who attended PWIs, Congressman Rush saw higher education as an opportunity to shape the mind and to gather the tools necessary for being successful in subsequent endeavors. Congresswoman Norton viewed college as an opportunity to break out of one's racial cocoon. Similarly, Congresswoman Plaskett described her PWI experience as helping her to learn how to move between different groups of people with greater ease.

On the other hand, among HBCU alumni, State Representative Gailliard noted a close connection between his experience at Morehouse and his interest in the overall improvement of society. He also connected it to the development of a powerful work ethic necessary for public service: "Morehouse really reinforced that work ethic, and I think that whatever you aspire to do, you have to have some grind and some grit to you to be able to be successful. And, I think that grind and grit were really required of us at Morehouse."

State Representative Smith described the HBCU experience as providing an academic and social experience that is sustaining. He once described his college experience as having "a spirit that permeates your soul once you set foot on a historically Black college that is true, is real, is genuine, and once you ever experience it, it will never leave you. It will be 'til the day you die . . . you will have that love, that feeling of love, for the HBCU because it's a place—it's probably the first place that many felt true love."

Conclusion

The data presented in this chapter corroborate the political science literature that describes educational attainment as a powerful determinant of political engagement, supporting the assertion that educational experiences often provide opportunities to acquire knowledge and skills—such as experience with public speaking or organizing events—that can prove valuable to one's future ability to engage in political activities.

Black elected officials who attended HBCUs and PWIs shared a range of political and politically relevant experiences during their undergraduate years that helped to create the foundation upon which they would build their careers as political leaders. However, an important distinction that emerged from the data is the nature of the higher educational experiences that elected officials who attended HBCUs and those who attended PWIs had. While the elected officials who attended PWIs often described engaging in activities geared toward improving the status of Black students on campus, fighting for equal citizenship on campus did not emerge from the data on those who attended HBCUs. The predominant theme among HBCU attendees was that their Black college campuses offered a welcoming environment in which they learned about politics and, more broadly, how to navigate life as Black Americans. Moreover, they described college experiences that offered an opportunity to delve into campus life while building lasting relationships and connections.

The youngest Black elected officials who attended PWIs also reported that social bonds forged during their college years were long-standing, but it is worth noting that such relationships were often forged from engaging in advocacy on behalf of Black and Brown students on campus. For the most senior PWI graduates, status as nontraditional students and an emphasis on moving through their degree programs as efficiently as possible resulted in a college experience characterized by fewer lasting relationships. In terms of the aspects of higher educational experiences that may facilitate movement into politics, elected officials who attended PWIs gained valuable advocacy and organizing skills from their work to fight for Black students on campus, while HBCU alumni gained powerful social networks that they called upon when they decided to run for office.

8

The Power of Black Excellence and the Future of Democracy

WHEN DR. ALVIN THORNTON WAS in high school, he had an experience that changed his life. In 1965, as a sophomore at an all-Black Rosenwald high school in segregated Alabama, he attempted to access public accommodations—a restaurant. The restaurant's White owner approached him with a gun, which he put in the teenager's face. He called Thornton the N-word and threatened to take his life for attempting to enter the Whites-only space. In the aftermath of the event, neither local law enforcement nor the county's judicial system would address the situation. Reflecting on the traumatizing experience, Thornton connects it to his engagement as a student at Morehouse College where he graduated in 1971, saying, "I'm sure it affected me because of the kinds of things that I subsequently engaged in as I went to Morehouse and then came to Howard, and then came into Prince George's County."

After studying political science at Morehouse College, Thornton joined the faculty in the Department of Political Science at Howard University in Washington, DC, where he eventually served as department chair, associate dean of the College of Arts and Sciences, associate provost, and interim provost. An inspiring leader, Thornton was also tapped to run for political office in nearby Prince George's County, Maryland, throwing his hat into the ring for state legislative and congressional races. He was elected to the school board and later appointed by the governor of Maryland to chair the state's Commission on Education Finance, Equity, and Excellence. He also chaired Prince George's County's Citizens for Representative Redistricting and Coalition Against Police Brutality committees. Thornton's distinguished career in political science, higher education administration, government, and civic life has earned him wide recognition and numerous accolades, including an NAACP Image Award.

On the significance of HBCUs for American political development, he says, "There would be no John Lewis without Fisk. There would be no Oprah Winfrey without Tennessee State, and there would be no Andrew Young without Howard. I can go on and on—Thurgood Marshall—clearly there would be no Thurgood without Lincoln and Howard University. So, HBCUs, in a sense, did that." He drives home the point by underscoring the vital role that HBCUs played in actualizing the potential of Reconstruction policies that have been essential to Black advancement since the nineteenth century: "I always say, initially the Thirteenth, Fourteenth, and Fifteenth Amendments are adopted but they sat there for more than fifty years, and HBCUs had to breathe life into them and extract from them the extended versions of privileges, due process, and equality. And, [they] produced students who did that."

Recalling a conversation that he had with Dr. Michael Lomax, president of the United Negro College Fund, Dr. Thornton describes a powerful observation that Dr. Lomax made regarding HBCUs' contributions to the fight for democracy in the United States: "He pointed out that from the beginning, [for HBCUs] the task of helping African Americans to move into their roles as citizens was really central. He argued that it's not been education for education's sake; it's been education with the purpose of empowerment, really."

Contemporary discussions about HBCUs often center on their effectiveness, with some questioning their relevance in the twenty-first century. For some, the end of legal segregation in the United States has rendered historically Black colleges and universities relics of the nation's past. Skeptics readily point to the widely reported institutional challenges that burden a number of HBCUs, such as the loss or threatened loss of accreditation, low graduation rates, high deficits, and administrative failures.[1] Nevertheless, as the United Negro College Fund notes in its advocacy for HBCUs, Black colleges provide affordable alternatives for many students seeking higher educational opportunity.[2] As such, HBCUs are critical for the nation's ambitious goal of increasing the proportion of Americans who have college degrees.

Given the role that the federal government has played in both creating the original necessity of HBCUs during the nineteenth century and shaping the trajectory of their development in the years since, the question remains as to the nature and extent of support that the federal government should be expected to devote to HBCUs in the future. Moreover, considering their rich history and tradition of, and continuing commitment to, educating Black Americans, how likely is it that HBCUs will be able to achieve the type of ecumenical recruitment and outreach necessary to attract and secure the support of groups that may not have felt historically invested in them, such as Whites and non-Black people of color? Ensuring the future of these institutions that have done so much for American educational and political development will require the broad support of a broad coalition of advocates committing to ensuring that their contributions are maximized during the twenty-first century.

HBCUs and a Model of Democracy-Enhancing Higher Education

For nearly two centuries, HBCUs have embraced an explicitly political mission of empowering Black people and promoting racial justice. They eschewed the "Ivory Tower" model of higher education that focuses on scholarly exploration in a way that is set apart from engagement in "real world" issues and broader social activism in favor of a model of education focused squarely on active engagement in the social and political landscape and helping students acquire knowledge and skills necessary for personal, community, and societal improvement. HBCUs have provided one of the most significant sources of higher educational opportunity—and pathways to democratic engagement—in the United States.

For generations of Black American students, scholars, and their communities, Black colleges have recognized, cultivated, empowered, and celebrated Black excellence. During the nineteenth century, at a time when there were intense debates about what education for Black people should look like and substantial variation as to the legitimacy or even legality of educating Black Americans in the first place, Black colleges offered a rare pathway to economic opportunity, enhanced social status, and prestige for Black Americans. They pioneered the creation of spaces that were dedicated to investing in Black people. Moreover, they were the standard bearers for Black excellence, embodying prominent, locally visible monuments to the talent, hard work, and brilliance of Black people, which existed in sharp contrast to dominant social narratives of Black incapacity and fecklessness that sought to prop up an economic order that relied on the cheap or entirely unremunerated labor of Black people.

Prior to and during the Civil War, Black colleges were a source of refuge and pride for the Black community. The Black community, in turn, rallied to marshal their often limited resources to support the often struggling Black colleges that they entrusted with the formidable task of racial uplift. This period saw the creation of multiple public policies that had a direct impact on both the necessity and shared mission of Black colleges. Anti-literacy laws and racial segregation severely limited Black people's access to education and their ability to acquire knowledge, skills, and experiences that could foster economic independence and mobility, as well as social and democratic inclusion.

Before the outbreak of the Civil War, the First Morrill Land-Grant Act brought the federal government into the business of higher education by devoting federal land to the establishment of flagship universities in every state. However, the benefits of that policy failed to reach Black Americans, as most colleges and universities created with the public support provided by the land grant policy excluded Black students. Despite their overwhelming exclusion from the benefits of the original educational land-grant policy, Black colleges were central institutional partners for a government working to habilitate formerly enslaved people and to help inaugurate them to a new relationship with the state as newly emancipated citizens. Not only were Black colleges an integral part of the nation's rebuilding efforts after the Civil War, the work that they had already done prior during the prewar period to educate Black teachers proved crucial to the nation's ability to deploy a capable teaching force to teach Black schoolchildren in the South.

During the post–Civil War Reconstruction period, important shifts in the racial dynamics of American political power fostered an increase in educational opportunity for Black Americans. With the passage of the Fifteenth Amendment extending suffrage to Black men, politicians interested in currying favor with Black voters devoted new attention to the provision of educational opportunities for Black people. Moreover, unprecedented political participation by Black men elected to serve in federal, state, and local government positions created a new cadre of empowered advocates for Black educational opportunity in the halls of power. These advocates played an important role in the inclusion of Black colleges as beneficiaries of the Second Morrill Land-Grant Act, which provided them with unprecedented support beginning in 1890.

In the ensuing decades, HBCU classrooms and libraries became the birthplace of many of the ideas and arguments that were used to challenge legally sanctioned racial discrimination and to advocate for civil rights for Black people. The strategies and resulting victories that emanated from these ideas provided powerful templates for subsequent rights movements. In addition to the thought leadership they provided, Black colleges also helped to cultivate the vanguard of leaders who would serve on the frontlines of the civil rights movement of the 1950s and 1960s, including activists Dr. Martin Luther King Jr., Ella Baker, and Rosa Parks, attorney and legal scholar Pauli Murray, and Supreme Court Justice Thurgood Marshall.[3] Moreover, they provided vital training grounds and bases of support for the student activists who were central to the movement's success.

This analysis has shown that, for many communities—especially in the southern region of the United States—HBCUs have represented empowering centers that have supported racial uplift by way of unprecedented educational, social, and cultural opportunity. Through unique campus cultures and traditions, HBCUs have provided what attendees frequently describe as an "oasis" where Black students can bring their complete, authentic selves to the task of learning, free of the macro- and microaggressions that many Black students face in predominantly White learning environments. Many Black college students gravitate toward HBCUs because they recognize them as uniquely invested in Black excellence.

HBCU faculty members may be the most important figures driving the role that their institutions play in helping to develop Black citizens and leaders. As the frontline implementers of HBCU programming and missions, they are often pioneers in their fields whose courses provide students with knowledge and skills that can unlock professional opportunities and foster civic engagement. Furthermore, HBCU faculty members act as valuable mentors who are attuned to the challenges that Black citizens face in the United States and more globally. They hold their students to high expectations and often go beyond the call of duty to marshal them through their academic programs. In this way, HBCU faculty help to create a culture on HBCU campuses that is almost familial—and where the collective takes precedence over the individual, resulting in students feeling as though others are watching out for them, expect them to be excellent, and are deeply invested in their success.

Moreover, this analysis has shown that HBCUs have made essential contributions to the fight for democracy. They offer programming and experiences that may be uniquely empowering for the development of politically and civically engaged citizens. For example, HBCUs offer unique academic environments where attention to Black history and the Black experience are woven into virtually every aspect of the curriculum. Many also have substantial community service requirements for graduation and they are frequently priority destinations for state, national, and international political leaders.

By offering academic experiences that offer careful attention to the contributions that Black people have made to the United States and promoting active engagement in civic and political life at the mass and elite levels, HBCUs have helped to power the advancement of citizens who, for generations, were excluded from mainstream educational, social, civic, and political institutions.[4] This analysis has shown that Black colleges have used education to promote full citizenship for Black Americans, thereby working to correct for the historical injustices and disparities wrought by slavery and segregation.[5]

The Value of Higher Education in the Twenty-First Century

In recent decades, as the cost of higher education has increased precipitously—along with the amount of debt that college students and their families assume to meet those costs—many have questioned the value of higher education in the twenty-first century. In addition to the tremendous sacrifice that students and families make in pursuit of advanced education, recent advances in technology have democratized access to information and online learning opportunities, leading many to second-guess the benefits of investing in expensive on-campus college programs.

Based on the analysis presented here, I argue that the democratic value of higher education and the potential that colleges and universities hold for fostering the development of politically engaged citizens represents one of the most compelling reasons to invest in HBCUs and their unique approach to the college experience. At a time when Americans are more educated than ever, yet mass-level engagement in politics has declined in recent decades, our democracy would greatly benefit from significantly increasing our investment in HBCUs and expanding the reach of their unique democracy work.

HBCUs specialize in making higher education accessible to a wide variety of students. They not only enroll a high proportion of students who are low-income, first-generation, and in need of higher levels of academic support, they also marshal them to degree completion and, in many cases, to high levels of educational attainment at particularly high rates.[6] HBCUs have also played a central role in contributing to the supply of Black teachers in the United States, a function that has important implications for Black students' experiences in the classroom and their persistence toward college degrees. This, in turn, has important implications for American democracy, which depends on a well-informed citizenry to perform the task of self-governance.

A significant portion of the lasting appeal and effectiveness of HBCUs lies in their success in providing inclusive, nurturing learning environments, which have proved particularly empowering to students hailing from a diverse array of racial and ethnic backgrounds.[7] In recent years, the proportion of non-Black students attending HBCUs has grown steadily. More than half of the students at historically Black colleges like Kentucky State University, Missouri's Lincoln University, and West Virginia State College are White.[8] More generally, approximately 13 percent of students at HBCUs are White, 3 percent are Latino, and 1 percent are Asian, Native American, or Pacific Islander.[9] While the original impetus for HBCUs—legally sanctioned racial segregation—is no longer permitted in US higher educational institutions, these trends demonstrate that they continue to provide vital educational opportunities to a substantial proportion of the nation's students.

Most important, HBCUs take a distinct approach to higher education. Their campus cultures serve as living reminders of Black resiliency and pride, as well as the significance of learning for achieving freedom and social progress. Faculty members make intentional efforts to familiarize students with the contributions that Black colleges and Black people, more broadly, have made to the educational, social, and political landscapes, fostering in students deep appreciation, respect, and a sense of responsibility for being a part of positive change moving forward. HBCUs also offer an array of campus mottos and traditions that contribute to distinctive campus cultures centered on a robust sense of community and linked fate.

HBCU faculty, administrators, and staff members are central players in the work of HBCUs, shaping campus cultures and routinely going beyond the call of duty to support their students and to marshal them to degree completion. In the course of completing these degrees, students gain the valuable opportunity to delve into a wide variety of disciplines through a lens that takes seriously Black perspectives and implications for Black people. If adopted broadly, this unique approach to higher education could provide college students studying in the United States with greater understanding of the relationship between racial inequity and our most pressing social challenges, potentially helping to alleviate the deep polarization that has come to characterize the nation's political landscape.

Moreover, all US higher educational institutions would do well to take lessons from HBCUs and the ways in which they have fostered democratic engagement during and after college, which has been central to their success in promoting a disproportionate number of Black political and civic leaders.[10] Having the opportunity to learn in an environment virtually free from racism and microaggressions is a central feature of the HBCU experience that has contributed to this strong sense of belonging, and it also has helped to give students greater mental space to explore ideas, activities, and projects that expand their horizons and contribute to their development as citizens. Moreover, by providing opportunities to participate in meaningful co-curricular activities and to build robust social networks that sustain them as they study, HBCUs give students unique opportunities to gain valuable knowledge and skills that provide a powerful foundation for democratic citizenship.

Ensuring That HBCUs Have What They Need to Continue Promoting Excellence and Democracy

During the mid-twentieth century, federal lawmakers issued a combination of legal rulings and policy interventions that required racial desegregation in higher educational institutions, thereby ending HBCUs' virtual monopoly on Black student recruitment and engendering a dramatic reimagining of their central purpose. Long entrusted with the task of educating Black students whose institutional options for higher education were heavily restricted, HBCUs had to adjust to a new postsecondary marketplace where they were required to compete with PWIs whose recruitment efforts had long benefited from higher levels of funding and assumptions of superiority. Since the 1960s, presidents and members of

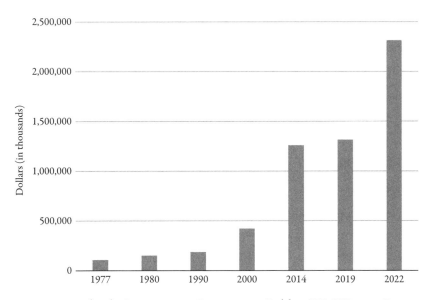

FIGURE 8.1 Federal Government Support to Public HBCUs in Current Dollars, 1977-2022

Source: "Historically Black Colleges and Universities, 1976 to 2001" (NCEA 2004-062). 2004; "Selected statistics on degree-granting historically Black colleges and universities, by control and level of institution: selected years, 1990 through 2022" (Table 313.30). U.S. Department of Education, National Center for Education Statistics, Integrated Postsecondary Education System (IPEDS).

Congress have lauded HBCUs for their legacy of extending equal opportunity to marginalized students; nevertheless, many HBCUs have continued to struggle with limited government and private support.

As Figure 8.1 shows, the amount of money that the federal government has allocated to historically Black colleges has increased steadily over time. However, if we consider federal support as a proportion of all revenues invested in HBCUs, we see that from the mid-1970s through 1989, the percentage of government support going to HBCUs declined precipitously. Since the early 1990s, federal support has come to represent a steadily increasing proportion of HBCU revenues (Figure 8.2), yet a history of modest government support has been particularly problematic, as aid from the federal and state governments represents a full 75 percent of the support that public HBCUs receive.[11] Historically, Black colleges have never received the same level support that their predominantly White counterparts have enjoyed. Education scholar Tiffany Jones notes that, "instead of steadily increasing funds to account for historical deficits, the

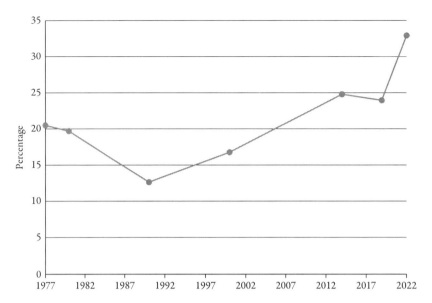

FIGURE 8.2 Federal Government Support as a Percentage of Current-Fund Revenues for Public HBCUs, 1977-2022.

Source: "Historically Black Colleges and Universities, 1976 to 2001" (NCEA 2004-062). 2004; "Selected statistics on degree-granting historically Black colleges and universities, by control and level of institution: selected years, 1990 through 2022" (Table 313.30). U.S. Department of Education, National Center for Education Statistics, Integrated Postsecondary Education System (IPEDS).

federal government has kept HBCU funding levels stagnant while at the same time increasing the funding of institutions of higher education as a whole."[12] Moreover, historically Black colleges operate with institutional endowments that are, on average, one-eighth the size of their historically White counterparts.[13]

Some HBCUs have struggled to provide high-quality postsecondary services in the face of dwindling resources. Such trends in the federal government's investment in HBCUs reflect important changes in the practices of US higher educational institutions, whereby PWIs have provided greater access to African Americans since the mid-1960s. In doing so, these institutions have become a formidable source of competition in the race to attract not only students but also government resources. Within this context, some HBCUs have struggled to survive in the face of challenges like declining enrollments, administrative difficulties, and student attrition.[14] Today only 13 percent of Black students attend HBCUs, compared to approximately 90 percent before 1964.[15]

Over the last fifty years, the continued existence of HBCUs has raised questions among those who feel that they unnecessarily duplicate the educational offerings that are now open to all students at colleges and universities that were once restricted. Others view them as relics of the nation's dark past that have simply outlived their usefulness. Such attitudes regarding HBCUs are only intensified by the popular media, which, according to education scholar Marybeth Gasman, often treats HBCUs like the "poor stepchildren of American higher education."[16] Indeed, high-profile news stories have long magnified the challenges facing HBCUs while downplaying their long-standing contributions to society. As a result of all of these factors, the future of HBCUs—which have provided generations of marginalized Americans with knowledge and skills that helped to facilitate their incorporation into social, economic, and political life—is uncertain.

The failure to address legacies of unequal support for HBCUs by states has contributed to a steady and persistent shrinking of educational opportunity for Black students. In states that established racially segregated, "separate but equal" public colleges and universities before the 1960s, the systematic failure of state governments to invest in Black educational institutions has had lasting consequences. Consider, for example, Mississippi, where it has taken decades for the courts to address whether the state has violated the Fourteenth Amendment's equal protection clause by not providing its HBCUs with the same level of support that its historically White colleges and universities receive.

In 1975, civil rights activist Jack Ayers Sr. sued the state of Mississippi in federal court on the grounds that it had not adequately supported HBCUs like Jackson State University where his son was a student.[17] The case became a class action suit, and congressman Bennie Thompson would join as a plaintiff. The suit held that before the University of Mississippi desegregated in 1962, Black residents of the state could only seek public education at HBCUs, which were systematically underfunded by the state legislature. In 1987 and 1990, the federal courts ruled that the desegregation of and use of race-neutral admissions policies in the state's public PWIs was rectification enough. But, in 1992, the US Supreme Court sent the case back to the district court, ruling that Mississippi was responsible for undoing inequalities in the higher educational system that can be

traced to the history of de jure segregation. In 2002 the state reached a settlement with the plaintiffs in which they agreed to award $503 million to
Mississippi's three HBCUs over a seventeen-year period.

The US Supreme Court's 2023 decision to outlaw the use of affirmative action in college admissions decisions offers a powerful contemporary
example of this ongoing phenomenon whereby Black college students are
systematically disadvantaged by policies that ultimately limit their access to higher educational opportunity. The demise of affirmative action
is likely to place greater demands on HBCUs, which have a rich legacy
of providing educational access to not only Black students but an increasingly diverse group of students who cannot access more-selective PWIs.[18]
The decline of affirmative action will likely translate into more pressure on
institutions like HBCUs that are committed to providing educational access to Black and Brown students who will be increasingly excluded from
other institutions.

Instead of developing programs targeted directly to HBCUs, lawmakers
have provided the most substantial support as part of the omnibus Higher
Education Act, which provided support to a range of beneficiaries. During
the late 1960s, the leaders of the nation's historically Black colleges began
to organize to advocate for HBCUs in the halls of government. In 1969,
they established the National Association for Equal Opportunity in
Higher Education to promote the interests of minority serving higher educational institutions in Washington, DC.[19] The following year, a group
of presidents from nine historically Black colleges criticized the Nixon administration for not supporting HBCUs.[20]

Such advocacy efforts led lawmakers to try to reimagine the role that
HBCUs could play in the United States at the end of the twentieth century.
In 1971, the Carnegie Commission on Higher Education issued a report
recommending that HBCUs serve as "custodians for the archives of Black
Americans," producing scholarly analyses focusing on the achievements of
and challenges faced by African Americans.[21]

As activists advocated for HBCUs in the post-desegregation United
States, institutional challenges reflecting the history of chronic under-
funding for HBCUs emerged in increasing numbers. The 1970s represented
a decade in which lawmakers faced difficult questions about institutional
quality and calls for enhanced federal support for HBCUs. Jack Ayers's
case against Mississippi, which became a class action lawsuit, remained active for nearly thirty years.[22] A 1992 Supreme Court decision held the state

of Mississippi responsible for chronically funding its HBCUs in violation of the Fourteenth Amendment's equal protection clause; and in 2002, the state reached a settlement with the plaintiffs, awarding $503 million to Jackson State University, Alcorn State University, and Mississippi Valley State University.

In 1979, HBCUs came under fire when a report from the General Accounting Office pointed to waste and mismanagement problems that severely tainted the reputations of HBCUs and other institutions benefiting from funding provided under Title III of the Higher Education Act. Such criticisms were intensified when a series of congressional hearings and newspaper articles implicated Black college administrators and shady educational consulting firms in taking advantage of government support.[23]

Since the 1980s, congressional gridlock has made it difficult for national lawmakers to substantially enhance or reimagine federal support for HBCUs. As a result, presidential leadership has been a central locus of the federal government's HBCU policymaking. In 1980, President Jimmy Carter signed Executive Order 12232, which created the White House Initiative on HBCUs with the goal of monitoring and increasing federal financial support for historically Black colleges and universities.[24] President Ronald Reagan also used the executive order approach to express support for HBCUs. In 1981, he signed Executive Order 12320, which established "a framework for federal agency accountability to HBCUs."[25] President George H. W. Bush followed suit, issuing Executive Order 12677 in 1989, which created the President's Advisory Board on Historically Black Colleges and Universities. This advisory board had the responsibility of advising the president and the secretary of education on historically Black colleges, producing annual reports analyzing the extent to which HBCUs benefit from federal support and weighing in on how to increase federal and private investment.[26] In 1993, President Bill Clinton signed Executive Order 12876, which reiterated federal interest in the continued strength and effectiveness of HBCUs.[27]

With the dawn of the new millennium, American presidents continued to use executive orders to convey their support for HBCUs. President George W. Bush created Executive Order 13225 in 2001, extending operation of the President's Advisory Board on Historically Black Colleges and Universities—which had been created during his father's administration—until September 2003.[28] In 2010, President Barack Obama issued Executive Order 13532, which worked to further enhance HBCUs' ability to provide effective education.[29] In 2017, President Donald Trump issued Executive Order 13779, which renewed the White House Initiative on Historically Black Colleges and Universities.[30] And in 2021 President Joe Biden issued Executive Order 14041, establishing a White House Initiative on Advancing Educational Equity, Excellence, and Economic Opportunity through HBCUs.[31] Since the mid-twentieth century, lawmakers have expressed an ongoing commitment to HBCUs, but this support often has been largely symbolic rather than material.

In recent decades, the federal government has offered some additional support to HBCUs. In 2001, the USDA, the Department of Defense, NASA, NSF, and other federal agencies allocated $404 million to HBCUs to support science and engineering—nearly double what federal agencies provided ten years prior.[32] However, this support has not been nearly enough to guarantee the continued operation of historically Black colleges or to ensure that they can effectively compete alongside their historically White counterparts. In 2015, Congresswoman Alma Adams (D-NC) founded the Congressional Bipartisan HBCU Caucus, which boasts more than 100 members committed to addressing the needs of HBCU campuses, their students, and their alumni.

The Vital Democratic Function of Higher Education

In recent decades, students of higher education have become increasingly concerned about a contemporary crisis in US education. Higher education has come under attack as colleges and universities are associated with escalating costs driven by runaway growth. These escalating costs have contributed to the often debilitating debt that college students and their families accrue to invest in education. With the nimble adjustments that many higher educational institutions made to withstand the onset of the COVID-19 pandemic, pivoting to the use of remote engagement technologies like Zoom videoconferencing software that allowed thousands of faculty members to continue teaching students joining from remote locations, many have questioned the relevance of a higher educational model centered on a residential experience.

Indeed, in recent years, many have questioned the contemporary relevance of higher education, more generally. As technological innovations have democratized access to education, higher educational institutions find themselves pressed to offer a clear articulation of their significance to society. I argue that higher education's democratic function is perhaps its most important contribution; and as this study has shown, HBCUs have long demonstrated the vital contributions that colleges and universities can make to American democracy. In doing so, they offer valuable lessons for other higher educational institutions, many of which are struggling to find purpose in the contemporary political and historical moment characterized by social unrest, declining political engagement, and increasingly acrimonious and polarized politics.

Policymakers have played an important role in shaping the relationship between HBCUs and democracy, and we can draw valuable lessons from landmark policies that have shaped not only Black Americans' access to democratically empowering education but also the creation and sustainment of institutions that have been essential to our nation's fight for democracy. Recognizing the role that policymakers have played in shaping HBCUs and their work since the nineteenth century underscores the value of policy feedback analysis for understanding the relationship between education and democracy. As this study has shown, policies shaping HBCUs offer a powerful example of how public policies can alter not only citizens but also the political landscape, more broadly.[33]

While this book's analysis has helped shed light on the important role that HBCUs have played in the fight for democracy, it has also raised some important questions that future research could help us explore. For example, do the democracy-promoting features of the HBCU higher educational experience see parallels across other educational institutions that have historically catered to historically marginalized groups? Is it possible that, in addition to HBCUs, women's colleges and Hispanic Serving Institutions provide higher educational experiences that are particularly valuable for promoting democratic citizenship? This analysis also prompts us to ask what role HBCUs will play as affirmative action policies promoting diversity in the nation's PWIs have come under attack. As Black college students and others seeking higher educational experiences that prioritize diversity, inclusion, and equity search for higher educational communities that take these values seriously, HBCUs will continue to serve a vital function on our educational and democratic landscape.

Lessons for Policymakers

As society grapples with the significance of higher education in the twenty-first century, HBCUs offer valuable lessons for how governmental and higher educational institutional policymakers can foster democratic citizenship. At the governmental level, policymakers should focus on policies that will provide equitable funding to support HBCU education, research, and top-of-the-line campus facilities to bridge the gap between the resources that HBCUs currently have and what they will need to maximize the impact of their work to cultivate leaders and promote democracy. In addition to direct funds to support campus infrastructure, funds to support democracy by promoting programming, research, and community extension programs would help extend the reach of HBCUs into their surrounding communities and the broader democratic landscape.

Another mechanism by which federal and state governments can ensure that HBCUs receive much-needed support to maintain and preserve their historic campus communities is to designate all HBCUs established before 1964 as national historic landmarks. Doing so could enhance their recognition as prominent parts of US history, attracting even greater attention to the impact that they have had on American political, social, and economic development. This could also help direct federal grants, tax incentives, and federal preservation supports—valuable benefits that are reserved for places listed in the national register.

To enhance the successful transition of students from K–12 education to college programs, lawmakers could provide support for HBCU pipeline programs like Upward Bound and the McNair Scholars, offering enhanced programming targeted toward helping prospective college students gain familiarity with HBCUs. Moreover, lawmakers could offer new financial aid opportunities for students who attend public and private HBCUs, such as tuition-free enrollment and loan-forgiveness programs for HBCU graduates. Lawmakers could also help HBCUs attract and retain the talented faculty who are their hallmark by offering student loan forgiveness or grants for continuing education for HBCU professors.

This analysis has demonstrated the value of distinctive higher educational experiences that provide students with nurturing and empowering campus cultures that are free of racism and microaggressions. At the institutional level, the broad community of American colleges and universities would benefit from bold efforts to address and eradicate hate, bias, and discrimination on their campuses.

For HBCU students, having the opportunity to live and learn in environments free of racial and ethnic bias helps to increase the energy and attention that they can apply to academic work, personal work, engagement with their campus communities, the outside world, and—more broadly—democracy. It stands to reason that articulating a clear institutional commitment to racial equity and nondiscrimination; devoting resources for equipping the campus community—students, faculty, and staff—with the knowledge and skills necessary to build a diverse, equitable, and inclusive culture; and establishing clear standards for evaluation, accountability, and constant improvement can help all higher educational institutions achieve that goal. College and university policymakers can also signal their institutions' commitment to building a campus culture that is free of hate and bias by incorporating it into their admissions process, academic curriculum, and in the criteria by which honors and other forms of academic or professional recognition and advancement are determined.

In addition to working actively to minimize hate and bias on campus, this study illustrates the value of cultivating a rich understanding of history that centers the voices and perspectives of traditionally marginalized and minoritized populations and that takes an asset-based—rather than a deficit-based—approach to grappling with the past. As HBCUs demonstrate, promoting a more nuanced understanding of Black history that ventures beyond the often superficial rendering that many Americans receive in elementary and secondary education programs may foster high levels of self-confidence, optimism, and democratic engagement among students. Moreover, offering more robust education regarding the history of racial oppression in the United States will be crucial for addressing the widespread polarization that has become a particularly troubling feature of our contemporary political landscape. Considerable division exists around whether and how to address inequality and historical discrimination in the United States, and integrating Black history requirements into college curricula will help ensure that—regardless of where students (and future leaders) stand on the issues—they can bring a robust understanding of history to bear as they consider the nature and causes of social problems and as they consider possible solutions.

In addition to requiring proficiency in Black history, including a substantial community service requirement for graduation is another way that institutional policymakers can promote long-term democratic engagement. Requiring students to venture beyond their campus walls to engage with, learn from, and contribute to the local community will enhance their intellectual experience by offering an opportunity to engage with the issues that they study in real time. Doing so will also increase the probability that students will connect with people who come from backgrounds different from their own and who have different lived experiences and drastically different perspectives than they do.

As society has become increasingly siloed, and as it becomes easier to exist within social "bubbles" where we spend virtually all of our time with people who look, think, and act like we do, educational institutions can do a great democratic service by following HBCUs in actively creating opportunities for conversation across differences. Community service requirements represent a powerful mechanism for fostering such conversations, and colleges and universities could make powerful contributions to democracy and civic society by making them a core part of their educational experience.

The Power of Black Excellence

HBCUs have played an important part in American political development. By providing a network of institutions devoted to the education and empowerment of Black people, they have boldly opposed the racial oppression that has been a chronic feature of the nation's history. As education scholar Gloria Ladson-Billings so powerfully noted, "African Americans . . . represent a unique form of citizen in the USA—property transformed into citizen. This process has not been a smooth one."[34]

Prior to 1964, Black colleges were central to that transformation, educating the vast majority of Black Americans who pursued postsecondary education. In the wake of the passage of laws ending racial segregation in college admissions across the educational landscape, HBCUs have continued this work, providing educational experiences geared toward identifying, cultivating, and celebrating Black excellence.

Moreover, they have continued to foster the development of generations of Black leaders whose contributions to the American civic and political landscape have been part and parcel of our fight for democracy. At a time when the cultivation of actively engaged citizens is crucial for the health of American democracy, political leaders and the broad landscape of higher educational institutions can learn a great deal from how HBCUs have empowered generations of people.

Given the central role that HBCUs have played and will continue to play in the fight for democracy, it is imperative that we invest in them and ensure that they have the resources necessary to continue their vital work in a changing society. As political polarization and rancor push many people to disengage with politics, and as people trust each other and institutions less and less, the health of our democracy depends on our capacity to foster active participation in political and civic activities.

Therein lies the vital role that higher education must play in the twenty-first century. Our ability to retain our democratic form of government requires that we deploy all of the resources at our disposal, and higher education's capacity to provide democracy promoting knowledge, skills, inclinations, and experiences at a vital moment in young people's personal development and political socialization represents perhaps the most promising resource of all. Just as HBCUs have been central to our past and present efforts to promote democracy, they will be vital to our work to maintain and improve democracy in the future.

APPENDICES

HBCUs Included in HBCU Alumni Study Interviews

Alabama A&M University
Bennett College
Bowie State University
Cheyney University
Claflin University
Clark Atlanta University
Delaware State University
Dillard University
Fayetteville State University
Florida A&M University
Grambling State University
Hampton University
Howard University
Jackson State University
Johnson C. Smith University
Lincoln University
Miles College
Morristown College
North Carolina A&T University

North Carolina Central University
Prairie View A&M University
St. Augustine's University
Savannah State University
Shaw University
Southern University and A&M College
Spelman College
Talladega College
Tennessee State University
Tuskegee University
University of Maryland–Eastern Shore
University of New Orleans
Virginia State University
West Virginia State University
Wilberforce University
Winston-Salem State University
Xavier University

College Experience Study Questions

Section 1.   Introduction

First, we have a few questions about your background.

1. What is the year of your birth?

2. Which of the following best describes your race?

    American Indian, Aleut, Eskimo
    Asian or Pacific Islander
    Black or African American
    Hispanic/Latino
    White or Caucasian
    Something else (please specify)

3. What is the highest level of education you have completed?
    a.   Less than high school degree
    b.   High school degree (Grade 12 or G.E.D. certificate)
    c.   Technical, trade, or vocational school AFTER high school
    d.   Some college, no degree
    e.   2 year college degree (Associates)

  f. 4 year college degree (BA, BS, Bachelors)
  g. Some post-graduate training or professional school AFTER college, no degree
  h. Master's degree
  i. Doctoral degree (PhD) or Professional degree (JD, DDS, MD, etc.)

4. [IF Q3=4/5/6/7/89] Thinking about the undergraduate college you attended, was it a private college or university, or was it a public college or university?

  Private College/University
  Public College/University

5. [IF Q3=4/5/6/7/89] Did you attend a community college for your undergraduate education?

  Yes
  No

6. [IF Q3==4/5/6/7/89] Did you attend a historically black college or university (HBCU) for your undergraduate education?

  Yes
  No

7. Did either of your parents attend college at a historically black college or university (HBCU)?

  Yes
  No

8. Did any of your grandparents attend college at a historically black college or university (HBCU)?

  Yes
  No

9. [IF Q3=4/5/6/7/89] Have you ever attended a for-profit college or university (examples include the University of Phoenix, DeVry University, Capella University, Grand Canyon University, Kaplan University, Walden University)?

  Yes
  No

10. [IF Q9=Yes] How did you learn about the for-profit college or university that you attended? (Select all that apply)

Television
Radio ad
Internet ad
Employer
High School
Family/Friend
Other

11. [If Q3=6/7/8/9] Were you a first generation college graduate? (Meaning that neither of your parents completed a four-year degree)

Yes
No

12. Thinking of when you were growing up, how much emphasis did your family place on education?

No emphasis at all
Not much emphasis
Some emphasis
A great deal of emphasis

Section 2. *Political Engagement*

Next we have a few questions about politics.

13. How often do you follow what's going on in government and public affairs?

Most of the time
Some of the time
Only now and then
Hardly at all

14. In the last 2 years, did any candidate for political office or anyone from a campaign or one of the political parties call you up or come around and talk to you about voting or engaging in other political activities?

Yes
No

15. Are you currently registered to vote?

1 Yes, I'm registered
2 Not sure if I'm currently registered
3 I could register but have not

4 I'm not registered because I'm not eligible

16. Thinking of the presidential elections since you were old enough to vote, have you voted in all of them, in most of them, in some of them, rarely voted in them, or have you never voted in a presidential election?

Voted in all
Voted in most
Voted in some
Rarely voted
Never voted

17. Have you ever worked or volunteered for a political candidate who is running for national, state, or local office? For instance, you might have made calls, distributed literature, prepared mailings, or gathered signatures.

Yes
No

18. Have you ever contributed money to an individual candidate, one of the political parties, or a political action committee?

Yes
No

19. Have you ever served in a voluntary capacity on any local governmental board, council, committee, or group that deals with community problems or issues?

Yes
No

20. Have you ever contacted a government official or someone on the staff of such an official—either in person, by phone, or by email—about problems or issues that you were concerned about?

Yes
No

21. Have you ever taken part in a protest, march, or demonstration on some national or local issue?

Yes
No

22. Have you ever considered running for political office?

Yes
No

23. Have you ever actually run for political office?

Yes
No

24. Have you ever held or been appointed to political office?

Yes
No

25. [IF Q3==4-9] During college, did you engage in any political activities (e.g., volunteering for a campaign or political cause, attending a political event, contacting an elected official, protesting, etc.)?

Yes
No

26. Generally speaking, do you think of yourself as a Republican, a Democrat, an independent, or something else?

   1 Republican
   2 Democrat
   3 Independent
   4 Other party
   5 Haven't thought much about it

27. [IF Q26==1/2] Generally speaking, do you think of yourself as a strong (Republican/Democrat) or not a very strong (Republican/Democrat), or haven't you thought much about this?

   Strong (Republican/Democrat)
   Not very strong (Republican/Democrat)
   Haven't thought much about this

28. [IF Q26==3] Would you say that you lean toward one of the two major parties—either Republican or Democratic—or haven't you thought much about this? If so, which party do you lean toward?

Republican
Democratic
Neither
Haven't thought much about this

Section 3. *Political Efficacy and Other Attitudes*

Please indicate whether you agree or disagree with each of the following statements (questions 29–38).

Agree strongly
Agree somewhat
Disagree somewhat
Disagree strongly

29. "Public officials care about what people like me think."

30. "I have a pretty good understanding of the important political issues facing this country."

31. "I consider myself well qualified to participate in politics."

32. "Generally, I feel like a full and equal citizen in this country with all the rights and protections that other people have."

33. "I am proud to be an American."

34. "We can trust lawmakers to help make our society more equitable."

35. "Government has given me opportunities to improve my standard of living."

36. "I am satisfied with the current political climate in the United States."

37. "Blacks have a great deal of power in American politics."

38. "My parents taught me about what it means to be black."

39. Do you believe that blacks should organize themselves only or work with other racial groups to achieve progress? Which of the following statements is closest to your view?

> Organize among themselves
> Organize with other racial groups
> Organize among themselves and with other racial groups

40. Do you feel that access to college in this country today is fair, or do you feel that higher educational access should be more evenly distributed among a larger percentage of the people?

> Access is very fair
> Access is moderately fair
> Access is slightly fair
> Access is not at all fair

41. Do you feel that the distribution of money and wealth in this country today is fair?

> Distribution is very fair
> Distribution is moderately fair
> Distribution is slightly fair
> Distribution is not at all fair

42. On the whole, how satisfied, if at all, are you with the way democracy works in the United States?

> Not at all satisfied
> Not that satisfied
> Somewhat satisfied
> Very satisfied

In general, how close do you feel to the following groups of people (questions 43–48)?
> Very close
> Moderately close
> Slightly close
> Not at all close

43. Black Americans

44. White Americans

45. Hispanic/Latino Americans

46. Asian Americans

47. Blacks in Africa

48. Whites in Europe

Section 4. Paying for College and the Value of Higher Education

[IF Q3=4–9] *Now, we have some questions about meeting the cost of college and the value of higher education.*

49. Did your parents, spouse, or other family members help to pay for your higher education?

Yes
No

50. Have you ever received scholarship/fellowship support to help pay for your higher education?

Yes
No

51. Did you receive any Pell Grants (or their precursors, Educational Opportunity Grants) to help pay for your higher education?

Yes
No

52. Did you receive any federal student loans (e.g., Stafford loans, Perkins loans, etc.) to help pay for your higher education?

Yes
No

53. Did you work for pay during college?

    Yes
    No

54. Did you participate in the federal work study program to help pay for your higher education?

    Yes
    No

55. In your own personal experience, to what extent, if at all, did government financial aid contribute to your ability to attend college?

    A great deal
    Quite a bit
    Some
    Very little
    Not at all

56. Did you receive any private student loans (e.g., loans from a bank) to help pay for your higher education?

    Yes
    No

57. Approximately how much student loan debt did you take on as a result of pursuing your college degree?

    a. None (0$)
    b. $1–$9,999
    c. $10,000–$24,999
    d. $25,000–$49,999
    e. $50,000–$74,999
    f. $75,000–$99,999
    g. $100,000–$149,999
    h. $150,000–$199,999
    i. $200,000+

58. [IF Q52 or 56=Yes] Are you currently repaying student loans?

    Yes
    No

59. [IF Q52 or 56=Yes] In your own personal experience, to what extent, if at all, did student loans burden you with debts that are or were difficult to repay?

A great deal
Quite a bit
Some
Very little
Not at all

60. [IF Q52 or 56=Yes] Do you agree or disagree with the following statement? "I am satisfied that the education I invested in with my student loan(s) was worth the investment for career opportunities."

Agree
Disagree

61. [IF Q52 or 56=Yes] Do you agree or disagree with the following statement? "I am satisfied that the education I invested in with my student loan(s) was worth the investment for personal growth."

Agree
Disagree

Section 5. Higher Educational Experience

Next, we have some questions about your experience in college.

62. What year did you graduate with your undergraduate degree?

63. How many years did it take to complete your undergraduate degree?

Please indicate how frequently you engaged in the following activities during college (questions 64–73).

Very often
Often
Occasionally
Never

64. Attended class.

65. Completed assignments

66. Contributed to class discussions.

67. Discussed your career plans with a faculty member.

68. Took remedial or developmental courses that did not count toward the degree.

69. Took online courses.

70. Took a course focusing on government, public policy, or politics.

71. Took a course in public speaking or otherwise gained substantial experience speaking in public.

72. Prepared a major written paper or report.

73. Studied abroad.

Please indicate how frequently you engaged in the following activities during college (questions 74–81).
     Very often
     Often
     Occasionally
     Never

74. Played a team sport (intramural, club, intercollegiate).

75. Participated in a campus club, organization, or student government group.

76. Managed or served as a leader for a club or organization, on or off campus.

77. Raised money for a club, organization, or project, on or off campus.

78. Discussed politics or current events.

79. Became acquainted with students whose family background (economic, social) was different from yours.

80. Became acquainted with students whose political opinions were very different from yours.

81. Became acquainted with students whose race or ethnic background was different from yours.

82. [If 2=1/3/4/6 AND 6=No] During college, did you ever feel that others assumed that you were the beneficiary of affirmative action (admissions policies that benefit traditionally underrepresented groups)?

    Yes
    No

83. Were you in a sorority or fraternity during college?

    Yes
    No

84. How often did you send money to support parents or other family members while you were in college?

    Very often
    Often
    Occasionally
    Never

85. Have you donated any money to the college or university where you earned your undergraduate degree?

    Yes
    No

Please indicate whether you agree or disagree with each of the following statements (questions 85–93).
    Agree strongly
    Agree somewhat
    Disagree somewhat
    Disagree strongly

86. "My high school prepared me well for college."

87. "My college or university was the best fit for me."

88. "I felt welcome on my college campus."

89. "My undergraduate college or university prepared me well for life outside of college."

90. "During college I had significant political experiences that have shaped my views of government."

91. "If I had it to do over again, I would attend the same college or university where I earned my undergraduate degree."

92. "Politics was a central part of life in my undergraduate college or university."

93. "During college, I gained friendships and social networks that I continue to draw upon today."

94. "I stay in close contact with classmates who I met in college."

Section 6.   Demographics

Finally, we have a few questions about you and your family's background. As a reminder, your responses to these and all questions are confidential.

95. What best describes you?

Male
Female

96. Do you have at least one parent who was born outside of the U.S.?

Yes
No

97. Which of the following best describes you:

   Employed now in a full-time, permanent or long-term position
   Employed now in a part-time or temporary position
   Temporarily laid off
   Unemployed
   Retired
   Permanently disabled
   Homemaker
   Student

98. Last year, in 2016, approximately what was your total household income from all sources, before taxes?

   Less than $10,000
   10 to under $20,000
   20 to under $30,000
   30 to under $35,000
   35 to under $40,000
   40 to under $50,000
   50 to under $75,000
   75 to under $100,000
   100 to under $150,000
   More than $150,000

99. Are you currently single, married, separated, divorced, or widowed?

   1 Single
   2 Married
   3 Widowed
   4 Divorced
   5 Separated
   6 Other

100. [IF Q99=2/3/4/5] Did you meet your spouse in college?

   Yes
   No

101. [IF Q99=2 or 5] Which of the following best describes your spouse's race?

   American Indian, Aleut, Eskimo
   Asian or Pacific Islander
   Black or African American
   Hispanic/Latino
   White or Caucasian
   Something else (please specify)

102. What is the highest level of education that your mother completed?

Less than high school degree
High school degree (Grade 12 or G.E.D. certificate)
Technical, trade, or vocational school AFTER high school
Some college, no degree
2 year college degree (Associates)
4 year college degree (BA, BS, Bachelors)
Some post-graduate training or professional school AFTER college, no degree
Master's degree
Doctoral degree (PhD) or Professional degree (JD, DDS, MD, etc.)

103. What is the last grade or class that your father completed in school or college?

Less than high school degree
High school degree (Grade 12 or G.E.D. certificate)
Technical, trade, or vocational school AFTER high school
Some college, no degree
2 year college degree (Associates)
4 year college degree (BA, BS, Bachelors)
Some post-graduate training or professional school AFTER college, no degree
Master's degree
Doctoral degree (PhD) or Professional degree (JD, DDS, MD, etc.)

104. Thinking about the time when you were 16 years old, compared with American families in general then, would you say your family income was above average, average, or below average?

Far below average
Below average
Average
Above average
Far above average

105. We are looking for survey respondents who are willing to have a follow-up interview by telephone at some point in the next year, so that we can ask you more about the topics covered in today's survey. Might you be willing to be interviewed in this way, and if so, could we contact you about it?

Yes
No

[If YES, continue:]

Please note that your responses to the previous survey questions are completely confidential. Any information that you provide below will not be tied to them.

Your name and identity will not be published anywhere or shared with other researchers. In order to contact you to set up the interview, however, could you please list your name and an email address and telephone number where we can reach you in the next year?

Name _____

Email Address _____

Telephone Number _____

106. Would you like to see a list of resources for learning more about running for political office?

    Yes

    No

Elite and Administrator Interview Questions

SEMI-STRUCTURED INTERVIEW QUESTIONS FOR AFRICAN-AMERICAN ELECTED OFFICIALS

1. In what year were you born?
2. Where are you from?
3. Where and when did you attend college? Were you the first person in your immediate family to attend college? How long were you enrolled in your college program?
4. Can you tell me about the factors that you considered when deciding where to attend college and how you selected [your college/university]?
5. For many students, securing the financial resources necessary to attend college is one of the central factors shaping where they go. What role did college costs play in shaping your decision? If you're comfortable with sharing, how did you and/or your family pay for your education?
6. Can you tell me about any ways in which your family and friends played a role in your decision about where to attend college?
7. If you had to do it again, would you make any changes to your decision to attend that college?
8. How would you describe your academic experience during college?
9. Before going to college, were you interested in politics? Were members of your family engaged in politics when you were growing up?
10. Did your undergraduate work include any training in politics and government? If so, what kind?
11. What types of social and/or extracurricular activities did you do during college?

12. How would you describe your relationship with your former college classmates? Are you still in touch with them?

13. Can you tell me about when you first became interested in politics/government?

14. Why did you decide to run for office? Did you always know that you wanted to get involved in public service?

15. When you first ran for office, what kind of support (if any) did you receive from your college network?

16. What are your priorities as a lawmaker?

17. Can you describe some of the legislation with which you've been most involved?

18. What do you feel are the biggest challenges facing the nation today?

19. Is there anything else that you'd like to share about your experience in higher education and how it has influenced your work as a policymaker?

SEMI-STRUCTURED INTERVIEW QUESTIONS FOR HBCU ADMINISTRATORS

1. How long have you worked at this university?

2. Can you tell me about your role as an administrator?

3. Could you tell me a bit about the history of the college/university?

4. What would you say makes this college/university unique?

5. What is the typical student experience here?

6. Has the college curriculum changed over time? If so, how?

7. How does the curriculum at this university contribute to students' development as citizens?

8. Would you say that helping to cultivate leaders is an important part of this college's mission? If so, what does the school do to achieve this goal?

9. Can you tell me about the alumni of this college? (E.g., what do they do?) How engaged are they?

10. How have internal influences (e.g., faculty, administrators, staff, students) shaped your university?

11. What role have external influences (e.g., alumni, philanthropy, government, etc.) played in shaping your university?

TABLE A.4.1 Variables Used in Analysis of the College Experience Study

Variable	Range	Coding
Birthyear	1936–2000	The respondent's year of birth
Female	0,1	The respondent's gender, coded as 1 for female and 0 for male
Household	1–12	Respondent's approximate household income in 2016 from all sources before taxes, coded into 12 categories from 1 ("Less than $10,000") to 12 ("More than $150,000")
Educational Attainment	4–9	Indicates highest level of education coded into six categories from (4) some college, no degree, (5) 2 year college degree (Associates), (6) 4 year college degree (BA, BS, Bachelors), (7) Some post-graduate training or professional school after college, no degree, (8) Master's degree (PhD) or Professional degree (JD, DDS, MD, etc.)
HBCU Attendees	0,1	Indicates whether respondent ever attended an HBCU (1) or not (0)
Efficacy	1–4	Indicates respondent's agreement with the statement "I consider myself well qualified to participate in politics," organized into four categories from (1) disagree strongly to (4) agree strongly
Considered Running	0,1	Indicates whether respondent has ever considered running for political office

Source: The College Experience Study.

TABLE A.4.2 Descriptive Statistics

	Mean or %	Std. Dev.	Min.	Max.
Birth Year	1971	16.10	1936	2000
Female	.52	.50	0	1
Youth SES	2.86	1.00	0	5
Educational Attainment	5.85	1.55	4	9
HBCU Attendees	.32	.47	0	1
Parent Attended HBCU	.24	.43	0	1
Grandparent Attended HBCU	.15	.36	0	1
$N = 1,140$				

Source: The College Experience Study—African Americans.

TABLE A.4.3 Paying for College: Government Financial Aid and Debt

	Not at All	Very Little	Some	Quite a Bit	A Great Deal	
"To what extent did government financial aid contribute to your ability to attend college?"						
HBCU Attendees	13%	9	24	21	34	=101%
Non-HBCU Attendees	19%	12	20	18	31	=100%
"To what extent did student loans burden you with debts that are or were difficult to repay?"						
HBCU Attendees	26%	10	18	20	26	=100%
Non-HBCU Attendees	34%	11	18	14	23	=100%

Notes: The sum of percentage in some rows may not equal 100% due to rounding. Difference in mean responses for each question is statistically significant at $\alpha = .01$.
Source: The College Experience Study—African Americans.

TABLE A.5.1 Variables Used in Analysis of College Experience Study Data

Variable	Range	Coding
HBCU Attendance	0,1	Whether the respondent attended an HBCU for undergraduate study (1) or not (0)
Educational Attainment	1–9	Indicates the highest level of education coded into nine categories: (1) less than high school; (2) high school diploma GED; (3) technical, trade, or vocational school after high school; (4) some college; (5) two-year degree; (6) four-year degree; (7) some post-graduate training after college; (8) master's degree; (9) Ph.D. or professional degree
Gender	0,1	The respondent's gender, coded as 1 for female and 0 for male
Year of Birth	1936–2000	The respondent's year of birth
Youth Socioeconomic Status	1–5	Respondent's family income compared to others at age sixteen; ranges from 1 ("far below average") to 5 ("far above average")
Household Income	1–10	Respondent's total annual income coded into ten categories from 1, which corresponds to less than $10,000 annually to 10, which corresponds to more than $150,000 annually
Parents' Education	2–18	A measure of parents' combined educational attainment as a sum of the highest level of education for each parent based on nine categories: (1) less than high school; (2) high school diploma GED; (3) technical, trade, or vocational school after high school; (4) some college; (5) two-year degree; (6) four-year degree; (7) some post-graduate training after college; (8) master's degree; (9) Ph.D. or professional degree
Parent Attended HBCU	0,1	Whether either of the respondent's parents attended an HBCU for undergraduate study (1) or not (0)
Grandparent Attended HBCU	0,1	Whether any of the respondent's grandparents attended an HBCU for undergraduate study (1) or not (0)

(continued)

TABLE A.5.1   Continued

Variable	Range	Coding
Family Emphasis on Education	1–4	Indicates respondent's perception of the emphasis that her or his family placed on education when she/he was growing up: (1) no emphasis at all; (2) not much emphasis; (3) some emphasis; or (4) a great deal of emphasis
College Prepared Me	1–4	Indicates respondent's agreement with the statement "My undergraduate college or university prepared me well for life outside of college": (1) disagree strongly; (2) disagree somewhat; (3) agree somewhat; or (4) agree strongly
Welcome on Campus	1–4	Indicates respondent's agreement with the statement "I felt welcome on my college campus": (1) disagree strongly; (2) disagree somewhat; (3) agree somewhat; or (4) agree strongly
Gov't/Politics/Policy Course	0,1	Whether the respondent took a course focusing on government, politics, or public policy during college (1) or not (0)
College Political Activity	0,1	Whether the respondent engaged in any political activities (e.g., volunteering for a campaign or political cause, attending a political event, contacting an elected official, protesting) during college (1) or not (0)
Political Participation Index	4 parts	Index consisting of whether respondents have ever volunteered on a political campaign, contributed money to a political candidate or cause, contacted a government official, and participated in a protest or demonstration
Political Efficacy Index	3 parts	Index consisting of feeling that public officials care about what people like the respondent think, the respondent has a good understanding of political issues, and feeling qualified to participate in politics
Resources for Running	0,1	Whether the respondent opted to see a list of resources for learning more about running for political office (1) or not (0)

Source: The College Experience Study.

TABLE A.5.2 Descriptive Statistics

	Mean or %	Std. Dev.	Min.	Max.
Birth Year	1971	16.10	1936	2000
Female	.52	.50	0	1
Youth SES	2.86	1.00	0	5
Educational Attainment	5.85	1.55	4	9
HBCU Attendees	.32	.47	0	1
Parent Attended HBCU	.24	.43	0	1
Grandparent Attended HBCU	.15	.36	0	1
N = 1,140				

Source: The College Experience Study—Black Respondents.

TABLE A.6.1 Determinants of Political Efficacy and Participation

	Efficacy	Participation
Gender	−.444***	−.104
	(.110)	(.113)
Year of Birth	−.007*	−.018***
	(.003)	(.004)
Household Income	.042*	.045*
	(.017)	(.018)
Educational Attainment	.089*	.150***
	(.037)	(.039)
HBCU Attendance	.072	.603**
	(.218)	(.225)
Public	−.327*	−.277†
	(.157)	(.159)
HBCU Attendance × Public	.258	−.179
	(.255)	(.265)
Log Likelihood	−2,243	−1,584
N	1,133	1,134

†$p \leq .1$; *$p \leq .05$, **$p \leq .01$, ***$p \leq .001$
Notes: Cells consist of ordinal logistic regression coefficients in the numerator and standard errors in parentheses. Analysis includes Black respondents who have completed at least "some college."
Source: The College Experience Study—Black Respondents.

TABLE A.6.2 Determinants of Engaging in Political Activity during College

	Model I	Model II	Model III	Model IV
Gender	−.074	−.040	−.029	−.039
	(.148)	(.149)	(.150)	(.151)
Year of Birth	.012*	.013**	.012*	.014**
	(.005)	(.005)	(.005)	(.005)
Youth Socioeconomic Status	.158*	.117	.106	.104
	(.076)	(.077)	(.078)	(.078)
Parents' Education	.069***	.043*	.039†	.034
	(.020)	(.021)	(.022)	(.022)
Parent Attended HBCU		.612***	.496**	.492**
		(.179)	(.189)	(.191)
Grandparent Attended HBCU			.400*	.391†
			(.201)	(.202)
HBCU Attendance	.881***	.742***	.729***	.815**
	(.149)	(.156)	(.156)	(.276)
Public				−.418*
				(.212)
HBCU Attendance × Public				−.158
				(.324)
Log Likelihood	−594	−588	−586	−582
N	1,134	1,134	1,134	1,134

Notes: Cells consist of binary logistic regression coefficients in the numerator and standard errors in parentheses. Analysis includes Black respondents who have completed at least "some college."

†$p \leq .1$; *$p \leq .05$, **$p \leq .01$, ***$p \leq .001$

Source: The College Experience Study—Black Respondents.

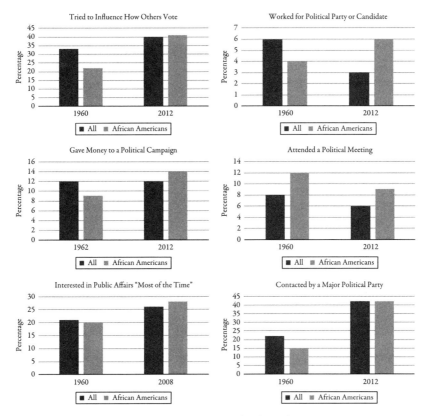

FIGURE A.1 The changing racial dynamics of political engagement.

Source: The American National Election Studies (ANES). The ANES Guide to Public Opinion and Political Behavior.

NOTES

Introduction

1. Public Law 89-329, The Higher Education Act of 1965.
2. Cynthia L. Jackson and Eleanor F. Nunn, *Historically Black Colleges and Universities: A Reference Handbook* (Santa Barbara, CA: ABC-CLIO, 2003).
3. See, e.g., Adam Harris, *The State Must Provide: Why America's Colleges Have Always Been Unequal—and How to Set Them Right* (New York: HarperCollins, 2021).
4. Derrick Bell, "Who's Afraid of Critical Race Theory," *University of Illinois Law Review* 1995, no. 4 (1995): 893–910, 893. As Tara J. Yosso notes, applying a Critical Race Theory lens to educational analysis provides space for acknowledging the strengths that communities of color bring to bear and the value that they hold for racial progress. By working to center and celebrate Black excellence and Black culture, HBCUs offer unique educational environments that provide their students with respite from the deficit mindsets about Black and Brown communities that they often encounter in other spaces. See Tara J. Yosso, "Whose Culture Has Capital? A Critical Race Theory Discussion of Community Cultural Wealth," *Race Ethnicity and Education* 8, no. 1 (2005): 69–91, 75.
5. Bell, "Who's Afraid of Critical Race Theory," 900.
6. Gloria Ladson-Billings and William F. Tate IV, "Toward a Critical Race Theory of Education," *Teachers College Record* 97, no. 1 (1995): 47–68, 50.
7. Walter Recharde Allen and Joseph O. Jewell, "A Backward Glance Forward: Past, Present, and Future Perspectives on Historically Black Colleges and Universities," *Review of Higher Education* 25, no. 3 (2002): 241–261, 242; Walter R. Allen, Joseph O. Jewell, Kimberly A. Griffin, and De'Sha S. Wolf, "Historically Black Colleges and Universities: Honoring the Past, Engaging the Present, Touching the Future," *Journal of Negro Education* 76,

no. 3 (2007): 263–280, 269; Robert Palmer, "The Perceived Elimination of Affirmative Action and the Strengthening of Historically Black Colleges and Universities," *Journal of Black Studies* 40, no. 4 (2010): 762–776, 763; Mariah Bohanon, "African American History: A Look Back at Early Student Activism," Insight into Diversity, webpage (2019), available at: https://www.insightintodiversity.com/african-american-history-a-look-back-at-early-student-activism/.

8.   Jelani M. Favors, *Shelter in a Time of Storm* (Chapel Hill: University of North Carolina Press, 2019).

9.   Steven J. Rosenstone and John Mark Hansen, *Mobilization, Participation, and Democracy in America* (New York: Longman, 1993); Sidney Verba, Kay Lehman Schlozman, and Henry E. Brady, "Civic Participation and the Equality Problem," in *Civic Engagement and American Democracy*, ed. Theda Skocpol and Morris P. Fiorina (Washington, DC: Brookings Institution Press/Russell Sage Foundation, 1999), 427–460.

10.   Allen and Jewell, "A Backward Glance Forward," 242; Allen et al., "Historically Black Colleges and Universities," 269; Palmer, "The Perceived Elimination of Affirmative Action and the Strengthening of Historically Black Colleges and Universities," 763.

11.   Thurgood Marshall College Fund, "Historically Black Colleges & Universities (HBCUs)," webpage (2016), available at: www.tmcf.org.

12.   See, e.g., Sidney Verba, Kay Lehman Schlozman, and Henry Brady, *Voice and Equality: Civic Volunteerism in American Politics* (Cambridge, MA: Harvard University Press, 1995); Claudia Goldin and Lawrence Katz, *The Race between Education and Technology* (Cambridge, MA: Harvard University Press, 2008).

13.   During the 2018–2019 academic year, HBCUs had a total revenue amount of $8.5 billion, $1.9 billion of which came from student tuition and fees. National Center for Education Statistics (NCES), "Fast Facts: Historically Black Colleges and Universities," website available at: https://nces.ed.gov/fastfacts/display.asp?id=667.

14.   St. Philip's College, North Carolina A&T State University, and Howard University are the largest HBCUs. "By the Numbers: How HBCUs Stack Up" (Washington, DC: United Negro College Fund, 2021), available at: https://uncf.org/the-latest/by-the-numbers-how-hbcus-stack-up.

15.   National Center for Education Statistics (NCES), "Fast Facts: Historically Black Colleges and Universities," website, available at: https://nces.ed.gov/fastfacts/display.asp?id=667.

16.   Allen and Jewell, "A Backward Glance Forward," 255; Jackson and Nunn, *Historically Black Colleges and Universities*, 2–3; Palmer, "The Perceived Elimination of Affirmative Action and the Strengthening of Historically Black Colleges and Universities," 762–763. National Center for Education Statistics (NCES), "Fast Facts: Back-to-School Statistics," website, available at: https://nces.ed.gov/fastfacts/display.asp?id=667.

17.   National Center for Education Statistics (NCES), "Fast Facts: Historically Black Colleges and Universities," website, available at: https://nces.ed.gov/fastfacts/display.asp?id=667.

18. "By the Numbers: How HBCUs Stack Up," United Negro College Fund (2021), website, available at: https://uncf.org/the-latest/by-the-numb ers-how-hbcus-stack-up.

19. C.K., "Why American Lost So Many of Its Black Teachers," *The Economist*, July 8, 2019; "Race and Ethnicity of Public School Teachers and Their Students," Data Point: U.S. Department of Education, National Center for Education Statistics (NCES), website, available at: https://nces.ed.gov/pubs2 020/2020103/index.asp#:~:text=In%20the%202017%E2%80%9318%20sch ool,were%20Black%20and%20non%2DHispanic.

20. Lavar Edmonds, "Role Models Revisited: HBCUs, Same-Race Teacher Effects, and Black Student Achievement," working paper (2022), available at: https://www.lavaredmonds.com/uploads/1/4/2/8/142800166/hbcus_ and_teacher_effects_draft_20220815.pdf; Seth Gershenson, Cassandra M. D. Hart, Joshua Hyman, Constance A. Lindsay, and Nicholas W. Papageorge, "The Long-Run Impacts of Same-Race Teachers," *American Economic Journal: Economic Policy* 14, no. 4 (2022): 300–342.

21. Mikyong Minsun Kim and Clifton F. Conrad, "The Impact of Historically Black Colleges and Universities on the Academic Success of African-American Students," *Research in Higher Education* 47, no. 4 (2006): 399–427, 421.

22. Monica Anderson, "A Look at Historically Black Colleges and Universities as Howard Turns 150," Pew Research Center, webpage (2017), available at: https://www.pewresearch.org/fact-tank/2017/02/28/a-look-at-historica lly-Black-colleges-and-universities-as-howard-turns-150/.

23. Anderson, "A Look at Historically Black Colleges and Universities as Howard Turns 150."

24. Walter R. Allen, Uma M. Jayakumar, Kimberly A. Griffin, William S. Korn, and Sylvia Hurtado, *Black Undergraduates from Bakke to Grutter: Freshman Status, Trends and Prospects, 1971–2004* (Los Angeles: Higher Education Research Institute, UCLA, 2005), 27–28.

25. Walter R. Allen, Channel McLewis, Chantal Jones, and Daniel Harris, "From *Bakke* to *Fisher*: African American Students in U.S. Higher Education over Forty Years," *RSF: The Russell Sage Foundation Journal of the Social Sciences* 4, no. 6 (2018): 47–48.

26. Allen et al., "From *Bakke* to *Fisher*," 56.

27. Allen et al., "From *Bakke* to *Fisher*."

28. Harold H. Wenglinsky, "The Educational Justification of Historically Black Colleges and Universities: A Policy Response to the U.S. Supreme Court," *Educational Evaluation and Policy Analysis* 18, no. 1 (1996): 91–103.

29. Jackson and Nunn, *Historically Black Colleges and Universities*, 22–23.

30. Keith V. Johnson and Elwood Watson, "The W. E. B. Du Bois and Booker T. Washington Debate: Effects upon African American Roles in Engineering and Engineering Technology," *Journal of Technology Studies* 30, no. 4 (2004): 65–70.

31. Johnson and Watson, "The W. E. B. Du Bois and Booker T. Washington Debate."
32. William L. Allen, "The Demise of Industrial Education for African Americans: Revisiting the Industrial Curriculum in Higher Education" (master's thesis, Wright State University, 2007), 2.
33. James D. Anderson, *The Education of Blacks in the South, 1860–1935* (Chapel Hill: University of North Carolina Press, 1988), 279–280; Allen, "The Demise of Industrial Education for African Americans," 65.
34. See, e.g., Jackson and Nunn, *Historically Black Colleges and Universities*, 2–3; Palmer, "The Perceived Elimination of Affirmative Action and the Strengthening of Historically Black Colleges and Universities," 763.
35. While the Constitution did not explicitly reserve its rights and privileges to men—in fact, it invoked the gender-neutral term "persons" when describing its targets—women's status as second-class citizens and essentially the property of their fathers and husbands under the British Common Law tradition on which the new government was based drove women's political and legal subordination under the document.
36. The Fourteenth Amendment, which was ratified in 1868, extended birthright citizenship to all born in the United States, included formerly enslaved people, while also mandating due process and equal protection under the law. The Fifteenth Amendment, which was passed in 1870, guaranteed that the right to vote would not be denied on the basis of race, color, or previous condition of servitude.
37. Allen and Jewell, "A Backward Glance Forward," 242; Allen et al., "Historically Black Colleges and Universities," 269; Michelle M. Espino and John J. Cheslock, "Considering the Federal Classification of Hispanic-Serving Institutions and Historically Black Colleges and Universities," in *Understanding Minority-Serving Institutions*, ed. Marybeth Gasman, Benjamin Baez, and Caroline Sotello Viernes Turner (Albany: State University of New York Press, 2008), 257–268; Marybeth Gasman and Roger L. Geiger, "Introduction: Higher Education for African-Americans before the Civil Rights Era, 1900–1964," in *Higher Education for African Americans before the Civil Rights Era, 1900–1964* (New Brunswick, NJ: Transaction Publishers, 2012); Jackson and Nunn, *Historically Black Colleges and Universities*; Bobby L. Lovett, *America's Historically Black Colleges & Universities: A Narrative History from the Nineteenth Century into the Twenty-first Century* (Macon, GA: Mercer University Press, 2011).
38. Allen et al., "Historically Black Colleges and Universities," 275.
39. Allen and Jewell, "A Backward Glance Forward," 255; Allen et al., "Historically Black Colleges and Universities," 268. HBCUs were at the vanguard of admitting women as well as men. It is also interesting to note that Black women benefited a great deal from the creation of HBCUs. According to Allen et al., Black women's access to HBCUs gave them greater access to higher educational institutions than White women had at historically White institutions (269).

40. Suzanne Mettler, *Soldiers to Citizens: The G.I. Bill and the Making of the Greatest Generation* (New York: Oxford University Press, 2005).

41. Deondra Rose, *Citizens by Degree: Higher Education Policy and the Changing Gender Dynamics of American Politics* (New York: Oxford University Press, 2018).

42. Allen, "The Demise of Industrial Education for African Americans"; see also Aldon D. Morris, *The Origins of the Civil Rights Movement: Black Communities Organizing for Change* (New York: Free Press, 1986), 2–4.

43. See, e.g., Andrea Louise Campbell, "Self-Interest, Social Security, and the Distinctive Participation Patterns of Senior Citizens," *American Political Science Review* 96, no. 3 (2002): 565–574; Theodore J. Lowi, "American Business, Public Policy, Case-Studies, and Political Theory," *World Politics* 16, no. 4 (1964): 677–715; Suzanne Mettler and Joe Soss, "The Consequences of Public Policy for Democratic Citizenship: Bridging Policy Studies and Mass Politics," *Perspectives on Politics* 2, no. 1 (2004): 55–73; Paul Pierson, "When Effect Becomes Cause: Policy Feedback and Political Change," *World Politics* 45, no. 4 (1993): 595–628; Theda Skocpol, *Protecting Soldiers and Mothers: The Political Origin of Social Policy in the United States* (Cambridge, MA: Harvard University Press, 1992).

44. Andrea Louise Campbell, "Self-Interest, Social Security, and the Distinctive Participation Patterns of Senior Citizens," *American Political Science Review* 96, no. 3 (2002): 565–574; Rose, *Citizens by Degree*.

45. Mettler, *Soldiers to Citizens*.

46. U.S. Department of Education, "White House Initiative on Historically Black Colleges and Universities," report (Washington, DC: Government Printing Office, 2002), 9.

47. Thurgood Marshall College Fund 2016; see also Palmer, "The Perceived Elimination of Affirmative Action and the Strengthening of Historically Black Colleges and Universities," 762; Katherine M. Saunders, Krystal L. Williams, and Cheryl L. Smith, "Fewer Resources More Debt: Loan Debt Burdens Students at Historically Black Colleges & Universities" (Washington, DC: UNCF Frederick D. Patterson Research Institute, 2016).

48. William Boland and Marybeth Gasman, "America's Public HBCUs: A Four State Comparison of Institutional Capacity and State Funding Priorities" (Philadelphia: Penn Center for Minority Serving Institutions, 2014); John Michael Lee Jr. and Samaad Wes Keys, "Land-Grant but Unequal: State One-to-One Match Funding for 1890 Land-Grant Universities," policy brief (Washington, DC: Association of Public and Land-Grant Universities, 2013); Krystal L. Williams and BreAnna L. Davis, "Public and Private Investments and Divestments in Historically Black Colleges and Universities," issue brief (Washington, DC: American Council on Education and United Negro College Fund, 2019).

Chapter 1

1. Greta Anderson and Susan Sawyer, *Ohio's Remarkable Women: Daughters, Wives, Sisters and Mothers Who Shaped History* (Guilford, CT: Globe Pequot, 2015), 60.
2. Anderson and Sawyer, *Ohio's Remarkable Women*, 59–60.
3. Anderson and Sawyer, *Ohio's Remarkable Women*, 61–62.
4. Before 1860, fewer than thirty Black Americans had earned bachelor's degrees at White colleges. See J. John Harris, Cleopatra Figgures, and David G. Carter, "A Historical Perspective of the Emergence of Higher Education in Black Colleges," *Journal of Black Studies* 6 (September 1975): 56; Manning Marable, *Black Leadership* (New York: Columbia University Press, 1998), 24.
5. John Dewey, *Democracy and Education* (New York: Free Press, 1997 [1917]); Amy Gutmann, *Democratic Education* (Princeton, NJ: Princeton University Press, 1999 [1987]); Deondra Rose, *Citizens by Degree: Higher Education and the Changing Gender Dynamics of American Citizenship* (New York: Oxford University Press, 2018); Suzanne Mettler, *Soldiers to Citizens: The G.I. Bill and the Making of the Greatest Generation* (New York: Oxford University Press, 2005); Sally A. Nuamah, *Closed for Democracy: How Mass School Closure Undermines the Citizenship of Black Americans* (New York: Cambridge University Press, 2022); Domingo Morel, *Takeover: Race, Education, and American Democracy* (New York: Oxford University Press, 2018).
6. Sidney Verba, Kay Lehman Schlozman, and Henry Brady, *Voice and Equality* (Cambridge, MA: Harvard University Press, 1995); Nancy Burns, Kay Lehman Schlozman, and Sidney Verba, *The Private Roots of Public Action: Gender, Equality, and Political Participation* (Cambridge, MA: Harvard University Press, 2001).
7. Steven J. Rosenstone and John Mark Hanson, *Mobilization, Participation, and Democracy in America* (New York: Longman, 1993).
8. Derrick Bell, "Who's Afraid of Critical Race Theory," *University of Illinois Law Review* 1995, no. 4 (1995): 893–910; Gloria Ladson-Billings and William F. Tate IV, "Toward a Critical Race Theory of Education," *Teachers College Record* 97, no. 1 (1995): 47–68; Adrienne D. Dixson and Celia K. Rousseau, "And We Are Still Not Saved: Critical Race Theory in Education Ten Years Later," *Race, Ethnicity and Education* 8, no. 1 (2005): 7–27; Walter R. Allen, Channel McLewis, Chantal Jones, and Daniel Harris, "From *Bakke* to *Fisher*: African American Students in U.S. Higher Education over Forty Years," *RSF: The Russell Sage Foundation Journal of the Social Sciences* 4, no. 6 (2018): 41–72, 42–45.
9. Ladson-Billings and Tate, "Toward a Critical Race Theory of Education," 60.
10. Gloria Ladson-Billings, "Just What Is Critical Race Theory and What's It Doing in a Nice Field Like Education?," *International Journal of Qualitative Studies in Education* 11, no. 1 (1998): 7–24, 20.
11. "The Declaration of Independence: A Transcription" (Washington, DC: The National Archives, 2022), available at: https://www.archives.gov/founding-docs/declaration-transcript.

12. Nany Kober and Diane Stark Rentner, "History and the Evolution of Public Education in the US," Center on Education Policy (Washington, DC, 2020), 1, available at: www.cep-dc.org.

13. Kober and Rentner, "History and the Evolution of Public Education in the US," 4.

14. Kober and Rentner, "History and the Evolution of Public Education in the US," 3.

15. James D. Anderson. *The Education of Blacks in the South, 1860–1935* (Chapel Hill: University of North Carolina Press, 1988), 148–149.

16. "African Americans and Education during Reconstruction: The Tolsons' Chapel Schools," National Park Service, accessed on May 31, 2021, available at: https://www.nps.gov/articles/african-americans-and-education-during-reconstruction-the-tolson-s-chapel-schools.htm.

17. Anderson, *The Education of Blacks in the South*, 193.

18. The five HBCUs created before the Civil War were: Cheyney University of Pennsylvania (1837), University of the District of Columbia (1851), Lincoln University of Pennsylvania (1854), Wilberforce University (1856), and Harris-Stowe State University in Missouri (1857).

19. William L. Allen, "The Demise of Industrial Education for African Americans: Revisiting the Industrial Curriculum in Higher Education" (PhD diss., Wright State University, 2007).

20. Hallie Quinn Brown, "Our Women: Past, Present, and Future." (Wilberforce, OH, 1925) *Alexander Street,* https://search.alexande rstreet.com/view/work/bibliographic_entity%7Cbibliographic_deta ils%7C3392103.

21. As Kim Tolley notes, the practice of hiring slaves out to work for others in the community extended the impact of slavery beyond the scope of benefiting slave owners. Tolley notes that "the wide range of employers hired slaves, from middle-class business owners who provided some training and hired individuals for several years to working-class individuals who hired slaves for short-term jobs lasting only several days, weeks, or months." Kim Tolley, "Slavery," in *Miseducation: A History of Ignorance-Making in America and Abroad*, ed. A. J. Angulo (Baltimore: Johns Hopkins University Press, 2016), 22. See also Christopher M. Span and Brenda N. Sanya, "Education and the African Diaspora," in *The Oxford Handbook of the History of Education*, ed. John L. Rury and Eileen H. Tamura (New York: Oxford University Press, 2019), 401.

22. Tolley, "Slavery," 14.

23. Anderson, *The Education of Blacks in the South*, 18.

24. Tolley, "Slavery," 15.

25. Maurice R. Berube, *American Presidents and Education* (New York: Greenwood Press, 1991), 20–22.

26. Thomas Adams Upchurch, *Legislating Racism: The Billion Dollar Congress and the Birth of Jim Crow* (Lexington: University Press of Kentucky, 2004), 47; Roger L. Williams, *The Origins of Federal Support for Higher*

Education: George W. Atherton and the Land-Grant Movement. (University Park: Pennsylvania State University Press, 1991), 35.

27. Williams, *The Origins of Federal Support for Higher Education*, 35.

28. Earle D. Ross, *Democracy's College: The Land-Grant Movement in the Formative Stage* (Ames: Iowa State College Press, 1942), 57.

29. Berube, *American Presidents and Education*, 20.

30. The choice between providing a broad-reaching education that included theory-centered classical and scientific study versus one that emphasized practical application represented one of the dominant debates of nineteenth-century discourse on higher education. Those embracing a "broad-gauge" educational philosophy viewed theory as central to a well-rounded education, while proponents of the "narrow-gauge" perspective supported an emphasis on application and a curriculum that centered on practical technical training. See, e.g., Ross, *Democracy's College*, 87–89.

31. Leedell W. Neyland, *Historically Black Land-Grant Institutions and the Development of Agriculture and Home Economics 1890–1990* (Tallahassee: Florida A&M University Foundation, 1990), 2.

32. Edward Danforth Eddy Jr., *Colleges for Our Land and Time: The Land-Grant Idea in American Education* (New York: Harper & Collins, 1957 [1956]), 34; Williams, *The Origins of Federal Support for Higher Education*, 139–141.

33. Eddy, *Colleges for Our Land and Time*, 35.

34. Span and Sanya, "Education and the African Diaspora," 401; Anderson, *The Education of Blacks in the South*, 16; Eric Foner, *Reconstruction: America's Unfinished Revolution, 1863–1877.* (New York: Harper & Row, 2014 [1988]), 96.

35. Neyland, *Historically Black Land-Grant Institutions and the Development of Agriculture and Home Economics.*

36. Neyland, *Historically Black Land-Grant Institutions and the Development of Agriculture and Home Economics*, 3, 16.

37. Eddy, *Colleges for Our Land and Time*, 44.

38. David Carleton, *Student's Guide to Landmark Congressional Laws on Education* (Westport, CT: Greenwood Press, 2002), 53; Williams, *The Origins of Federal Support for Higher Education*, 3.

39. In his analysis of the dramatic shifts in the racial dynamics of political representation that occurred during the post–Civil War period, Richard Valelly says that "Black office-holding emerged very rapidly. About half of the lower house of South Carolina's legislature during the first reconstruction was black, 42 percent of Louisiana's lower house and 19 percent of its upper house was black, and Mississippi's house was 29 percent black and its senate 15 percent black. Even Virginia, which did not experience a 'radical' phase in its reconstruction, had for a brief period a lower house that was 21 percent black and an upper house that was 6 percent black." Valelly, *The Two Reconstructions*, 3.

40. Foner, *Reconstruction*, 97.

41. John W. Blassingame, "The Union Army as an Educational Institution for Negroes, 1862–1865," *Journal of Negro Education* 34, no. 2 (1965): 152–159, 159.

42. Thavolia Glymph, *The Women's Fight: The Civil War's Battles for Home, Freedom, and Nation* (Chapel Hill: University of North Carolina Press, 2020), 238–239, 320.

43. Bobby L. Lovett, *America's Historically Black Colleges & Universities* (Macon, GA: Mercer University Press, 2015), 25–26.

44. Jackson and Nunn, *Historically Black Colleges and Universities*, 7–8; Juan Williams and Dwayne Ashley, *I'll Find a Way or Make One: A Tribute to Historically Black Colleges and Universities* (New York: HarperCollins, 2004), 72. President Andrew Johnson, who had consistently blocked liberal Republicans' efforts to extend civil rights to Black Americans, opposed the charter that would establish Howard University in the nation's capital. Nevertheless, Congress approved its charter in March of 1867. Williams and Ashley, *I'll Find a Way or Make One*, 72.

45. Stephen R. Robinson, "Rethinking Black Urban Politics in the 1880s: The Case of William Gaston in Post-Reconstruction Alabama," *Alabama Review* 66, no. 1 (2013): 3–29, 10–11.

46. Robinson, "Rethinking Black Urban Politics in the 1880s," 11.

47. Anderson, *The Education of Blacks in the South*, 2–3.

48. Valelly, *The Two Reconstructions*, 1.

49. Judy Bussell LeForge, "Alabama's Colored Conventions and the Exodus Movement, 1871–1879," *Alabama Review* 63, no. 1 (2010): 3–29, 12.

50. Valelly, *The Two Reconstructions*, 1–2.

51. LeForge, "Alabama's Colored Conventions and the Exodus Movement," 3.

52. Neyland, *Historically Black Land-Grant Institutions and the Development of Agriculture and Home Economics*, 16–17.

53. Lucius J. Barker, Mack H. Jones, and Katherine Tate, *African Americans and the American Political System*, 4th ed. (Upper Saddle River, NJ: Prentice Hall, 1999), 17.

54. Kimberley Johnson, *Reforming Jim Crow: Southern Politics and State in the Age before Brown* (New York: Oxford University Press, 2010), 117–118.

55. Neyland, *Historically Black Land-Grant Institutions and the Development of Agriculture and Home Economics*, 19.

56. Deondra Rose, "Race, Post-Reconstruction Politics, and the Birth of Federal Support for Black Colleges," *Journal of Policy History* 34, no. 1 (2022): 25–59. Efforts to support the creation of higher educational institutions during the nineteenth century were made more difficult by uneven access to elementary and secondary education throughout the United States. As Edward Danforth Eddy notes, there were only 2,526 public high schools in the United States in 1890, and not all students enjoyed access to them. See Eddy, *Colleges for Our Land and Time*, 83–84.

57. Williams, *The Origins of Federal Support for Higher Education*, 3.

58. Rose, "Race, Post-Reconstruction Politics, and the Birth of Federal Support for Black Colleges."

59. Williams, *The Origins of Federal Support for Higher Education*, 138, 141–142.

60. The Grange was a particularly interesting advocacy group because while it supported gender equality in educational access, the organization was adamantly opposed to racial equality in the provision of educational opportunity. As James Ferguson notes in his analysis of the Grange's support for farmer education in Mississippi in the late nineteenth century, objections to the state's Republican-led government's efforts to provide segregated public school education for White and Black children were rooted in objections to using White tax dollars to educate Black children. See James S. Ferguson, "The Grange and Farmer Education in Mississippi," *Journal of Southern History* 8, no. 4 (1942): 497–512, 500.

61. Williams, *The Origins of Federal Support for Higher Education*, 82.

62. Theodore Saloutos, "The Grange in the South, 1870–1877," *Journal of Southern History* 19, no. 4 (1953): 473–487, 485; Scott M. Gelber, *The University and the People: Envisioning American Higher Education in an Era of Populist Protest* (Madison: University of Wisconsin Press, 2011), 25–26.

63. Eddy, *Colleges for Our Land and Time*, 83–84, 101.

64. Gelber, *The University and the People*, 56.

65. Gelber, "The Populist Vision for Land-Grant Universities, 1880–1900," in *The Land-Grant Colleges and the Reshaping of American Higher Education*, ed. Roger L. Geiger (New York: Routledge, 2017), 165–194, 173.

66. Gelber, *The University and the People*, 57; see also Johnson, *Reforming Jim Crow*, 15.

67. Eddy, *Colleges for Our Land and Time*, 83–84, 102; Neyland, *Historically Black Land-Grant Institutions and the Development of Agriculture and Home Economics*, 21.

68. Brown, "Our Women."

69. Thousands of northern teachers descended on the South to teach in freedmen's schools. In 1869, for example, there were approximately 10,000 missionary teachers working throughout the region. Berube, *American Presidents and Education*, 20.

70. Anderson and Sawyer, *Ohio's Remarkable Women*, 63–66.

71. "A Sketch of the Life of Miss Hallie Quinn Brown," *A.M.E. Church Review* 6, no. 3 (January 1890): 257–261.

72. Laurie F. Maffly-Kipp and Kathryn Lofton, *Women's Work: An Anthology of African-American Women's Historical Writings from Antebellum America to the Harlem Renaissance* (New York: Oxford University Press, 2010), 218–219.

73. Hallie Quinn Brown, "The Black Mammy Statue," *National Association Notes* 25, no. 7 (April 1923): 3–4.

74. Hallie Quinn Brown, "An Educational Awakening!" *The National Notes* 28, no. 9 (June 1926): 3.

75. Maffly-Kipp and Lofton, *Women's Work,* 219; Dorothy Salem, "Hallie Quinn Brown: Leading through Example" (Alexandria, VA: Alexander Street, 2016), 1–9.

76. Span and Sanya, "Education and the African Diaspora," 399.

77. Tolley, "Slavery," 15. Span and Sanya, "Education and the African Diaspora," 404.
78. Robinson, "Rethinking Black Urban Politics in the 1880s."
79. Foner, *Reconstruction*, 96.
80. The Black clergy played a particularly important role in helping to shape efforts to promote equal opportunity and racial uplift in their communities. See, e.g., Robinson, "Rethinking Black Urban Politics in the 1880s."
81. Millington Bergeson-Lockwood, "No Longer Pliant Tools: Urban Politics and Conflicts over African-American Partisanship in 1880s Boston, Massachusetts," *Journal of Urban History* 44, no. 2 (2018): 169–186, 182.
82. Bergeson-Lockwood, "No Longer Pliant Tools," 171–172.
83. Robinson, "Rethinking Black Urban Politics in the 1880s," 10–11.
84. David Joens, "Illinois Colored Conventions of the 1880s," *Journal of the Illinois State Historical Society* 110, no. 3–4 (2017): 305–324, 319–320.
85. Foner, *Reconstruction*, 359.
86. Johnson, *Reforming Jim Crow*, 148.

Chapter 2

1. Walter Recharde Allen and Joseph O. Jewell, "A Backward Glance Forward: Past, Present, and Future Perspectives on Historically Black Colleges and Universities," *Review of Higher Education* 25, no. 3 (2002): 241–261; Cynthia L. Jackson and Eleanor F. Nunn, *Historically Black Colleges and Universities: A Reference Handbook* (Santa Barbara, CA: ABC-CLIO, 2003), 3.
2. M. Christopher Brown and James Earl Davis, "The Historically Black College as Social Contract, Social Capital and Social Equalizer," *Peabody Journal of Education* 76, no. 1 (2001): 31–49, 33.
3. See, e.g., Autumn A. Arnett, "Separate and Unequal," *Diverse Issues in Higher Education* 32, no. 8 (2015): 12–14, 13; Brown and Davis, "The Historically Black College as Social Contract, Social Capital and Social Equalizer."
4. See, e.g., F. Erik Brooks and Glenn L. Starks, *Historically Black Colleges and Universities: An Encyclopedia* (Santa Barbara, CA: ABC-CLIO, 2011), 171–175; Bobby L. Lovett, *America's Historically Black Colleges & Universities* (Macon, GA: Mercer University Press, 2015); Brian McClure, "Heart and Soul of the Movement: Influence of Historically Black Colleges and Universities on the Civil Rights Movement" (2013), webpage, available at: https://stateofhbcus.wordpress.com/2013/08/26/heart-and-soul-of-the-movement-influence-of-historically-black-colleges-and-universities-on-the-civil-rights-movement/.
5. "The Jubilee Singers," *The Christian Recorder* 16, no. 3 (Philadelphia, January 17, 1878).
6. Marybeth Gasman and Roger L. Geiger, "Introduction: Higher Education for African-Americans before the Civil Rights Era, 1900–1964," in *Higher Education for African Americans before the Civil Rights Era, 1900–1964*, ed. Marybeth Gasman and Roger L. Geiger (New Brunswick, NJ: Transaction

Publishers, 2012), 10; Louis Ray, "Competing Visions of Higher Education: The College of Liberal Arts Faculty and the Administration of Howard University, 1939–1960," in *Higher Education for African Americans before the Civil Rights Era, 1900–1964*, ed. Gasman and Geiger, 154–155.

7. Arthur E. James, "Richard Humphreys and Cheyney State College," *Friends Journal* 8, no. 8 (1962): 170–172, 170.

8. Milton Morris James, "A Note on Richard Humphreys," *Negro History Bulletin* 23, no. 1 (1959): 4.

9. Henry Barnard, ed., "Institute for Colored Youth," *American Journal of Education, Vol.* 19 (1870), p. 379, accessed July 9, 2022.

10. "Graduates of the Institute for Colored Youth: Teachers in the African American Community," Falvey Memorial Library, Villanova University (2022), webpage, available at: https://exhibits.library.villanova.edu/institute-colored-youth/community-moments/icy-graduates-teachers.

11. James, "Richard Humphreys and Cheyney State College," 170.

12. James, "Richard Humphreys and Cheyney State College," 170.

13. Benjamin C. Bacon, "Statistics of the Colored People of Philadelphia" (Philadelphia: Pennsylvania T. E. Chapman, 1856), 6; James, "Richard Humphreys and Cheyney State College," 171.

14. "Objects of the Institute for Colored Youth, with a List of the Officers and Students, and the Annual Report of the Board of Managers, for the Year 1864" (Philadelphia: Sherman & Co., 1864), 8–9.

15. Bacon, "Statistics of the Colored People of Philadelphia," 5; Isaac Collins and John S. Powell, "A List of Some of the Benevolent Institutions of the City of Philadelphia and their Legal Titles" (Philadelphia: Henry B. Ashmead Book and Job Printer, 1859), 30.

16. John Thomas Scharf and Thompson Westcott, *History of Philadelphia, 1609–1884*, 3 vols. (Philadelphia: L. H. Everts & Co., 1884), 3:1475.

17. Bacon, "Statistics of the Colored People of Philadelphia," 9.

18. "Lectures by Frederick Douglas [sic]," *The Christian Recorder* (Philadelphia), March 21, 1863; "National Hall—Frederick Douglas [sic]," *The Christian Recorder* (Philadelphia), April 11, 1863; "Objects of the Institute for Colored Youth," 15–16.

19. "The Debating Society of the Institute for Colored Youth," *The Christian Recorder* (Philadelphia), November 8, 1900.

20. Bacon, "Statistics of the Colored People of Philadelphia," 12.

21. Henry Barnard, ed., "Legal Status of the Colored Population," *American Journal of Education* 3 (1870): 379.

22. See "Graduates of the Institute for Colored Youth."

23. Barnard, ed., "Legal Status of the Colored Population," 378.

24. "Philadelphia Institute for Colored Youth," *The American Freedman* 1, no. 11 (1867): 165.

25. "Philadelphia Institute for Colored Youth," 165.

26. "Graduates of the Institute for Colored Youth."

27. Barnard, ed., "Legal Status of the Colored Population," 474.

28. "Graduates of the Institute for Colored Youth."
29. "Graduates of the Institute for Colored Youth"; John W. Blassingame, "The Union Army as an Educational Institution for Negroes, 1862–1865," *Journal of Negro Education* 34, no. 2 (1965): 154.
30. "Political Opinions: Views of the Prominent Colored Men in and about Philadelphia on the Status of the Colored Race in the Event of Cleveland's Election," *The Christian Recorder* (Philadelphia), November 13, 1884.
31. "A Good Movement," *The Christian Recorder* (Philadelphia), March 9, 1867.
32. "Ex-Minister Bassett," *The Christian Recorder* (Philadelphia), June 6, 1878.
33. "Local News," *The Christian Recorder* (Philadelphia), July 5, 1883.
34. "Work among the Freedmen," *The Christian Recorder* (Philadelphia), June 25, 1885.
35. J. Henry Bartlett, "The Institute for Colored Youth, a Normal School," *The Friend* 78 (October 1904): 92.
36. James, "A Note on Richard Humphreys," 4; James, "Richard Humphreys and Cheyney State College," 171.
37. During the 1961–1962 school year, 10 percent of students and 19 percent of the staff at Cheyney State College were White. James, "Richard Humphreys and Cheyney State College," 172.
38. "Wilberforce University: Its Utility and Designs," *The Christian Recorder* (Philadelphia), November 21, 1863.
39. Henry Barnard, "In Respect to Schools and Education," *American Journal of Education* 19 (1856–1882): 373. link.gale.com/ apps/doc/CY0103857681/ SABN?u=duke_perkins&sid=bookmark-SABN&xid=38b13796&pg=21 (Accessed 8 July 2022).
40. Cheyney University, Wilberforce University, and Lincoln University were founded before the Civil War. All other Black colleges and universities were established after the war.
    Matthew Simpson, ed., "Wilberforce University," in *Cyclopaedia of Methodism: Embracing Sketches of Its Rise, Progress, and Present Condition with Biographical Notices and Numerous Illustrations* (Philadelphia: Everts & Stewart, 1878), 945; Barnard, "In Respect to Schools and Education," 373.
41. Greta Anderson and Susan Sawyer, *Ohio's Remarkable Women: Daughters, Wives, Sisters and Mothers Who Shaped History* (Guilford, CT: Globe Pequot, 2015), 62–63.
42. Barnard, "In Respect to Schools and Education," 319.
43. "General Summary," *The National Era* (Washington, DC), October 14, 1858.
44. "A Letter for a Soldier of the 55th Mass.," *The Christian Recorder* (Philadelphia), October 24, 1863.
45. "Wilberforce University," *The Christian Recorder* (Philadelphia), July 13, 1861.
46. "Wilberforce University," *The Christian Recorder* (Philadelphia), September 26, 1863. This sentiment emerged as a theme in the newspaper's coverage of Wilberforce University during late 1863. Another article offered a similarly compelling appeal for support, noting that "The Wilberforce University, when properly founded, will exert an influence that shall be felt by our

people every where. The ministers and instructors, who shall go forth from this college, we hope may be found in every part of the United States, in the Republics of South America, in Asia, Africa—*all over the globe.*" "Wilberforce University," *The Christian Recorder* (Philadelphia), December 26, 1863.

47. "Wilberforce University," *The Christian Recorder* (Philadelphia), October 2, 1863.

48. "The Necessity of Wilberforce University for Our Youth—The Demands for Such an Institution," *The Christian Recorder* (Philadelphia), November 26, 1864.

49. "Wilberforce University Destroyed by Fire," *New York Times*, April 21, 1865, 4; "An Appeal in Behalf of Wilberforce University," *The Christian Recorder* (Philadelphia), September 2, 1865.

50. Society for the Promotion of Collegiate and Theological Education at the West, "Annual Report of the Society for the Promotion of Collegiate and Theological Education at the West," Vol. 23 (New York: John F. Trow & Co., 1866).

51. Elizabeth Keckley, First Lady Mary Todd Lincoln's dressmaker during President Lincoln's years in the White House, received a number of the president's and first lady's clothing items after Lincoln's death, which she donated to support Wilberforce after it was ravaged by fire. Elizabeth Keckley, *Behind the Scenes: Thirty Years a Slave, and Four Years in the White House* (New York: G. W. Carleton & Co.), 203.

52. "For the Christian Recorder: Wilberforce University," *The Christian Recorder* (Philadelphia), April 7, 1866.

53. "Princeton College," *The Christian Recorder* (Philadelphia), November 7, 1868.

54. "Wilberforce University," *The Christian Recorder* (Philadelphia), June 12, 1869.

55. Elizabeth Cady Stanton and Parker Pillsbury, eds., "The Howard University at Washington," *The Revolution* (New York), September 17, 1868.

56. "Howard University: Its Past and Future," *The Christian Recorder* (Philadelphia), September 10, 1874.

57. Sydney Howard Gay, Oliver Johnson, and Edmond Quincy, eds., "The Howard University," *New York Evening Post* and the *National Anti-Slavery Standard* (New York), January 2, 1869.

58. Jackson and Nunn, *Historically Black Colleges and Universities*, 7–8.

59. Juan Williams and Dwayne Ashley, *I'll Find a Way or Make One: A Tribute to Historically Black Colleges and Universities* (New York: HarperCollins, 2004), 72.

60. "Education," *The Christian Recorder* (Philadelphia), July 24, 1869.

61. Sydney Howard Gay, Oliver Johnson, and Edmond Quincy, eds., "Howard University," *New York Evening Post* and the *National Anti-Slavery Standard* (New York), October 23, 1869.

62. Caroline Wells Healey Dall, "The College, the Market, and the Court or Women's Relation to Education, Labor, and Law" (Boston, MA: Lee & Shepard, 1867), 380.

63. "Personal and General," The 19th Amendment Victory: A Newspaper History, 1762–1922, from *Frank Leslie's Weekly*, June 3, 1871.

64. "Gerritt Smith Gives Howard University a Thousand Dollars," *The Christian Recorder* (Philadelphia): September 3, 1874.

65. Aaron Powell, ed., "The National Standard" (New York), November 11, 1871.

66. South Carolina General Assembly, *Reports and Resolutions of the General Assembly of the State of South Carolina*, Vol. 1871–72 (Columbia, SC: Republican Print Co., 1872), 193.

67. Sydney Howard Gay, Oliver Johnson, and Edmond Quincy, eds., "Howard University," *New York Evening Post* and the *National Anti-Slavery Standard* (New York), October 23, 1869.

68. Walter Dyson, "A History of the Federal Appropriation of Howard University 1867–1926," *Howard University Studies in History* 8, no. 1 (1927): 12–22.

69. Henry Barnard, "Education of the Colored Race," *American Journal of Education* 29 (1878): 35–36.

70. Sydney Howard Gay, Oliver Johnson, and Edmond Quincy, eds., "Howard University," *New York Evening Post* and the *National Anti-Slavery Standard* (New York), October 23, 1869.

71. Albert Gallatin Riddle, "The Philosophy of Political Parties and Other Subjects: Eight Lectures Delivered before the Law Department of Howard University" (Washington, DC: W. H. & O. H. Morrison, 1873), 41

72. Riddle, "The Philosophy of Political Parties and Other Subjects," 180–181.

73. Charles Sumner, *The Works of Charles Sumner*, 15 vols. (Boston: Lee & Shepard, 1883), 14:148.

74. "Two Speeches to Colored Men, Frederick Douglass and President Hayes at Howard University," *The Christian Recorder* (Philadelphia), February 28, 1878.

75. *The American Cyclopaedia and Register of Important Events of the Year 1872* (New York: D. Appleton & Co., 1873), 123.

76. "For the Christian Recorder: Grand Presentation to Professor John M. Langston," *The Christian Reorder* (Philadelphia), February 19, 1870.

77. Will H. Thomas, "Saunterings," *The Christian Recorder* (Philadelphia), October 23, 1873.

78. "Howard University," *The Christian Recorder* (Philadelphia), March 25, 1875.

79. Dyson, "A History of the Federal Appropriation of Howard University," 12–22.

80. Lovett, *America's Historically Black Colleges & Universities*, 88.

Chapter 3

1. "An Appeal for Human Rights," Advertisement in the *Atlanta Constitution* (1960), Constance W. Curry papers, Manuscript, Archives, and Rare Book Library, Robert W. Woodruff Library, Emory University, 0818-010.tif, 1–4.

2. HBCUs have long been central nodes of democratic engagement in their communities as well as valuable resources for policymakers. During the New Deal era, for example, government officials used Black colleges as conduits for distributing federal resources in the form of poverty relief and training opportunities to local communities. Bobby Lovett, *America's Historically Black Colleges & Universities: A Narrative History from the Nineteenth Century into the Twenty-First Century* (Macon, GA: Mercer University Press, 2011), 108.

3. As Walter Allen and Joseph O. Jewell note, HBCU faculty and students were central to the movements for both civil rights and Black power. See Walter Recharde Allen and Joseph O. Jewell, "A Backward Glance Forward: Past, Present, and Future Perspectives on Historically Black Colleges and Universities," *Review of Higher Education* 25, no. 3 (2002): 241–261, 249.

4. Marybeth Gasman and Roger L. Geiger, "Introduction: Higher Education for African-Americans before the Civil Rights Era, 1900–1964," in *Higher Education for African Americans Before the Civil Rights Era, 1900–1964*, ed. Marybeth Gasman and Roger L. Geiger (New Brunswick, NJ: Transaction Publishers, 2012), 11–12.

5. Cynthia L. Jackson and Eleanor F. Nunn, *Historically Black Colleges and Universities: A Reference Handbook* (Santa Barbara, CA: ABC-CLIO, 2003), 86–87.

6. Christopher P. Loss, *Between Citizens and the State: The Politics of American Higher Education in the 20th Century* (Princeton, NJ: Princeton University Press, 2012), 116; Ira Katznelson, *When Affirmative Action Was White: An Untold History of Racial Inequality in Twentieth-Century America* (New York: W. W. Norton, 2006). To be sure, the G.I. Bill contributed to a boost in Black college enrollments, as beneficiaries enrolled in record numbers. In 1945 when the G.I. Bill was first rolling out, approximately 44,000 students attended Black colleges. One year later, that number had reached nearly 57,000 students, with World War II veterans making up nearly a third of students studying at Black colleges. This, in turn, contributed to the emergence of a class of Black professionals who were able to work through legal, social, and political institutions to advocate boldly for civil rights. Nevertheless, the nation's tradition of racial segregation and discrimination ultimately limited the number of Black Americans who would reap the benefits of the G.I. Bill, as the extent to which this influx of federal financial support was limited by the educational infrastructure that would accommodate students. In the midst of institutional segregation that persisted into the 1960s, Black G.I. Bill recipients could only take advantage of their education benefits if they could secure a spot in a college or university. Unfortunately, there were only so many seats available for students entering Black colleges, and they could only accommodate a portion of the veterans who applied for those seats.

7. Booker T. Washington, "Atlanta Exposition Address, 1895," *Black History Bulletin* 68, no. 1 (Winter 2006): 18–20, 20.

8.   W. E. B. Du Bois, *The Souls of Black Folk*, Open Road Integrated Media, Inc.
     (1994), *ProQuest Ebook Central*, https://ebookcentral.proquest.com/lib/
     duke/detail.action?docID=1806378, 50–52.

9.   William L. Allen, "The Demise of Industrial Education for African
     Americans: Revisiting the Industrial Curriculum in Higher Education"
     (master's thesis, Wright State University, 2007), 6.

10. Allen, "The Demise of Industrial Education for African Americans," 33.

11. Jacqueline M. Moore, *Booker T. Washington, W. E. B. Du Bois and
     the Struggle for Racial Uplift* (Wilmington, DE: Scholarly Resources,
     2003), 11–13.

12. Allen, "The Demise of Industrial Education for African Americans," 62.

13. Robert A. Gibson, "Booker T. Washington and W. E. B. DuBois: The
     Problem of Negro Leadership," *Curriculum Units by Fellows of the Yale–New
     Haven Teachers Institute* 2 (1978): 1–11, 3.

14. Kimberlé Crenshaw, "Mapping the Margins: Intersectionality, Identity
     Politics, and Violence against Women of Color," *Stanford Law Review* 43, no.
     6 (1991): 1241–1299.

15. Anna J. Cooper, "Colored Women as Wage-Earners," *The Southern Workman*
     28, no. 8 (August 28, 1899): 295–298, 298.

16. Mary Eliza Church Terrell, "Citizenship," *Howard University Journal* 7
     (January 29, 1910): 5–6, 6.

17. Ida B. Wells, "Our Country's Lynching Record," *The Survey* 29, no. 18
     (February 1, 1913): 573–574, 574.

18. Carter G. Woodson, *The Mis-education of the Negro* (Washington,
     DC: Associated Publishers, 1933), 115.

19. Woodson, *The Mis-education of the Negro*, 114–115.

20. Alain Locke, "The Dilemma of Segregation," *Journal of Negro Education* 4,
     no. 3 (1935): 406–411, 407.

21. Travis J. Albritton, "Educating Our Own: The Historical Legacy of HBCUs
     and Their Relevance for Educating a New Generation of Leaders," *Urban
     Review* 44, no. 3 (2012): 311–331, 327.

22. Juan Williams and Dwayne Ashley, *I'll Find a Way or Make One: A Tribute
     to Historically Black Colleges and Universities.* (New York: HarperCollins,
     2004), 213.

23. Lovett, *America's Historically Black Colleges & Universities*, 88.

24. Juan Williams, *Thurgood Marshall: American Revolutionary*
     (New York: Three Rivers Press, 1998), 55; see also Genna Rae McNeil,
     Groundwork: Charles Hamilton Houston and the Struggle for Civil Rights
     (Philadelphia: University of Pennsylvania Press, 1983), 76, 82–83.

25. Williams, *Thurgood Marshall*, 53.

26. Williams, *Thurgood Marshall*, 57.

27. Pauli Murray, *Song in a Weary Throat: Memoir of an American Pilgrimage*
     (New York: Liveright Publishing Corporation, 2018 [1987]), 235.

28. Murray, *Song in a Weary Throat*, 236.

29. Murray, *Song in a Weary Throat*, 236.

30. Walter R. Allen, Joseph O. Jewell, Kimberly A. Griffin, and De'Sha S. Wolf, "Historically Black Colleges and Universities: Honoring the Past, Engaging the Present, Touching the Future," *Journal of Negro Education* 76, no. 3 (2007): 263–280, 268–269.

31. Rosalind Rosenberg, *Jane Crow: The Life of Pauli Murray* (New York: Oxford University Press, 2017), 4, 115–119.

32. Rosenberg, *Jane Crow: The Life of Pauli Murray*, 4, 171.

33. Clayborne Carson, ed., *The Autobiography of Martin Luther King, Jr.* (New York: Abacus, 2000), 13.

34. Barbara Ransby, *Ella Baker and the Black Freedom Movement: A Radical Democratic Vision* (Chapel Hill: University of Chapel Hill Press, 2003), 55.

35. Ransby, *Ella Baker and the Black Freedom Movement*, 60–61.

36. Joy Ann Williamson, *Radicalizing the Ebony Tower: Black Colleges and the Black Freedom Struggle in Mississippi.* (New York: Teachers College Press, 2008), 36.

37. John Britton, "A Partial Transcript of a Recorded Interview with Miss Ella Baker, Staff-Member-Consultant with Southern Conference Educational Fund (SCEF)," Washington, DC (June 19, 1968), available at: https://www.crmvet.org/nars/baker68.htm.

38. Britton, "A Partial Transcript of a Recorded Interview with Miss Ella Baker."

39. In reflecting on the reasons why Martin Luther King embraced a prominent leadership role in the civil rights struggle, Ella Baker noted the strong force of King's background and a parallel between willingness to embrace high-profile leadership positions and higher educational achievement within the Black middle class. "Martin had come out of a highly competitive black, middle-class background," Baker noted. "You know, the bragging about whose child got a master's degree first and whose child, maybe, was the first Ph.D. Out of a background like that, the business of becoming a chairman of an important movement or a movement that symbolizes a certain amount of prestige is something you don't resist easily." Britton, "A Partial Transcript of a Recorded Interview with Miss Ella Baker."

40. Interview with Diane Nash, conducted by Blackside, Inc., on November 12, 1985, for "Eyes on the Prize: America's Civil Rights Years (1954–1965)." Washington University Libraries, Film and Media Archive, Henry Hampton Collection, Eyes on the Prize Interviews.

41. Oral History Interview with Julian Bond, interviewed by Elizabeth Gritter, November 1 and 22, 1999, Interview R-0345, Southern Oral History Program Collection in the Southern Oral History Program Collection (#4007), Southern Historical Collection, Wilson Library, University of North Carolina at Chapel Hill. Published by Documenting the American South: docsouth.unc.edu/sohp/R-0345/menu.html.

42. Lovett, *America's Historically Black Colleges & Universities*, 155.

43. Lovett, *America's Historically Black Colleges & Universities*, 155.

44. Lovett, *America's Historically Black Colleges & Universities*, 142.

45. Lovett, *America's Historically Black Colleges & Universities*, 138.

46. Lovett, *America's Historically Black Colleges & Universities*, 156.
47. Williamson, *Radicalizing the Ebony Tower*, 39.
48. Oral History Interview with Julian Bond, November 1 and 22, 1999.
49. John Lewis, *Walking with the Wind: A Memoir of the Movement* (New York: Simon & Schuster, 2015), 72.
50. Oral History Interview with Julian Bond, November 1 and 22, 1999.
51. The student activism that reached a fever pitch during the early 1960s was a continuation of efforts that had started during the previous decades. For example, students studying at Spelman College organized a club devoted to fighting for civil rights during the late 1950s. In 1958, club members traveled to the Georgia State Capitol to protest segregation; and the following year they worked to dismantle segregation at public libraries in Atlanta. Lovett, *America's Historically Black Colleges & Universities*, 144.
52. Lovett, *America's Historically Black Colleges & Universities*, 145.
53. Oral History Interview with Julian Bond, November 1 and 22, 1999.
54. Oral History Interview with Julian Bond, November 1 and 22, 1999.
55. "An Appeal for Human Rights," Advertisement in the *Atlanta Constitution* (1960), 1–4.
56. "An Appeal for Human Rights," Advertisement in the *Atlanta Constitution* (1960), 2.
57. Williamson, *Radicalizing the Ebony Tower*, 49.
58. Interview with Diane Nash, November 12, 1985.
59. Lewis, *Walking with the Wind*, 83.
60. Interview with Diane Nash, November 12, 1985.
61. Lewis, *Walking with the Wind*, 92–93.
62. Lewis, *Walking with the Wind*, 197.
63. Lewis, *Walking with the Wind*, 197–198.
64. Williamson, *Radicalizing the Ebony Tower*, 60.
65. Interview with Diane Nash, November 12, 1985.
66. Lewis, *Walking with the Wind*, 76, 182–184.
67. During their work with the SNCC, both Julian Bond and Diane Nash took leave of their studies to devote all of their time to the movement. While Bond would return to Morehouse ten years later in 1971, Nash did not complete her studies at Fisk. Oral History Interview with Julian Bond, November 1 and 22, 1999; Interview with Diane Nash, November 12, 1985.
68. Interview with Diane Nash, November 12, 1985.
69. Oral History Interview with Julian Bond, November 1 and 22, 1999.
70. Lovett, *America's Historically Black Colleges & Universities*, 88.
71. Numan V. Bartley, *The Rise of Massive Resistance: Race and Politics in the South during the 1950's* (Baton Rouge: Louisiana State University Press, 1997), 230.
72. Bartley, *The Rise of Massive Resistance: Race and Politics in the South During the 1950's,* 231–236.
73. Lewis, *Walking with the Wind*, 102.
74. Williamson, *Radicalizing the Ebony Tower*, 68.

75. Williamson, *Radicalizing the Ebony Tower*, 62.
76. Williamson, *Radicalizing the Ebony Tower*, 64.
77. Lewis, *Walking with the Wind*, 220.
78. Oral History Interview with Julian Bond, November 1 and 22, 1999; see also Lewis, *Walking with the Wind*, 221–228.

Chapter 4

1. See, e.g., Kara Mayer Robinson, "Are HBCUs Still Relevant?" Minority Corporate Counsel Association, available at: https://mcca.com/mcca-arti cle/are-hbcus-still-relevant-pt1/.
2. See, e.g., Pearl Stewart, "HBCU Merger Proposals Persist Despite Fervent Opposition," Diverse Issues in Higher Education, available at: https://www. diverseeducation.com/demographics/african-american/article/15090345/ hbcu-merger-proposals-persist-despite-fervent-opposition.
3. Prior to conducting the College Experience Study, I conducted a pilot of the survey using Amazon's Mechanical Turk (mTurk) service to ensure that the questions were clear and that the survey could completed in 15–20 minutes. mTurk workers engaged to pretest my questionnaire received $1.40 to complete the survey. Respondents who completed the Qualtrics survey received compensation in the form of Qualtrics eRewards currency, which is redeemable for a variety of benefits, such as points toward airline and hotel rewards and sweepstakes entries. The survey also included an item asking respondents if they would be willing to participate in a 20-minute follow-up telephone interview to further discuss their college experience, political attitudes, and political engagement. This second phase of the study yielded 100 follow-up interviews that offer in-depth responses to some of the questions posed in the first phase of the study.
4. Youth socioeconomic status is a measure of respondent's self-reported family income at age sixteen compared to other families. For detailed variable coding information, please see Table A.4.1.
5. Figure 4.1 illustrates the distribution of HBCU and non-HBCU attendance for College Experience Study participants across four birth-year cohorts. For members of the most senior cohorts of respondents, HBCUs were a dominant higher educational option. For the cohort that was born between 1952 and 1967, 31.3 percent went to an HBCU, compared to 26.6 percent who did not. And among the most senior cohort of respondents, 13 percent attended an HBCU, compared to 15.2 percent who did not. For the cohort born between 1968 and 1983, the proportions are practically identical, with 29.6 percent reporting that they attended an HBCU, and 29.5 percent indicating that they did not. Among the most junior cohort of respondents who were born between 1984 and 2000, 25.5 percent of respondents attended an HBCU, compared to 28.5 percent who attended PWIs.
6. Throughout this analysis, I use pseudonyms to protect the identities of survey participants.

7. Terris Ross, Grace Kena, Amy Rathbun, Angelina Kewal-Ramani, Jijun Zhang, Paul Kristapovich, and Eileen Manning, "Higher Education: Gaps in Access and Persistence Study" (2012), NCES 2012046, available at: https://nces.ed.gov/pubsearch/pubsinfo.asp?pubid=2012046.

8. Robert T. Palmer and Estelle Young, "The Uniqueness of an HBCU Environment: How a Supportive Campus Climate Promotes Student Success," in *The Evolving Challenges of Black College Students: New Insights for Practice and Research*, ed. Terrell L. Strayhorn and Melvin C. Terrell (Sterling, VA: Stylus, 2010), 139, 763; see also Cynthia L. Jackson and Eleanor F. Nunn, *Historically Black Colleges and Universities: A Reference Handbook* (Santa Barbara, CA: ABC-CLIO, 2003), 86–87.

9. "Fast Facts: Historically Black Colleges and Universities," National Center for Education Statistics, available at: https://nces.ed.gov/fastfacts/display.asp?id=667.

10. Gerald David Jaynes and Robin M. Williams Jr., eds., *A Common Destiny: Blacks and American Society* (Washington, DC: National Academy Press, 1989); Michael C. Dawson, *Behind the Mule: Race and Class in African American Politics* (Princeton, NJ: Princeton University Press, 1994); Claudine Gay and Katherine Tate, "Doubly Bound: The Impact of Gender and Race on the Politics of Black Women," *Political Psychology* 19, no. 1 (1998): 169–184.

11. Ramon B. Goings, "Investigating the Experiences to Two High-Achieving Black Male HBCU Graduates: An Exploratory Study," *Negro Educational Review* 67, no. 4 (2016): 54–75; Palmer and Young, "The Uniqueness of an HBCU Environment," 140; Rachelle Winkle-Wagner and Dorian L. McCoy, "Feeling Like an 'Alien' or 'Family'?: Comparing Students and Faculty Experiences of Diversity in STEM Disciplines at a PWI and an HBCU," *Race, Ethnicity, and Education* 21, no. 5 (2016): 593–606.

Chapter 5

1. See, e.g., Deondra Rose, *Citizens by Degree: Higher Education Policy and the Changing Gender Dynamics of American Citizenship* (New York: Oxford University Press, 2018); Suzanne Mettler, *Soldiers to Citizens: The G.I. Bill and the Making of the Greatest Generation* (New York: Oxford University Press, 2005); Sidney Verba, Kay Lehman Schlozman, and Henry Brady, *Voice and Equality* (Cambridge, MA: Harvard University Press, 1995); Sidney Verba and Norman H. Nie, *Participation in America: Political Democracy and Social Equality* (New York: Harper & Row, 1972). In 1940, 1.3 percent of Black Americans over the age of twenty-four held a bachelor's degree. In 1980, that number reached 7.9 percent; and by 2017, 24.3 percent of African Americans held at least a bachelor's degree. At all points, HBCUs provided a substantial proportion of those degrees. Before 1964, HBCUs awarded an estimated 90 percent of the college degrees earned by Black Americans. In 2014, HBCUs enrolled 10 percent of Black college students in the United States and awarded 17 percent of the bachelor's degrees that Black students earned that year. See "HBCUs Make America Strong: The Positive Economic

Impact of Historically Black Colleges and Universities," The United Negro College Fund, available at: UNCF.org/HBCUsMakeAmericaStrong.

2. Verba et al., *Voice and Equality*; Raymond E. Wolfinger and Steven J. Rosenstone, *Who Votes?* (New Haven, CT: Yale University Press, 1980), 18; Louis Menand, "Re-imagining Liberal Education," in *Education and Democracy: Re-imagining Liberal Learning in America*, ed. Robert Orrill (New York: College Entrance Examination Board 1997): 1–19, 3; Bruce A. Kimball, "Naming Pragmatic Liberal Education," in *Education and Democracy: Re-imagining Liberal Learning in America*, ed. Robert Orrill (New York: College Entrance Examination Board, 1997), 45–68.

3. Michael Anft, "How Colleges Ignite Civic Engagement," Chronicle of Higher Education, January 8, 2018.

4. Elizabeth Beaumont, Anne Colby, Thomas Ehrlich, and Judith Torney-Purta, "Promoting Political Competence and Engagement in College Students: An Empirical Study," *Journal of Political Science Education* 2, no. 3 (2006): 249–270; D. Sunshine Hillygus, "The Missing Link: Exploring the Relationship between Higher Education and Political Engagement," *Political Behavior* 27, no. 1 (2005): 25–47; Richard G. Niemi and Jane Junn, *Civic Education: What Makes Students Learn* (New Haven, CT: Yale University Press, 1998); Jo-Ann Amadeo, Judith Torney-Purta, Ranier Lehmann, Vera Husfeldt, and Roumiana Nikolova, *Civic Knowledge and Engagement: An IEA Study of Upper Secondary Students in Sixteen Countries* (Amsterdam: International Association for the Evaluation of Educational Attainment, 2002).

5. For the variables and descriptive statistics used in this analysis, see Tables A.5.1 and A.5.2.

6. As Gershenhorn (2010) notes, although Thorpe worked part-time as a professor of Black history at Harvard during the 1970s, and although he—like other HBCU college professors during the era—was offered positions at PWIs like Harvard and Ohio State University, he remained committed to teaching Black history at HBCUs. Jerry Gershenhorn. "Earlie Thorpe and the Struggle for Black History, 1949–1989," *Souls* 12, no. 4 (2010): 376–397, 390–391.

Chapter 6

1. See, e.g., Robert D. Putnam, *Bowling Alone: The Collapse and Revival of American Community* (New York: Simon & Schuster, 2000); Patricia Snell, "Emerging Adult Civic and Political Development: A Longitudinal Analysis of Lack of Involvement with Politics," *Journal of Adolescent Research* 25, no. 2 (2010): 258–287, 260; The American National Election Studies 2018.

2. See Figure A.6.1.

3. Sidney Verba, Kay Lehman Schlozman, and Henry Brady, *Voice and Equality* (Cambridge, MA: Harvard University Press, 1995); Nancy Burns, Kay Lehman Schlozman, and Sidney Verba, *The Private Roots of Public Action: Gender, Equality, and Political Participation* (Cambridge, MA: Harvard University Press, 2001).

4. Sidney Verba and Norman H. Nie, *Participation in America: Political Democracy and Social Equality* (New York: Harper & Row, 1972); Verba et al., *Voice and Equality*; Sidney Verba, Kay Lehman Schlozman, Henry Brady, and Norman H. Nie, "Citizen Activity: Who Participates? What Do They Say?," *American Political Science Review* 87, no. 2 (1993): 303–318; Raymond E. Wolfinger and Steven J. Rosenstone, *Who Votes?* (New Haven, CT: Yale University Press, 1980). Colleges use a variety of programs, such as internships, service learning, deliberative discussion, racial/cultural awareness workshops community organizing, and voter registration efforts to encourage students to participate in politics. Some colleges have even added voting precincts on campus. Michael Anft, "How Colleges Ignite Civic Engagement," *Chronicle of Higher Education*, January 7, 2018; Nicholas A. Bowman, Nida Denson, and Julie J. Park, "Racial/Cultural Awareness Workshops and Post-College Civic Engagement: A Propensity Score Matching Approach," *American Educational Research Journal* 53, no. 6 (2016): 1556–1587; Adam H. Hoffman, "Institutionalizing Political and Civic Engagement on Campus," *Journal of Political Science Education* 11 (2015): 264–278.

5. Norman H. Nie, Jane Junn, and Kenneth Stehlik-Barry, *Education and Democratic Citizenship in America* (Chicago: University of Chicago Press, 1996); Steven J. Rosenstone and John Mark Hansen, *Mobilization, Participation, and Democracy in America* (New York: Longman, 1993).

6. Travis J. Albritton, "Educating Our Own: The Historical Legacy of HBCUs and Their Relevance for Educating a New Generation of Leaders," *Urban Review* 44 (2012): 311–331, 323.

7. Marybeth Gasman, Dorsey Spencer, and Cecilia Orphan, "'Building Bridges, Not Fences': A History of Civic Engagement at Private Black Colleges and Universities, 1944–1965," *Higher Education Quarterly* 55, no. 3 (2015): 346–379, 359.

8. Gasman et al., "'Building Bridges, Not Fences,'" 351.

9. To explore the possibility that the results differ for students who attend public versus private HBCUs, I conducted additional analysis incorporating an interaction term into the model to examine whether attending public versus private HBCUs reveals significant differences in terms of engaging in political activities during college. As the analysis in Table A.6.2 shows, the interaction reveals no significant association.

10. Many campus student voter registration efforts emerged in the wake of the 1971 passage of the Twenty-sixth Amendment to the US Constitution, which granted eighteen-year-olds the right to vote.

11. Gasman et al., "'Building Bridges, Not Fences,'" 364.

12. Gasman et al., "'Building Bridges, Not Fences,'" 366.

13. According to the Tennessee State University website, the motto is formally rendered as, "Think. Work. Serve." See "Tennessee State University: Vision and Mission," webpage, available at: https://catalog.tnstate.edu/content.php?catoid=4&navoid=176.

Chapter 7

1. "About HBCUs," Thurgood Marshall College Fund, available at: https://www.tmcf.org/about-us/member-schools/about-hbcus/.

2. See, e.g., Richard L. Fox and Jennifer L. Lawless, "Entering the Arena?: Gender and the Decision to Run for Office," *American Journal of Political Science* 48, no. 2 (2004): 264–280.

3. Sidney Verba, Kay Lehman Schlozman, and Henry E. Brady, *Voice and Equality: Civic Voluntarism in American Politics* (Cambridge, MA: Harvard University Press, 1995).

4. Nancy Burns, Kay Lehman Schlozman, and Sidney Verba, *The Private Roots of Public Action: Gender Equality, and Political Participation* (Cambridge, MA: Harvard University Press, 2001).

5. Sydney Verba and Norman H. Nie, *Participation in America* (New York: Harper & Row, 1972).

6. James E. Conyers and Walter L. Wallace, *Black Elected Officials: A Study of Black Americans Holding Government Office* (New York: Russell Sage Foundation, 1976), 44.

7. Conyers and Wallace, *Black Elected Officials*, 61–63.

8. See, e.g., Jane Mansbridge, "Should Blacks Represent Blacks and Women Represent Women? A Contingent 'Yes,'" *Journal of Politics* 61, no. 3 (1999): 628–657; Carol M. Swain, *Black Faces, Black Interests: The Representation of African Americans in Congress* (Cambridge, MA: Harvard University Press, 1995); Katherine Tate, "The Political Representation of Blacks in Congress: Does Race Matter?," *Legislative Studies Quarterly* 26, no. 4 (2001): 623–638.

9. Lawrence Bobo and Franklin D. Gilliam Jr., "Race, Sociopolitical Participation, and Black Empowerment," *American Political Science Review* 84, no. 2 (1990): 377–393.

10. Dianne Pinderhughes, *Race and Ethnicity in Chicago Politics* (Urbana: University of Illinois Press, 1987); Swain, *Black Faces, Black Interests*, 5.

11. Paula D. McClain and Jessica D. Johnson Carew, *"Can We All Get Along?": Racial and Ethnic Minorities in American Politics*, 7th ed. (New York: Routledge, 2017), 236.

12. McClain and Carew, *"Can We All Get Along?,"* 236.

13. Richard F. Fenno, *Going Home: Black Representatives and Their Constituents* (Chicago: University of Chicago Press, 2003), 5–6.

14. The former mayor's city had a population of approximately 26,000 people when the mayor was in office during the early 1970s.

15. "HBCU Caucus."

Chapter 8

1. Gasman acknowledges these challenges but cautions that data indicating that HBCUs trail their predominantly White counterparts "reflects less on the institutions themselves than on the tendency in the United States to invest

in students who need the least help instead of those who need the most"—
the group that HBCUs disproportionately serve. Marybeth Gasman, "The
Changing Face of Historically Black Colleges and Universities," Penn Center
for Minority Serving Institutions (2013), 3. http://repository.upenn.edu/gse_
pubs/335.

2.   Marybeth Gasman, *Envisioning Black Colleges: A History of the United Negro
     College Fund* (Baltimore: Johns Hopkins University Press, 2007), 97.

3.   Walter Recharde Allen and Joseph O. Jewell, "A Backward Glance
     Forward: Past, Present, and Future Perspectives on Historically Black
     Colleges and Universities," *Review of Higher Education* 25, no. 3 (2002): 241–
     261, 242; Walter R. Allen, Joseph O. Jewell, Kimberly A. Griffin, and De'Sha
     S. Wolf, "Historically Black Colleges and Universities: Honoring the Past,
     Engaging the Present, Touching the Future," *Journal of Negro Education* 76,
     no. 3 (2007): 263–280, 269; Robert Palmer, "The Perceived Elimination of
     Affirmative Action and the Strengthening of Historically Black Colleges and
     Universities," *Journal of Black Studies* 40, no. 4 (2010): 762–776, 763.

4.   Cynthia L. Jackson and Eleanor F. Nunn, *Historically Black Colleges and
     Universities: A Reference Handbook* (Santa Barbara, CA: ABC-CLIO,
     2003), 3.

5.   M. Christopher Brown and James Earl Davis, "The Historically Black College
     as Social Contract, Social Capital and Social Equalizer," *Peabody Journal of
     Education* 76, no. 1 (2001): 31–49, 33. See also Autumn A. Arnett, "Separate
     and Unequal," *Diverse Issues in Higher Education* 32, no. 8 (2015): 12–14, 13.

6.   Thurgood Marshall College Fund, "Historically Black Colleges &
     Universities (HBCUs)," webpage (2016), available at: www.tmcf.org.

7.   Allen et al., "Historically Black Colleges and Universities," 271; Robert T.
     Palmer, Ryan J. Davis, and Marybeth Gasman, "A Matter of Diversity, Equity,
     and Necessity: The Tension between Maryland's Higher Education System
     and Its Historically Black College and Universities over the Office of Civil
     Rights Agreement," *Journal of Negro Education* 80, no. 2 (2011): 121–133, 122.

8.   Jackson and Nunn, *Historically Black Colleges and Universities.*

9.   Gasman, "The Changing Face of Historically Black Colleges and
     Universities," 6.

10. According to the Thurgood Marshall College Fund (2016), 80 percent of
     Black judges, half of Black lawyers and professors teaching at predominantly
     White colleges and universities, and 40 percent of Black engineers were
     educated at historically Black colleges and universities.

11. Tiffany Jones, "A Historical Mission in the Accountability Era: A Public
     HBCU and State Performance Funding," *Educational Policy* 30, no. 7
     (2015): 1–43, 5.

12. Jones, "A Historical Mission in the Accountability Era," 5; see also Lawrence
     E. Gladieux and Thomas R. Wolanin, *Congress and the Colleges: The National
     Politics of Higher Education* (Lexington, MA: Lexington Books, 1976), 19;
     Kenneth E. Redd, "Historically Black Colleges and Universities: Making a
     Comeback," *New Directions for Higher Education* 102 (1998): 33–43, 33.

13. Thurgood Marshall College Fund, "Historically Black Colleges & Universities (HBCUs)"; see also Palmer, "The Perceived Elimination of Affirmative Action and the Strengthening of Historically Black Colleges and Universities," 762.

14. Marybeth Gasman, "How to Paint a Better Portrait of HBCUs," *Academe* 97, no. 3 (2011): 24–27, 25.

15. Marybeth Gasman, "Minority-Serving Institutions: A Historical Backdrop," in *Understanding Minority-Serving Institutions*, ed. Marybeth Gasman, Benjamin Baez, and Caroline Sotello Viernes Turner (Albany: State University of New York Press, 2008), 22. Although some point to *Brown v. Board of Topeka* as the point at which US education was entirely desegregated, higher education continued to be segregated throughout the South well into the 1960s. The passage of the Civil Rights Act in 1964 dealt a decisive blow against segregation in US higher educational institutions. See Jackson and Nunn, *Historically Black Colleges and Universities*, 97; Palmer, "The Perceived Elimination of Affirmative Action and the Strengthening of Historically Black Colleges and Universities," 768; Jeanita W. Richardson and J. John Harris III, "Brown and Historically Black Colleges and Universities (HBCUs): A Paradox of Desegregation Policy," *Journal of Negro Education* 73, no. 2 (2004): 365–378, 365. As Espino and Cheslock note, "[t]he language used in the Civil Rights Act focused on the PWIs that were not adhering to the Brown v. Board ruling against segregation." Michelle M. Espino and John J. Cheslock, "Considering the Federal Classification of Hispanic-Serving Institutions and Historically Black Colleges and Universities," in *Understanding Minority-Serving Institutions*, ed. Gasman, Baez, and Turner (Albany: State University of New York Press, 2008), 258–259.

16. Gasman, "How to Paint a Better Portrait of HBCUs," 25.

17. Crystal R. Sanders, "*Ayers v. Fordice*," *Mississippi Encyclopedia* (University, MS: Center for Study of Southern Culture, 2017), available at: http://mississippiencyclopedia.org/entries/ayers-v-fordice/.

18. Walter R. Allen, Channel McLewis, Chantal Jones, and Daniel Harris, "From *Bakke* to *Fisher*: African American Students in U.S. Higher Education over Forty Years," *RSF: The Russell Sage Foundation Journal of the Social Sciences* 4, no. 6 (2018): 41–72, 58.

19. Bobby L. Lovett, *America's Historically Black Colleges & Universities: A Narrative History from the Nineteenth Century into the Twenty-First Century* (Macon, GA: Mercer University Press, 2011), 193.

20. Juan Williams and Dwayne Ashley, *I'll Find a Way or Make One: A Tribute to Historically Black Colleges and Universities* (New York: HarperCollins, 2004), 193, 270.

21. Jackson and Nunn, *Historically Black Colleges and Universities*, 23.

22. Jackson and Nunn, *Historically Black Colleges and Universities*, 100.

23. Hugh Davis Graham, *The Uncertain Triumph: Federal Education Policy in the Kennedy and Johnson Years* (Chapel Hill: University of North Carolina Press, 1984), 217.

24. Gasman, "Minority-Serving Institutions," 22; Jackson and Nunn, *Historically Black Colleges and Universities*, 87.

25. Lovett, *America's Historically Black Colleges & Universities*, 195.

26. Jackson and Nunn, *Historically Black Colleges and Universities*, 88.

27. Gasman, "Minority-Serving Institutions: A Historical Backdrop," 22; Jackson and Nunn, *Historically Black Colleges and Universities*, 88. This era also saw the continuation of important legal activity related to HBCUs. In 1992, the *United States v. Fordice* case reached the US Supreme Court. The Court ruled that postsecondary institutions were permitted to factor race into admissions decisions, as long as doing so helped to correct the legacy of inequality that was wrought by the history of dual education systems in the United States (Gasman, "Minority-Serving Institutions," 22; Jackson and Nunn, *Historically Black Colleges and Universities*, 100).

28. Gasman, "Minority-Serving Institutions," 22; Jackson and Nunn, *Historically Black Colleges and Universities*, 88.

29. Lovett, *America's Historically Black Colleges & Universities*, 199.

30. "About Us: Historical Overview." White House Initiative on Advancing Educational Equity, Excellence, and Economic Opportunity Through Historically Black Colleges and Universities (U.S. Department of Education, 2021) https://sites.ed.gov/whhbcu/about-us/.

31. Joseph R. Biden, Executive Order 14041—White House Initiative on Advancing Educational Equity, Excellence, and Economic Opportunity Through Historically Black Colleges and Universities. Gerhard Peters and John T. Woolley, eds. *The American Presidency Project* (2021) https://www.presidency.ucsb.edu/node/352090.

32. Lovett, *America's Historically Black Colleges & Universities*, 197.

33. See, e.g., Andrea Louise Campbell, "Self-Interest, Social Security, and the Distinctive Participation Patterns of Senior Citizens," *American Political Science Review* 96, no. 3 (2002): 565–574; Theodore J. Lowi, "American Business, Public Policy, Case-Studies, and Political Theory," *World Politics* 16, no. 4 (1964): 677–715; Suzanne Mettler and Joe Soss, "The Consequences of Public Policy for Democratic Citizenship: Bridging Policy Studies and Mass Politics," *Perspectives on Politics* 2, no. 1 (2004): 55–73; Paul Pierson, "When Effect Becomes Cause: Policy Feedback and Political Change," *World Politics* 45, no. 4 (1993): 595–628; Theda Skocpol, *Protecting Soldiers and Mothers: The Political Origin of Social Policy in the United States* (Cambridge, MA: Harvard University Press, 1992).

34. Gloria Ladson-Billings, "Just What Is Critical Race Theory and What's It Doing in a Nice Field Like Education?," *International Journal of Qualitative Studies in Education* 11, no. 1 (1998): 7–24, 16.

INDEX